D1603636

Missing a BEAT

Judaic Traditions in Literature, Music, and Art
Ken Frieden *and* Harold Bloom, *Series Editors*

Fred W. McDarrah, Seymour Krim, 1961.
Premium Archive, Getty Images.

Missing a BEAT

The Rants and Regrets of

Seymour Krim

Edited and with an Introduction by **Mark Cohen**

With a Foreword by **Dan Wakefield**

Syracuse University Press

Copyright © 2010 by Syracuse University Press
Syracuse, New York 13244-5290

All Rights Reserved

First Edition 2010
10 11 12 13 14 15   6 5 4 3 2 1

The following material reprinted courtesy of the Estate of Seymour Krim:
"What's *This* Cat's Story?"; "Milton Klonsky: My Favorite Intellectual"; "The
American Novel Made Me"; "The 215,000 Word Habit: Should I Give My Life
to *The Times?*"; "Remembering Harold Rosenberg"; "On Being an Anglo";
"Anti-Jazz: Unless the Implications Are Faced"; "Ask for a White Cadillac";
"Making It!"; "Norman Mailer, Get Out of My Head!"; "Mario Puzo and
Me"; "The One & Only Million-Dollar Jewboy Caper"; "For My Brothers
and Sisters in the Failure Business"; "The Menahem Begin Image"; "Sitting
Shiva for Henry Miller"; "My Sister, Joyce Brothers"; "Epitaph for a Canadian
Kike"; and "Black English, or the Motherfucker Culture."

∞ The paper used in this publication meets the minimum requirements of
the American National Standard for Information Sciences—Permanence of
Paper for Printed Library Materials, ANSI Z39.48-1992.

For a listing of books published and distributed by Syracuse University
Press, visit our Web site at SyracuseUniversityPress.syr.edu.

Library of Congress Cataloging-in-Publication Data
Krim, Seymour, 1922–
    Missing a beat : the rants and regrets of Seymour Krim / edited and
with an introduction by Mark Cohen ; with a foreword by Dan Wakefield.
— 1st ed.
        p. cm. — (Judaic traditions in literature, music, and art)
    Includes bibliographical references and index.
    ISBN 978-0-8156-0948-3 (cloth : alk. paper)
    I. Cohen, Mark. II. Title.
    PS3521.R557A6 2010
    814'.54—dc22   2009048977

Manufactured in the United States of America

For my father

Mark Cohen's work on Jewish literature and culture has appeared in *American Jewish History, Midstream, Modern Judaism, ANQ Journal, Saul Bellow Journal,* and other publications. He is the author of *Last Century of a Sephardic Community.*

Contents

Foreword, DAN WAKEFIELD   *ix*

Acknowledgments   *xiii*

Editor's Introduction, MARK COHEN   *xvii*

PART ONE **Intellectuals**

1. What's *This* Cat's Story?   *3*

2. Milton Klonsky, My Favorite Intellectual   *28*

3. The American Novel Made Me   *58*

4. The 215,000 Word Habit
Should I Give My Life to The Times?   *78*

5. Remembering Harold Rosenberg   *83*

PART TWO **Whites and Blacks**

6. On Being an Anglo   *91*

7. Anti-Jazz
Unless the Implications Are Faced   *94*

8. Ask for a White Cadillac   *100*

9. Black English, or the Motherfucker Culture   *117*

PART THREE **Success and Failure**

10. Making It!   *131*

11. Norman Mailer, Get Out of My Head!   *138*

12. Mario Puzo and Me   *161*

13. The One & Only Million-Dollar Jewboy Caper   *169*

14. For My Brothers and Sisters in the Failure Business   *177*

PART FOUR **Jews**

15. The Menahem Begin Image   *193*

16. Sitting *Shiva* for Henry Miller   *196*

17. My Sister, Joyce Brothers   *201*

18. Epitaph for a Canadian Kike   *207*

Appendix
Seymour Krim Bibliography   *223*

Works Cited   *225*

Index   *231*

Foreword

DAN WAKEFIELD

Seymour Krim described his nonfiction articles or essays or "pieces" (whichever term you prefer) as "grapplings with life, desperate bids for beauty and truth and the slaking of personal need, hot mortal telegrams from writer to reader however disguised by subject-matter." No better description of his offbeat, on-the-mark work could be made, and that work not only lit up the consciousness of writers, artists, musicians, hipsters, and freelance intellectuals who came of age in New York in the 1950s, it still shines understanding on the world today.

My friendship with Krim began in the most inauspicious of ways, but in the most appropriate literary setting of the era—the back room of The White Horse Tavern on Hudson Street, hallowed by the poet Dylan Thomas, who imbibed his last drink at one of its tables before being taken across the street to St. Vincent's Hospital to die of complications brought on by acute alcoholism. Soused myself in that very back room one night, I doused my pint of 'arf and 'arf on the head of a young woman at another table who had screamed, "I just can't *stand* Murray Kempton," thus taking in vain the name of one of my journalistic/literary heroes of the time.

After I had poured out (literally) my response to such sacrilege, I calmly sat down at my own table of friends as if there would be no consequence to my oafish action, but of course there was. Two chivalrous knights from the table of the besoaked blonde stood up to avenge her honor, one of them grabbing me by the scruff of my tattered sport coat and lifting me up to upbraid and challenge me. When face to face, we began shouting at each other, "Why you goddamn—who the hell do you think you are!" Then one of my antagonists, a tall, intellectual-looking guy wearing black-rimmed glasses and a black corduroy sport coat grabbed me by the collar and said, "I know who you are, Wakefield—I've seen you around, I never thought you'd. . . ." Now I grabbed his collar and demanded, "Who the hell are you?" When he said he was Seymour Krim, I said "Yeah? I read your stuff in *The Village Voice*," and he said, "Yeah? I read your stuff in *The Nation*. We were still gripping each other by the collar and snarling through our teeth, in the classic pose of a Western barroom showdown. "Great piece you did on Bellevue," I said, and he said, "I dug the one you did on Kerouac," but everyone was watching and we couldn't release ourselves from our roles as ferocious antagonists. We both admitted later how relieved we were when a big waiter came over and broke us apart, which allowed us to disengage without losing face.

I was already an admirer of Krim's writing, and after our encounter he became a friend. He had a great sense of humor as well as a personal and literary style I enjoyed. He always seemed to be out in front of whatever new wave was coming along, coining the term "radical chic" before Tom Wolfe picked it up and made it famous, and writing a terrific essay on "Making It" before the critic and editor Norman Podhoretz wrote a whole memoir with the title. It was fitting that Norman Mailer praised Krim's work in a foreword to *Views of a Nearsighted Cannoneer*, Krim's first book of his published pieces, since Mailer's own nonfiction style owes a great deal to what Krim was doing in *The Village Voice* that both of them were writing for in the Fifties.

"I think sometimes," wrote Mailer in his foreword, that Krim, in the matter of style, "is *the* child of our time, he is New York in the middle of the 20th century, a city man, his prose as brilliant upon occasion as the electronic beauty of our lights, his shifts and shatterings of mood as searching and true as the grinding of wheels in a subway train."

The kind of nonfiction pieces that Mailer made famous and that reached a wider audience in the *Esquire* of the Sixties—like "Superman Comes to the Supermart," his impressionistic riff on JFK—owe their jazz, souped-up, incisive style to the kind of prose that Krim was turning out for *The Village Voice, The Evergreen Review, Commentary,* and *Commonweal* in the Fifties.

It was not just his sparks-flying style that made Krim's writing so memorable, it was the sensibility it expressed, the ability to capture and articulate the deep-down fears and hopes and feelings of thinking people, the taboo subjects of professional jealousy, burning ambition, the need to grab and to flout the badges of status, to consume the goods being sold us in this consumer society's nonstop assault on every sense until we are rendered senseless. The labels may have changed but the desires have not, and the vast apparatus of advertising, the never-ceasing sales pitch coming at us through every orifice is only increasing, becoming more slick and sophisticated. Yet Krim, without sentimentality ("He has the guts of New York, old Krim," wrote Mailer), after depicting all the devil's temptations and the slick slides to downfall, offers up hard-earned affirmation, as he writes in his classic essay "The Insanity Bit" that "we can be grateful that the human soul is so constructed that it ultimately bursts concepts once held as true out of its terrible need to live and creates the world anew just in order to breathe in it."

Amen, old Krim. Amen.

Acknowledgments

Thanks are gratefully extended to the Estate of Seymour Krim for rights to publish his works. The following essays appear here Courtesy of the Estate of Seymour Krim: "What's *This* Cat's Story?"; "Milton Klonsky: My Favorite Intellectual"; "The American Novel Made Me"; "The 215,000 Word Habit: Should I Give My Life to *The Times?*"; "Remembering Harold Rosenberg"; "On Being an Anglo"; "Anti-Jazz: Unless the Implications Are Faced"; "Ask for a White Cadillac"; "Making It!"; "Norman Mailer, Get Out of My Head!"; "Mario Puzo and Me"; "The One & Only Million-Dollar Jewboy Caper"; "For My Brothers and Sisters in the Failure Business"; "The Menahem Begin Image"; "Sitting *Shiva* for Henry Miller"; "My Sister, Joyce Brothers"; "Epitaph for a Canadian Kike"; and "Black English, or the Motherfucker Culture."

Thanks are also owed to *Commentary* magazine for permission to reprint "Remembering Harold Rosenberg," by Seymour Krim, *Commentary*, November 1978; to Judson Memorial Church, New York, NY, for permission to reprint "Ask for a White Cadillac," by Seymour Krim, *Exodus*, 1959; to Holt, Rinehart and Winston for permission to reprint "For My Brothers and Sisters in the Failure Business" and "The One & Only Million-Dollar Jewboy Caper" from *You & Me* by Seymour Krim, copyright © 1974 by Holt, Rinehart and Winston, used by permission of Houghton Mifflin Harcourt Publishing Company; to *The Nation* for permission to reprint "The 215,000 Word Habit: Should I Give My Life to the *Times?*" by Seymour Krim, from the April 23, 1988, issue of *The Nation*; and to DeWitt Clinton High School, Bronx, New York, for permission to quote from "Two Photographers in Search of a Subject," by Seymour Krim, *The Magpie*, June

1938. I am also grateful for access to "Black English," by Seymour Krim, held with the Seymour Krim Papers, The University of Iowa Libraries, Iowa City, Iowa.

"What's *This* Cat's Story?" appeared in slightly different form in *The Noble Savage* 3 (June 1961) as the introduction to the original edition of *Views of a Nearsighted Cannoneer* (New York: Excelsior Press, 1961); to the new, enlarged edition of the same title (New York: E. P. Dutton, 1968); and to *What's This Cat's Story? The Best of Seymour Krim*, edited by Peggy Brooks (New York: Paragon House, 1991). It also appeared in *Editors: The Best from Five Decades*, edited by Saul Bellow and Keith Botsford (London: Toby Press, 2001).

"Milton Klonsky" appeared in shorter form under the title "Two Teachers—Nuts, Two Human Beings!" in the original 1961 edition of *Views of a Nearsighted Cannoneer;* and in its present form in the 1968 enlarged edition of the same title and in *What's This Cat's Story? The Best of Seymour Krim*, edited by Peggy Brooks.

"The American Novel Made Me" appeared in different form in *Playboy* magazine, June 1969, as "The American Novel Made Us"; and under its present title in *Shake It for the World, Smartass* (New York: Dial Press, 1970) and in *What's This Cat's Story? The Best of Seymour Krim*, edited by Peggy Brooks.

"The 215,000 Word Habit: Should I Give My Life to *The Times*?" first appeared in the *Nation*, April 23, 1988. It was reprinted in *Best American Essays 1989*, edited by Geoffrey Wolff and Robert Atwan (Boston: Ticknor & Fields, 1989), and in *What's This Cat's Story? The Best of Seymour Krim*, edited by Peggy Brooks.

"Remembering Harold Rosenberg" first appeared in *Commentary*, November 1978.

"On Being an Anglo" first appeared in *Stroker*, January 1978.

"Anti-Jazz: Unless the Implications Are Faced" first appeared in the *Village Voice*, October 30, 1957, as "Anti-Jazz/Question of Self-Identity"; in the original edition of *Views of a Nearsighted Cannoneer;* and in the 1968 enlarged edition of the same title.

"Ask for a White Cadillac" first appeared in *Exodus*, 1959; in the original edition of *Views of a Nearsighted Cannoneer;* in the 1968 enlarged edition of the same title; and in *What's This Cat's Story? The Best of Seymour Krim*, edited by Peggy Brooks.

"Black English, or the Motherfucker Culture" is published here for the first time. The manuscript is held in the Seymour Krim Papers, The University of Iowa Libraries, Iowa City, Iowa.

"Making It!" appeared in the *Village Voice*, September 9, 1959; in the original edition of *Views of a Nearsighted Cannoneer*; in the 1968 enlarged edition of the same title; and in *What's This Cat's Story? The Best of Seymour Krim*, edited by Peggy Brooks.

"Norman Mailer, Get Out of My Head!" appeared in *New York* magazine, April 21, 1969, and in *Shake It for the World, Smartass* (New York: Dial Press, 1970) as "Ubiquitous Mailer vs. Monolithic Me."

"Mario Puzo and Me" first appeared in the *Chicago Sun-Times*, April 1972, as "The Godfather Papers & Other Confessions." It was reprinted as "Two Hermit Gamblers: One Who Scored (Puzo), One Who Is Still Playing and Sort of Losing (Krim)" in *You & Me: The Continuing One-on-One Odyssey of a Literary Gambler* (New York: Holt, Rinehart and Winston, 1974).

"The One & Only Million-Dollar Jewboy Caper" first appeared in *Changes*, November 1973, and in *You & Me: The Continuing One-on-One Odyssey of a Literary Gambler*.

"For My Brothers and Sisters in the Failure Business" appeared in *You & Me: The Continuing One-on-One Odyssey of a Literary Gambler*. It was reprinted in *The Art of the Personal Essay: An Anthology from the Classical Era to the Present*, edited by Phillip Lopate (New York: Anchor Books, 1994).

"The Menahem Begin Image" appeared under the title "The Begin Image" in the *New York Times*, July 15, 1977.

"Sitting *Shiva* for Henry Miller" appeared under the title "Sitting Shiva for Henry" in the *Village Voice*, June 23, 1980.

"My Sister, Joyce Brothers" first appeared in the *Soho News*, April 9, 1980, and in *What's This Cat's Story? The Best of Seymour Krim*, edited by Peggy Brooks.

"Epitaph for a Canadian Kike" appeared in *Evergreen Review*, April 1970, and in *You & Me: The Continuing One-on-One Odyssey of a Literary Gambler*.

Editor's Introduction

MARK COHEN

In 1993 I became the customer of a near-lunatic who guarded the most dejected, flimsy, poorly stocked book table in New York. In hindsight, it was the perfect setting for a fairy tale discovery. The vendor displayed barely a dozen items, including a yellowing 1961 paperback called *Views of a Nearsighted Cannoneer,* by someone named Seymour Krim. The attraction was immediate. Its cover featured a black-and-white photo of the author kneeling behind a cannon and dressed in the hip formality of the day: suit jacket and tie, short hair, and glasses with black frames sturdy enough to jack up a car. What was in it? The cover said it all: Sex Suicide Homosexuality Sportswriting Jews Negroes Jazz Genius Insanity New York: The Literary/Lower Depths.

What a grab bag. I bought my copy for a dollar and read Krim's "Making It!" piece on the downtown number 1 train—the ideal spot in which to soak up his gleeful blowtorching of the art-tinged and money-mad world of infinite New York. "Making It!" is not a short story, not traditional reportage. Instead it is a guided tour of Krim's book-stuffed mind as he debates his contradictory desires for nobility and the big money. By 1965, this kind of writing became known as New Journalism. That's when writers such as Tom Wolfe and Joan Didion ran with the style. The approach allowed them to fuse fictional techniques with reporting and make the writer's experience of an event as integral to the story as the event itself. Such a future moment was unanticipated when "Making It!" appeared in 1958, but Krim knew he was onto something original that begged for description and so he called his articles "hot mortal telegrams from writer to reader" ("What's *This* Cat's Story?"). Krim was angry but he wasn't a scold. He was titillated even as he held his nose. And he wrote exciting untrammeled wised-up city talk as good as that found in the mouths of A. J. Liebling's downtown operators and Saul Bellow's tough guys. Like those writers, Krim brought a connoisseur's ear to the language of the street. He celebrated its masterpieces, and in "Making It!" he caressed a new phrase: "*You've got it made.* How the words sing a swift jazz poem of success, hi-fi, the best chicks (or guys), your name in lights, pot to burn, jets to L.A. and London, bread in the bank, baby, and a fortress built around your ego like a magic suit of armor!"

Not bad.

I had never heard of Krim and neither had anyone else I excitedly rushed to speak with about this new discovery, but I did recognize the rush of exaltation I got reading him. The same sense of a new territory opening up hit me when I watched Billy Wilder's *Ace in the Hole,* read Bellow's *Humboldt's Gift,* or watched Twyla Tharp and Mikhail Baryshnikov glide and dance to the sounds of Frank Sinatra. Krim's writing harnessed and rode the same released bolt of energy as those other marvelous works, and like them his pieces seemed to derive their strength from direct contact with big-city cement. Norman Mailer felt the same way. *Cannoneer* sports a brief foreword by Mailer that offers generous praise. Krim's style made him "*the* child of our time," wrote Mailer. His prose is "as brilliant upon occasion as the electronic beauty of our lights, his shifts and shatterings of mood as searching and true as the grinding wheels in a subway train" (6). This evidence that Krim once enjoyed respect and recognition deepened the mystery surrounding the writer. He was born May 11, 1922, died in 1989, and published at least this one collection of ready-for-action pieces that Mailer once stood up for but that now nobody seemed to know. Who was this Krim?

Seymour Krim was thirty-five when he appeared on the Greenwich Village writing scene in 1957 with breakthrough personal journalism in the *Village Voice.* His first piece, "Anti-Jazz," stomped on the touchy subject of race, declaring that whites construct false selves when they borrow the black style and slang of jazz ("are they ultimately entitled to love this music so enthusiastically"?). "Making It!" hacked open America's dollar-soaked culture to show how the rot had spread to the arts. And in other articles he mocked the democratization of the notion of genius and invented a gay persona who deflated arguments against homosexual rights ("Editorial-page gas!" is the homosexual's retort to charges that the family would wither) (Krim 1961, 92, 77). The *Voice*, born just a few years earlier in 1955, was created to print this kind of rule-breaking journalism. Krim's articles were long, employed bouncy street slang and rough if not obscene language (at least not in the beginning), and made no attempt to be objective. But Krim also was no typical alternative writer. He toed no ideological line. He was independent, objected to almost everything he saw and heard, and came at things from his singular point of view with his dukes up. That was okay with the *Voice*. As founding publisher Ed Fancher told the *New Yorker*, "Ideology bored us—not simply the Communist line but the anti-Communist line too" (Menand 2009, 39). That was perfect, because neither category had anything to do with what Krim wanted to say. Editor Jerry Tallmer published Krim's work and was rewarded for it in the currency that editors love best: circulation. Krim generated an "extraordinary response from readers," wrote Tallmer. "Seymour was provocative" (1989, 21). Critical acclaim followed. *Cannoneer* collected Krim's articles from the *Voice* and other publications and garnered the foreword by Mailer and a strong review by James Baldwin. It also brought a fan letter from William Styron. The novelist wrote that *Cannoneer*'s "What's *This* Cat's Story"— which chronicles Krim's attempt to escape New York Jewish intellectualism and just say something—was "one of the most profound, truthful, courageously honest forays into the territory of necessary enlightenment that I have ever read" (Krim 1968, back cover). Saul Bellow liked the essay too, and published it in his own journal, *The Noble Savage*.

Those early essays and the *Cannoneer* book opened the way for Krim's next twenty years of writing, which had its ups and downs and catastrophes. Nearly always a freelancer, nearly always in need of money, and nearly always tough to get along with, he easily lost friends and made enemies. For instance, Mailer may have written the foreword to *Cannoneer*, but Krim had something important to say about the suffocating scale of Mailer's fame and he was going to say it even if it meant losing Mailer's support. He did and it did. But readers of the 1969 article "Norman Mailer, Get Out of My Head!" make out like bandits. The piece blames Mailer for ruining Krim's sex life, making such a racket he couldn't write, and in general screwing up the literary age. "Did Mailer ever stop to think that his gigantic personal needs for being indiscriminately admired would help smear up a standardless period?" In a tantrum of frustration with his overeducated and undercompensated position, Krim offers an anatomy of a new kind of contagious disease—one spread by contact with celebrities—that is today an epidemic. Like a pioneering researcher, Krim infected himself with celebrity envy to study its effects and publish his findings.

Another one. Legendary newspaper reporter Jimmy Breslin was a pal, but Krim quoted Breslin as privately saying he sold the movie rights to his novel *The Gang That Couldn't Shoot Straight* for a quarter of a million bucks to "two Jewboys." That ended that relationship. The quote was to appear in a 1970 article about Breslin's book for the *New York Times.* Breslin threatened to sue everyone, the *Times* panicked, and Krim's new job at the *International Herald Tribune* in Paris came to a quick end because it was almost impossible to be a newspaperman and also have an enemy named Breslin. The ostensible point of Krim's article was to find Breslin guilty of the crime of writing a novel. Krim didn't believe the novel was up to the challenge of reflecting the mad and outsized state of contemporary America, and he wanted Breslin to stick to nonfiction. (In addition to writing some of the earliest New Journalism, Krim developed a theoretical framework to defend it.) But in the Breslin piece Krim overplayed his hand. He was superior, dismissed Breslin's novel without reading it, and lost another friend and contact in the publishing world. But again, Krim's readers profit. Three years later he wrote an article about the Breslin escapade called "The One & Only Million-Dollar Jewboy Caper." It takes aim at jewboys and goyboys, the Jewish culture of the *Times,* success and failure—you name it—and hits bull's-eyes.

Krim had other bad habits. A sometime speed freak and gambler, he was virtually unemployable. "Sometimes he just might tell you to go fuck yourself," said Joanna Ney, who had a relationship with Krim. Yet he could write, and nobody else could do what he could do. In a sign of his growing reputation, *Cannoneer* was reissued in 1968 in an expanded edition that included his early literary criticism pieces so readers could see what he had left behind. But it was his New Journalism that won admirers. He published in some of the best publications in the country, including the *New York Times, Los Angeles Times, Playboy, New York, Washington Post,* and even *Vogue.* Many of these pieces appeared in two more books, *Shake It for the World, Smartass* (1970) and *You & Me* (1974). He taught writing at Columbia University, the University of Iowa, Pennsylvania State University, and the University of Puerto Rico; won a Guggenheim Fellowship in 1976 and in 1985 a Fulbright to teach at the University of Haifa, Israel. It amounted to an impressive but spotty résumé that often made Krim feel like a failure. But he never lost sight of his one great success—discovering how to write like Seymour Krim.

Accidental Intellectual

That wasn't how he started out. The new writing he debuted in the *Voice* was a rubber-burning getaway from the work he had done the previous ten years: intelligent and professional literary criticism destined for oblivion upon publication. Worse, the form's rules and regulations enforced a tight-lipped code of limited candor. And it demanded feats of mental gymnastics that Krim always found difficult and eventually found pointless. At first, he admired it. In his essay about Village poet and intellectual Milton Klonsky, he salutes Klonsky as a Village all-star who could hit and field. Klonsky knew "the most formidable of the contemporary headache-makers like Kafka, Eliot, Pound, Auden, Joyce, Yeats, Stevens and critics like Coleridge, Blackmur, Tate." Krim gave it a try. He published articles on Walt Whitman, Hemingway, Theodore Dreiser, and other heavyweights for *Partisan Review, Commentary, Commonweal,* and *Hudson Review.* He studied up and tried to be profound, because as he jibed in "What's *This* Cat's Story?" in the rarefied world of the literary journals it was made clear that "a person who had the wit to be intelligent should realize that the age demanded nothing less than genius as the bare minimum, and good taste itself required at least brilliance."

High-toned profundity rubbed Krim the wrong way. His prose had to arrive decked out in "Englishy airs, affect all sorts of impressive scholarship and social-register unnaturalness" ("What's *This* Cat's Story?").

Just that kind of writing is on display in a representative mouthful from a 1951 *Hudson Review* article on Mary McCarthy, Irwin Shaw, and William Faulkner. "Considered in a broader perspective for a moment, Miss McCarthy might be taken as a not entirely fair example of a school of fiction-writers which *Partisan Review* has, by its temper if not its express wish, encouraged, and whose self-conscious"—but that's enough (1968, 214). Such constraints drove Krim to a mental collapse in 1955 and then a new direction that allowed him to write like he does in "What's *This* Cat's Story?" about the devil's bargain he made with criticism. "I was sucking the sugar-tit of local snob success and didn't want to let go for nothing, momma, not even the cry of perplexity and sadness that came up from the being of the man who had once wanted to be a big stubborn writer in the grand tradition that laid waste to crap and lying everywhere." That's not the kind of writing they wanted in the *Hudson Review*.

But until Krim's breakdown and then breakthrough into proto–New Journalism, a literary critic seemed like the only kind of writer he could be. In fact, once it became clear that Krim did not have the instincts of a fiction writer (he published a fragment of a novel and a short story or two in the late 1940s), literary criticism seemed like what he had been preparing for his whole life. Krim had been a precocious teenaged Jewish intellectual in 1930s New York, and also one scarred by the death of both parents by the time he was ten. His father, Abraham Krim, was a Russian-Jewish immigrant who along with three brothers ran a successful chain of Hanover Lunch & Restaurant cafeterias. Through Krim Realty Corp. the brothers also developed New York real estate. They made money, and Seymour was born into a prosperous family in Manhattan's Washington Heights neighborhood. But Abraham died of a heart attack in February 1930. Seymour turned eight that May. Soon after her husband died, Ida Goldberg Krim, Seymour's mother, began to lose her sanity.

"She became indifferent to Seymour," remembered his sister Blanche Levie, who was thirteen years older than Seymour. "It was very disturbing, I can tell you. It affected him very deeply. Her behavior was strange, to put it mildly."

Ida Krim suffered a breakdown, was institutionalized, and was later released under the care of a nurse. In November 1932, she committed suicide by leaping from the roof of a six-story building that adjoined the Krim family's own. Seymour, born into an affluent and apparently stable family, was at age ten an orphan who shuttled between his maternal grandparents in Newark, New Jersey, and his older sister in Manhattan. Brother Norman was at MIT, beginning a brilliant career as a computer scientist. He apparently inherited his gift from his mother, who kept calculus books for bedtime reading. The oldest brother, Herbert, received a less benign maternal gift. He also suffered from mental instability and died in 1953 as the result of a lobotomy that Seymour signed to allow along with his sister and brother.

"There's a pattern in the family of mental aberration," said Levie.

In high school Seymour buried himself inside a bunker of books. Then he read his way out. Thomas Wolfe, Hemingway, William Faulkner, James T. Farrell, John Steinbeck, Richard Wright, and John Dos Passos made him fall in love with literature and America. As he wrote in "The American Novel Made Me," those novelists bridged the divide between his unhappy Jewish world and "the America OUT THERE and more than anything I wanted to identify with that big gaudy continent and its variety of human beings who came to me so clearly through the pages of these so-called fictions." America was "out there" because Krim, like other New York intellectuals described by Alexander Bloom in *Prodigal Sons,* felt that as a Jew and the child of immigrants he stood, in Alfred Kazin's words, "outside America" (Bloom 1986, 25). Literature was a way in. Besides, being a literary critic was not so ludicrous an idea for Depression-era intellectuals. "It was taken for granted that one would be unemployed" regardless of what one did, remembered Irving Howe. And so a luftmensch outlook developed. Bright young men with impractical interests were content to float along on a cloud of ideas, swooping down to feed on books and conversation (Bloom 1986, 36). Few were as cut loose from firm ground as the orphaned Krim. Writing anchored him and, most important, he was good.

DeWitt Clinton High School in the Bronx supported a student literary magazine, *The Magpie,* in addition to a school newspaper, and in June 1938 Krim, a junior just one month past his sixteenth birthday, published literary criticism there alongside work by the future playwright Paddy

Chayefsky and other budding writers and illustrators. In "Two Photographers in Search of a Subject," Krim reviewed and found wanting two new novels by Sinclair Lewis and Hemingway. *To Have and Have Not* showcases "*the* Ernest Hemingway. He roars and staggers and loves like the Hemingway of old." But in this novel Hemingway "has capitalized on his ability as a delineator, and has made a quick, insincere sketch that lacks mental strength and vitality." Lewis's *Prodigal-Parents* is not much of a novel either, but Krim amuses himself and the reader with the political predicament Lewis encounters by presenting a Communist character in a negative light. "Poor Mr. Lewis is now being classed as a reactionary because of his condemnation of the communist, and scalded as being inconsistent because in his previous writings he leaned towards liberalism, and was more the proletariat than the capitalist. But after all the smoke clears, and Mr. Lewis is worn haggard defending his intellectual integrity, I believe that this novel should be taken in stride as an exception to a good rule." Krim sums up both disappointing works. "Two main cogs in the evolution of American literature have lost prestige this year. They have taken a writing picnic that has produced nothing but banana peels and other left-overs that have been sold to a gullible public at the same price as the banana itself" (Krim 1938, 20). The piece displays confidence and style, and also the boredom of a literary mind impatient with the humdrum of predictable political positions. The writer who later won plaudits from as diverse a group as the critics Pauline Kael and Irving Malin, novelists James Baldwin and James Dickey, and journalists David Halberstam and Murray Kempton had already shown up for work.

So it was not surprising that after just one year of college at the University of North Carolina—but with a jumbo-sized reading list under his belt—Krim moved to Greenwich Village in 1943 to meet, hear, and imitate the now legendary New York intellectuals. Excused from military service because of poor eyesight and flat feet, Krim supported himself by working as a writer for the Office of War Information and in other jobs, and in 1947 he began reviewing books for the *New York Times*, benefiting from what Bellow called the "post-war cultural boom" (1976b, 16). During the summer of 1947 he and his wife, Eleanor Goff, a dancer with the Martha Graham Dance Company, were awarded a stay at the Yaddo artist's colony in Saratoga, New York. The marriage was brief and produced no children. By 1951, Krim began publishing in *Commentary, Commonweal,* and other prestigious journals, and in 1954 he marshaled his intellectual credentials and lifetime love affair with American realist fiction to edit *Manhattan: Stories from the Heart of a Great City.* The paperback anthology presented a broad range of writers that testified to Krim's undoctrinaire approach. There's the garrulous and unbuckled narrator of Damon Runyon and the hesitant and brittle one of John Cheever, plus Truman Capote and Edith Wharton, Jerome Weidman and Pietro Di Donato. If literary criticism had suited him, he might have been on his way. Instead it stunted his growth as a writer. Inhaling "the killing standards of the superintellectual community" turned out to be worse for him than cigarettes ("What's *This* Cat's Story?").

The Beats

Kerouac's *On the Road,* published in September 1957, changed all that. It affected Krim the same way Elvis Presley did Bob Dylan, and at about the same time. Hearing Elvis was "like busting out of jail," said Dylan (Dean 2003, 272). Kerouac sprung Krim. "I should have gotten out of criticism, said to hell with it, but one turned scared at the thought because where could you go?" Then "the beats came along," wrote Krim in "What's *This* Cat's Story?" and "revived through mere power and abandonment and the unwillingness to commit death in life some idea of a decent equivalent between verbal expression and actual experience." For Krim, it was the "catalytic figure of Kerouac" that was behind "the revivifying power of the Beats and I can testify in court if need be to the actuality of the Beat messianic excitement" (1970, 189). Court testimony was unnecessary. Krim's excitement can be gleaned from his writing. As late as 1956 he published a long article on Theodore Dreiser in *Commonweal.* Then on October 30, 1957, less than two months after the appearance of *On the Road,* Krim published "Anti-Jazz," his first article for the *Voice* and the first to feature his own unshackled style. From that point onward Krim's *Village Voice* articles, "dinky, book-erupting studio apartment" on East 10th Street, patronage of the White Horse Tavern—legendary Village watering hole for writers—and spitfire writing made him part of the then fluid Beat world (Wakefield 1992, 133–34). In 1960 he edited a classic collection, *The Beats,* and the same year "Making It!" was reprinted in *The Beat Scene.* That collection's cover listed the names of just twenty-one of its forty-five contributors, with Krim appearing near the top, bested only by Beat brand names Ginsberg, Ferlinghetti, and Kerouac. In 1961 Krim published *Cannoneer,* which collected the Beat-inspired writings he had published over the previous four years in the *Voice,* the short-lived *Exodus,* and the high-minded flesh-peddling *Swank,* which Krim briefly edited in his no-apologies effort to make a living in New York City as a talented but never a headline writer who could do nothing more than obey his instincts, whatever the meager payoff.

Krim's vital need for release into a new kind of writing that could accommodate his bursting desire to discuss an infinite array of personal and social issues led him into the arms of the Beats. *On the Road* showed him a way to escape the established forms that were not elastic enough to contain the wonderfully inelegant language he had to write. But the Beats were not the only ones to pioneer a new way of writing. Saul Bellow's *The Adventures of Augie March,* published in 1953, was an equivalent experiment in unregulated first-person narrative, a subterranean deposit of words that surfaced in a gusher. It was a form whose time had come. The experience of a new generation demanded it. And though Krim's journalistic version of this new style first found a home with the Beats, that literary school has in recent years eschewed it in favor of poetry, which is a better fit for the contemplative, nature-oriented, Buddhist-flavored strain that was always a core element in Beat writing. Collections such as *The Portable Beat Reader* (Charters 1992), *The Beat Book* (Waldman 1996), *The Birth of the Beat Generation* (Watson 1995), *The Rolling Stone Book of the Beats* (George-Warren 1999), and others make no room for Krim. This omission could have been predicted. The fit between Krim and the Beats was never smooth. It squeaked from the beginning.

Jazz and black jazz musicians were the craze in the 1950s Village, and the *Voice* ran scads of articles extolling the jazz life. So when Krim's "Anti-Jazz" appeared in the paper it almost made him a Beat heretic before his reputation was established as a believer. The article warned white hipsters that the black jazz music and cool style they loved stemmed from a "wild, violent, bitterly unjust life" that should not be emulated. He also skewered Beat pretensions to deep knowledge of the soul's bad neighborhoods. Beautiful sentiments went into jazz, but so too did ugly sides of life that white listeners were too squeamish to investigate. Jazz might be "especially attractive to young people who are disillusioned with the values of white society. But no matter how beat they are themselves, the majority have literally no idea of the conditions of life that lie behind this music." It seems half the Village did a spit-take over their morning espressos when they read Krim's face-slapping article. They had fled to the Village to escape such parental-type rebukes, and now they get a talking-to from the *Voice?* So many letters berating Krim flooded into the paper that it was forced to run a special letters section devoted solely to "Anti-Jazz." But Krim later won the kind of vindication that most wounded writers secure only in their dreams, the kind that Woody Allen enacted in a fantasy sequence in *Annie Hall* when he refuted a Marshall McLuhan–quoting academic by producing McLuhan, who dealt the professor the ultimate put-down. Krim's McLuhan was James Baldwin, the uncontradictable authority on the black experience. In Baldwin's *Village Voice* review of Krim's *Cannoneer* collection, he called Krim, "God bless him, almost the only writer of my generation who has managed to release himself from the necessity of being either romantic or defensive about Negroes." After building up Krim, Baldwin tore down his enemies. "'Anti-Jazz' ought to be required reading by every hipster who can read (on the evidence, there are not many)" (1961, 6). About his Marshall McLuhan revenge Woody Allen asked, "Why can't life be like this?" For Krim, for a moment, it was.

Jewish New Journalism

In retrospect, "Anti-Jazz" held a hint that Krim's interests might be more at home in another literary community that emerged parallel to that of the Beats in the late 1950s. While analyzing the trend and problem of whites copying the black jazz style, Krim introduced the example of Mezz Mezzrow, "a Jewish man who did everything but paint his face black in his effort to behave and be like a Negro." It was an unexpected and obscure reference. Krim had to inform his readers that Mezzrow was the subject of a book by Bernard Wolfe called *Really the Blues*. Published in 1946, it was out of print by 1957. Mezzrow fit nicely into Krim's thesis, but the mention of Mezzrow's Jewish origins strikes the reader as superfluous, even fishy. What's he getting at? Then before the reader can forget the mention of the delicate Jewish issue Krim criticizes boosters of the jazz philosophy such as the *Voice* jazz columnist, Mr. Reisner, whose name now sounds unavoidably Jewish. Krim doesn't go any further. Any Jewish topic that may have been pecking at his mind for the article never emerged. But it is important as the first appearance of a Jewish theme that surfaced more and more often and more and more extensively until a significant body of Krim's work became a renegade branch of Jewish cultural criticism or social history.

Krim's first effort to address the Jewish aspect of the black-white cultural nexus may have been short-circuited by a lack of literary models, oppressive Jewish social norms, Jewish public self-consciousness, or all the above. There was no shortage of any of them. From today's perspective it is difficult to remember the underdeveloped Jewish-American cultural world of 1957, but reactions to Philip Roth's relatively tame collection *Goodbye, Columbus,* published in 1959, offer reminders. In an essay published that same year, Theodore Solotaroff complained that Roth's honest treatment of Jewish life "is what has gotten him into trouble, in a depressingly predictable way, with a number of Jews and liberals." Roth's stories were a harsh rebuke to an American-Jewish fiction that had typically been "very literal, claustral, repetitive, and rather dull" (1959/1963, 354–55). Roth himself looked into the hornet's nest he disturbed to see what all the buzzing was about. In 1961 he found that the popular depictions of Jews sold by successful writers Harry Golden and Leon Uris worked, like a snake-oil salesman's elixir, to soothe gentile consciences and boost Jewish self-esteem. He was especially antagonistic toward the "swallowing up of difference that goes on around us continuously, that deadening 'tolerance' that robs—and is designed to rob—those who differ, diverge, or rebel of their powers" (1985, 201).

Roth's emphasis on Jewish difference is exactly to the point for an appreciation of Krim's experimental, at first tentative but then determined examination of Jewish anger, ambitions, insecurities, intellectualism, and cool. It is what earns Krim a place as a Jewish social historian before that school burgeoned in the 1970s, and what makes him a precursor of the Jewish cultural critics who arrived on the scene even later. Both approaches broadened the realm accessible to Jewish inquiry, and so did Krim. As Todd M. Endelman argued in his 2001 article "In Defense of Jewish Social History," that discipline "legitimized new avenues of research and expanded the content of the modern Jewish experience" (57). In 1997, Jonathan and Daniel Boyarin, in their aptly named *Jews and Other Differences: The New Jewish Cultural Studies,* wrote that the aim of Jewish cultural studies is to counter "the devaluation of Jewish difference" (vii). By the end of the twentieth century, scholars and critics had the advantage of standing atop a mountain of riotous Jewish creativity that had permeated America over the previous forty years, including the writings of Saul Bellow, Philip Roth, and Bernard Malamud, the movies of Woody Allen and Mel Brooks, and the blockbuster *Seinfeld* television hit, to name only the most obvious examples. Alerted by this unambiguous announcement of Jewish distinction, the cultural critics, like forensic accountants, went back over the books and records of American cultural life to point out where entries originally defined as American should be credited to Jews. Work by academics such as Stephen J. Whitfield, Andrea Most, Josh Kun, Michael Rogin, Jeffrey Shandler, and Donald Weber, along with journalists such as Neal Gabler and J. Hoberman, have made a commonplace of the notion that Jewish creativity is responsible for many of America's greatest films and Broadway musicals, the most clever and sly lyrics of the American songbook, and nearly all of contemporary comedy, in addition to furnishing impressive manpower in the fight for black civil rights while at the same time borrowing, popularizing, and perhaps exploiting black culture.

Krim began commenting on some of these same aspects of Jewish culture in the late 1950s, decades before works of Jewish social history and cultural criticism appeared. He was attuned to the importance of Jewish culture even before the most respected manifestation of that culture—Jewish-American literature—was recognized as an important new phenomenon. A milestone anthology of that literature, Irving Malin and Irwin Stark's *Breakthrough: A Treasury of Contemporary American-Jewish Literature,* did not appear until 1963. But for Krim, the relative scarcity of

Jewish cultural artifacts was no handicap. He learned from the great fiction writers he loved as a boy that a writer's strength and worth came from the trust he put in his own experience, and from the conviction that this experience can be made to yield true and far-reaching insights. Novelists tap into the "great ton of submerged American experience locked inside themselves," he wrote in "The American Novel Made Me." Krim was no novelist, so he folded a literary sensibility into journalism to document the Jewish difference locked inside him and took that difference seriously, applying his mind and emotions to it despite a cultural atmosphere that was hostile to the undertaking. As he spelled it out in his 1960 piece on his friend Klonsky, "I know from experience that my swinging non-Jewish friends, occasional girlfriends, even detractors, feel this whole Jew business comes out of left field, is a private obsession, in today's interscrewing world where the name and rank you carry means nothing compared to what you can lay down. But I would lie to myself and to you if I said that my life has not been conditioned by my enormous wrestling with this historical mountain on my back."

Krim's intuition about where the Jewish cultural gold was buried led him to dig first into how Jewishness figured into relations between blacks and whites. Today the study of blacks and Jews is so robust that one critic calls it the "'Black-Jewish relations' industry" (Itzkovitz 2005, 3). In the late 1950s, it was just a mom-and-pop shop. Norman Podhoretz's "My Negro Problem—and Ours" would not appear until 1963 and Norman Mailer's famous 1957 essay "The White Negro" avoided the Jewish angle. In fact, it contributed to the swallowing up of Jewish difference that Roth condemned in the literature of the 1950s. Mailer's opening line takes for granted that "the concentration camps and the atom bomb" equally caused the postwar psychic wounds that engendered the hipster as white Negro (1957/1959, 338). During the Bomb-obsessed 1950s this equivalence feels more like an assertion than a self-evident truth, a piece of flattery that commends the reader for a pain he would be feeling if only someone would remind him.

Krim's "Anti-Jazz" appeared almost simultaneously with Mailer's article. Both essays recognize that jazz is what attracted whites to black style and slang, but only Krim hints that the phenomenon might contain a Jewish angle. Krim touched on Mezzrow a second time in "Anti-Jazz" when he entertained the notion that some adopt black style to give their identities "a bigger and perhaps better dimension," anticipating arguments made forty years later by critics such as Maria Damon, who also sees Mezzrow as an intriguing Jewish figure in the story of blacks and Jews (1997, 150–74). But it is best not to make too much of the Jewishness in Krim's early essay. Its treatment is brief, its scope limited. After "Anti-Jazz," however, Krim was off to the races. Jewishness appeared everywhere in his work. Whether writing about the New York intellectual scene peopled by the alternately self-adoring and self-loathing "brillianteers" in "What's *This* Cat's Story?" and "Milton Klonsky"; wrestling with his own perceived failure and the success of others in articles about Norman Mailer, Mario Puzo, and Jimmy Breslin; continuing his investigation of blacks and Jews in "Ask for a White Cadillac"; or going beyond that subject with premonitions of what is today awkwardly called Whiteness Studies in his brief, enticing, and shrewd essay "On Being an Anglo," Krim never failed to wonder at the role played by his own or others' Jewish identity, history, culture, taste, prejudice, ugliness, and even pride. Mailer fascinated Krim as a "New York Jewish novelist who had crashed out of the parochial Brooklyn–Washington Heights-tea-and-wisdom orbit which was our mutual ethnic hashmark into the splendid chaos of everyone's U.S.A." Puzo's edge was due in part to his unbroken link with Italian peasant culture while Krim had weakened himself because he "wiped the ancient Hebrew out of myself to become an American." Klonsky's streetwise Brooklyn example of Jewish manhood—"the unconscious pride and soldierliness he showed in ordinary life"—directed Krim to the exits from his stifling childhood world of uptown Jewish respectability among "White Jews." The desperate struggle to achieve genius and originality among the intellectuals he remembered in "What's *This* Cat's Story?" also had a Jewish explanation. "We were Americans who loved our country and its experience (being writers who thrive off the real) but we were also Jews who because of Christian society's traditional suspicion and our own heartbreaking self-awareness became almost fanatical within ourselves to try and triumph over this blotch of birth by transcending it in brilliant individualism." And in "Making It!" the voice of the amoral go-getter defends his valueless power-grab way of life with the glib "isn't it obvious that it's better to be miserable as a storm-trooper than as a Jew?" hinting at how the Holocaust was beginning to seep into postwar life and steer it in a cynical direction.

But even this prevalence of Jewish musings understates Krim's attention to the subject. From the late 1950s through the 1960s, the Jewish topic sprouted up in essays devoted to other issues like a suppressed urge that announces itself in a Freudian slip. In the 1970s, however, Krim surrendered to it. The slips became full-blown disquisitions. Krim was undoubtedly affected by the changed American cultural climate that was coming to accept and even embrace the idea of ethnicity, and especially Jewish ethnicity. As Moses Rischin pointed out, the idea of cultural pluralism first championed by Jewish-American philosopher Horace Kallen in the 1920s had by the 1970s become "self-evident" (1978, 80). And Norman Podhoretz saw that by the mid-1960s Bellow's and Malamud's success encouraged young writers to "affect a stronger connection with Jewishness" than they actually had in order to cash in with "novels and stories about life on the Lower East Side" (1978, 148).

Krim exploited this new and more openly Jewish moment differently, to say the least. Producing appealing portraits of a long-ago world was not his bag. Instead he dug deeper into that submerged ton of Jewish experience inside him and produced original articles on the most unfashionable Jewish topics imaginable. He discovered a connection between himself and the popular, earnest, and defiantly un-hip psychologist Dr. Joyce Brothers. In "My Sister, Joyce Brothers," she is the flip side of Krim's smug Jewish bohemianism, the straight arrow whose achievement he is forced to acknowledge and respect. On the eve of Israeli prime minister Menahem Begin's 1977 visit to the United States, Krim admired the right-wing leader that right-thinking American Jews loved to hate. "Here is the intact, unashamed, brilliant and sometimes scathing old-world relative" that American middle-class Jews did "their best to forget." But like him or not, when Begin starts talking the "Jew suppressed in all of us steps forward, alert. Agree or disagree with Menahem, intelligence ignites in the ears."

Krim's masterpiece of Jewish New Journalism is "Epitaph for a Canadian Kike," a frank, outrageous, and comic look at his own Jewish discomfort. The 1970 essay is Krim's attempt to come to terms with the late Sam Goodman, a founding member of the rejectionist, scatological, and ugly No!Art movement who represented—to Krim—everything vulgar, unseemly, offensive, and unattractive about being Jewish. Krim was painfully aware that his aversion to Goodman had less to do with Goodman than it did with his own insecurities and fears, and in "Epitaph" all of the rage and insult he directs at Sam only makes Krim look worse, and Krim knew it. It is Krim's ruthless honesty and abandonment of respectability that gives the essay its power and makes it a valuable testimony. "I could accept being 'Jewish' very nicely if I didn't look like one, 'act' like one," writes Krim. Then along came Goodman, "short, belly sticking out, hooked schnozzola," to bring "me back to my own self-persecution dreads." Krim admired Goodman's anti-art sculptures for the offensive 1964 "Shit Show": "I was always to be fascinated by those dextrous, deadly hands and eyes of Sam's as they showed their vicious skill in the artifacts he turned out," he admitted. "But the man, oh dearie me, the man! THAT was something else, wasn't it? First, foremost, most obvious I guess and therefore unworthy—but then I am as unworthy as you, my hypocrite readers, and as ninetenths of humanity, so we all make a team, don't we?—there was this eerie likeness to the Hitler caricature of the slimy Jew about Sam."

Jewish discomfort doesn't get any more vivid than that, but Krim then goes beyond himself to understand Goodman as a deliberate offender, in life and art, in reaction to the Holocaust. Goodman and the other Jewish artists of the early 1960s No!Art movement "tossed their bum stinkbombs at U.S. life from the experience of the war in Europe, with charred Jews down at the bottom of the entire pyramid that ended with Uncle Sam boogie-woogieing before the whole globe on the triumphant top. They were inflamed Jewish WAR artists."

Krim and Jewish Studies

The steady drumbeat of Jewish topics in Krim's work is almost certainly what has made him unwelcome in Beat anthologies. Allen Ginsberg's role as a Beat icon does not refute this argument. Where Krim wrestled with Jewish issues that confronted him in his daily life, Ginsberg, though of the same American-born generation, wrote immigrant literature when he wrote on Jewish themes. His masterpiece, *Kaddish* (1961), is a memorial to a dead Jewish world, as is *To Aunt Rose*. For Ginsberg, Jewish concerns were not contemporary concerns. They were historical matters. For Krim, it was the opposite.

If Krim's absence from the pages of Beat collections is no surprise, the failure of Jewish studies to adopt him is one. He has all the necessary credentials. Krim was part of that first generation of American-born Jews who, beginning in the 1950s, produced the fiction that soon emerged as the dominant form of American regionalism. The genre offered the most exciting novels and authors of the day. Jewish literature of previous decades included powerful works by Charles Reznikoff, Abraham Cahan, Leo Rosten, Henry Roth, and Daniel Fuchs, but they described an immigrant experience that had come to an end. Legal reforms largely halted Jewish immigration in 1924, and the intense pressure to assimilate that marked the 1930s and 1940s produced a new kind of American, a Jewish American, who reached adulthood in an affluent and confident time. Ironically, that period of confidence allowed American-born Jewish writers to explore their unease. Herbert Gold, Wallace Markfield, Isaac Rosenfeld, Bruce Jay Friedman, Kate Simon, Saul Bellow, Cynthia Ozick, Grace Paley, and Philip Roth were among those who wrote about how Jewish Americans struggled to feel at home in—and create a natural style of spoken English for—postwar American life.

Krim was repeatedly and powerfully drawn to the same Jewish subjects as the Jewish novelists. He recognized that his own experience was marked by the legacy of the immigrant experience and anti-Semitism, feelings of Jewish inferiority and superiority, a Jewish affinity for blacks as a persecuted minority and a revulsion toward black violence, intellectual ambition, ambivalent attitudes toward white culture, cravings for success and respectability, and resentment of and love for the America he was both part of and apart from. His writing also revels in the "yoking of opposites, gutter vividness with university refinement," and it delivers the "rapid, nervous, breathless tempo" that for Irving Howe is a hallmark of the Jewish-American writing style (1977, 15). Howe took no notice of Krim, but another Irving did. Literary critic Irving Malin called attention to Krim's "brilliant, energetic prose rhythms" on display in sentences such as this one from "The American Novel Made Me": "Do I therefore mean, to hit it squarely, that writing fiction for me and my breed was a pimply kind of revenge on life, an outcast tribe of young non-Wheaties failures getting their own back, all the shrimpy, titless, thicklensed, crazy-headed dropouts and sore losers of American youth resolving in the utter misery of the dateless Saturday nights to shoot down their better-favored peers in the pages of a novel?" (1996, 490). That freedom-loving, high-octane, testosterone-spiked says who? voice is the voice found in some of the great works of Jewish-American literature, a voice that has remained at the center of Jewish writing until today. Not a straight line but a jagged, cardiac-arrest line of passionate spikes and depressive dips connects Krim to J. D. Salinger's Holden Caulfield, Joseph Heller's Yossarian, journalist Sidney Zion, Norman Mailer, playwright David Mamet, and also to the authors of today's comic and often frankly autobiographical Jewish screeds produced by Michael Wex *(Born to Kvetch)*, Shalom Auslander *(Foreskin's Lament)*, and Steve Almond *(Not That You Asked)*.

Krim's nonfiction was a fateful distinction when it came to exploring Jewish themes. Fictional creations allowed Jewish novelists to distance themselves from the Jewish concerns expressed in their books. Bellow was famous for his rejection of the label "Jewish writer." But Krim did not have the luxury of a fictional remove. When he wrote about the anxieties of Jewish identity, when over the course of his work he helped invent the scathing, mocking, obscene, and comic Jewish primal scream that Roth made legendary in *Portnoy's Complaint*, well, Krim was doing something gutsy and unheard of, except in the manic spritzes of Lenny Bruce. A quick look at the nonfiction included in the 1963 *Breakthrough* reveals what Krim was up against when he wrote his jazzy, vibrant literary journalism that tackled contemporary Jewish life. The contributions, whatever their lasting value, resort almost by automatic reflex to an earnest and solemn engagement with the Jewish past. There is an excerpt from Alfred Kazin's *A Walker in the City* called "The Kitchen" that focuses on that moment "at dusk that my mother's loneliness came home most to me" (Kazin 1963, 258). Issac Rosenfeld's essay "America, Land of the Sad Millionaire" evaluates Abraham Cahan's *The Rise of David Levinsky*, published in 1917 (Rosenfeld 1963). Shlomo Katz begins his article with

xxxvi   •   Editor's Introduction

"My father was always an old man" (Katz 1963, 267). Pieces by Podhoretz and Howe discuss Yiddish literature. By contrast, Krim in his 1959 "Ask for a White Cadillac" writes about his adventures in Harlem and the piece is packed with up-to-the-minute language that touches on a new Jewish world that novelists had just begun to dig their teeth into. Harlem's "ads and shops for hair-straightening and beauty treatments" were "not so unlike my nose-bobbing . . . in the attempt to gleam like a clean-cut White Protestant beauty." And Krim's 1960 "Milton Klonsky" pulses with excitement about the new Jews created on the poor but alive streets of New York City: "These unashamed (because they couldn't help it), often bitterly slanted and harsh-talking Jewish boys knew chicks without Cole Porter romanticization and could throw a mature lay in the sunlight as well as the Scotch-dripping hi-fied dark—Klonsky himself made 16-year-old time under the boardwalks of Coney Island and Brighton Beach—knew the tough classics instead of the latest Salinger or Hemingway or Graham Greene confection, knew the sharp outlines and brick anatomy of human life in the twentieth (and last! it often seemed) century instead of some wistful-schmaltzy sentimentalization of it." Irving Malin did not include Krim's writing in *Breakthrough*, but he seemed to recognize his mistake decades later when he called Krim "without doubt one of the best writers of that [Beat] generation" (1996, 490).

In the decades since this early 1960s breakthrough period, Jewish fiction has engaged fully with the present reality and been fully embraced. Nonfiction has made less progress. Little nonfiction has been included in recent Jewish anthologies, such as the 2001 *Jewish American Literature: A Norton Anthology*. Perhaps editors feel, with Groucho Marx, that nonfiction is unreliable. In a piece included in Abraham Chapman's *Jewish-American Literature: An Anthology* (1974), Marx maintains that autobiography and truth occupy two separate and opposing camps. "The private thoughts that percolate through the minds of individuals remain in deep, dark recesses and never come to the surface" (1974, 260). That is another point in Krim's favor. He owned up to his experience without evasion. When Krim wrote about his Jewish self, it was on the record.

One of Krim's persistent themes is his childish innocence, which he felt was due to assimilationist social surgery that had early removed something vital and Jewish from his soul. Yet the surgery was not completely successful. Signs of an older, primitive Jewish essence sometimes surfaced. In the spring of 1971, while teaching writing at the University of Iowa, Krim befriended the playwright Kenneth H. Brown, who persuaded Krim to perform a role in a production of Brown's *The Green Room*. Krim's character, called Solomon, was a "contemporary wise man in a small, closed society," wrote Brown. "As rehearsals proceeded, this character emerged from somewhere deep within Krim's being, this medieval Polish Orthodox fellow who wore all the trimmings that announced his religious fervor. Where Krim got the accessories for his costume I never knew, but they showed up on his person like remittances direct from God. By the time the show opened, he was so good at it that you could almost see the Wailing Wall behind him. It was a shame that there was nobody there besides myself who could appreciate it. In the reviews of the play, nobody even mentioned his performance. No one knew what he was doing. There wasn't a Jew for miles around" (Brown 2001, 18).

Rants and Regrets

In the years after his 1974 *You & Me* collection, Krim devoted himself to writing an experimental and epic American prose-poem called *Chaos*. With his 1976 Guggenheim grant, he traveled to all the forty-eight contiguous states to gather material for the proposed 1,000-page work, which strove for a mixed tone of jauntiness and sobriety that Krim in a recorded interview called "drastic fun" (1984). The writing of it took eight years. It was never published. His old friend and Dutton editor Peggy Brooks regarded *Chaos,* also called *Siege,* as a failure. "It was really sort of heartbreaking," Brooks told me. "He wanted something so badly. But it wasn't there on the page." Others disagreed. Krim's friend Morris Renek, a novelist, considered it Krim's masterpiece, and Village activist Nancy Macdonald, wife of intellectual Dwight Macdonald, liked a reading of *Chaos* that she attended. Perhaps she heard these lines about America that attempt to fashion salesman lingo and commercial jingle into literature: "Yes, sure, agreed, decreed!, it's not us alone, the whole planet's speeding like that Friday night bar-fight bleeding in the St. Vince emergency room, but we were the mod pioneers numero uno, we were the first to scream hallelujah on the seats of the human rollercoaster, snap to the pop of a Westinghouse toaster!" (Krim 1991, 178). Six pages of *Chaos* were printed in the posthumous collection *What's This Cat's Story? The Best of Seymour Krim.*

While teaching in Israel on a Fulbright in 1986, Krim suffered a heart attack, and the resulting congestive heart failure continued to weaken him until he could barely rise from a chair (Nicosia 1989, 10). Rather than decline into complete helplessness, Krim planned his own death. But even the prospect of eternity could not lull him into a mood of acceptance and tranquility. When he sent a friend out onto to the streets to buy the barbiturates he needed, the bill appalled him. "Why can't we get a couple of dollars off if we're buying so many?" Krim complained. He committed suicide by overdosing on the too-expensive drugs on August 30, 1989.

It first occurred to me to say that the essays in this book present Krim in his many moods. But that is just a cliché that gets tossed up when the mind spins in a mental rut. Krim had only two moods, rants and regrets, and that volatility is typical of the Jewish-American writer. On the first page of Bellow's first novel, *Dangling Man,* the narrator rejects verbal restraint with a "To hell with that!" Any anthology of Jewish writing could be called "Howl." Bob Dylan captured the condition that led to such outbursts when he sang, "I got a head full of ideas / that are drivin' me insane" (Dylan 1985, 166). But that lyric only tells half the story. The other half is the announcement itself. If you have a head full of ideas that are driving you insane, the cure is to vent them and let them drive someone else insane for a while. And also to get some mileage out of them. Perhaps turn a "small mental profit" (Bellow 1976b, 83). Nobody better captures this state—the insatiable need for release from a mind that won't quit, the unreasonableness, and the desire to turn it all into an acceptable offering that will bring love and success—than Seymour Krim.

All that howling and ranting sooner or later leads to a moment of reckoning, a tallying of the bill, and the total can be staggering. But Jewish-American fiction has done such a good job of documenting the uproarious rants that in spite of itself the regrets are overshadowed. *Portnoy's Complaint* is regret *as* rant, but the rant is what emerges triumphant. Nonfiction has done a better job of forcing readers to take the regrets seriously. Mailer's *Armies of the Night* manages this, and so does James Atlas's biography of Delmore Schwartz and the journalistic Objectivist fiction of Charles Reznikoff's *By the Waters of Manhattan.* So does Krim. One of the great values of Krim's work is that he wrote well about rants *and* regrets, thoughtlessness and thoughtfulness, talking and thinking. On success he could slug out the take-no-prisoners "Making It!" that condemns all compromise made for worldly gain and also, years later, the plaintive "For My Brothers and Sisters in the Failure Business," which admits of more complexity. The same holds true for the intellectuals. "What's *This* Cat's Story?" waves the banner and bangs the drum against New York's Jewish intellectuals. "Remembering Harold Rosenberg" salutes one. When it comes to race, "Anti-Jazz" admits no ambiguity about such identities. "On Being an Anglo" confesses that there is something to be said for role-playing. And as for the Jews, well, when a Kerouac-inspired writer can embrace Dr. Joyce Brothers as a Jewish sister, that is what is called enlightenment.

If Krim could conjure up such high-mindedness for Brothers, Jewish Studies departments should be able to do the same for Krim. The canon always looks complete when someone new shows up. But there is room on the bookshelf. Put him next to another lover of New York, like Louis Lozowick the printmaker, or a journalist like Mark Singer, or the dyspeptic comedian S. J. Perelman, or Nicolas Slonimsky, another self-identified failure, or Greenwich Village veteran Hettie Jones, née Cohen. It doesn't matter where you put him. He won't be comfortable anywhere. But that's how to tell he belongs.

PART ONE

Intellectuals

Chris Felver, Seymour Krim, 1991.
Photograph © Chris Felver.

What's *This* Cat's Story?

When someone finally writes a book about New York's Jewish anti-intellectuals, "What's This Cat's Story?" should get top billing. There has been so much written about New York's Jewish intellectuals—and so much written by them—that the very existence of an anti-intellectual trend among Jewish writers in post–World War II New York is hardly recognized. But in addition to the writers of Partisan Review, Dissent, and Commentary there were Jewish novelists and journalists who found that these intellectual stomping grounds only brought out their desire to stomp intellectuals. Norman Mailer felt that his "deepest detestation was often reserved for the nicest of liberal academics" (1968, 26). Saul Bellow loved the life of the mind but felt that "the intellectuals one meets are something else again" (1976b, 57). And the great New Yorker writer A. J. Liebling loved to sneak in swipes at intellectuals. In one of his boxing pieces he wrote how attending a prizefight and remarking that "[t]hey don't make fighters like Al anymore" marks you as the kind of guy who "enjoys what the fellows who write for quarterlies call a frame of reference" (1982, 17).

This Krim essay is an attack on the bloated language and thinking of New York's Jewish intellectuals, "self-chosen brillianteers." He recalls how he was bullied into adopting that intellectual style until he "sounded and sometimes wrote like a bastard encyclopedia." This essay is Krim's good-bye to all that. It appeared almost simultaneously in 1961 as the opening essay to Krim's Views of a Nearsighted Cannoneer and in Saul Bellow's journal, The Noble Savage. Forty years later Bellow included it in a collection of the best essays he ever published (Bellow 2001, 367–87).

The publication of this book of pieces—actually grapplings with life, desperate bids for beauty and truth and the slaking of personal need, hot mortal telegrams from writer to reader however disguised by subject matter which seems to be at a remove—marks the end of a long shipwrecked journey for me and the beginning of a new one. I am going to try and devote the writing time left to the more openly and explicitly creative expression that I always wanted to do from the age of 17 to 37. After literally 20 lousy years of doubting, agonizing, poeticizing, speculating, criticizing, fantasying, I still do not know whether this work will be the traditional novel or play or a necessity-inspired homemade form of my own invention—yet I must bring it into being or my tumultuous days will have been wasted in cowardly amateurism.

But I had to live through two decades of the wildest confusion to reach this firing-line of commitment. I traveled all the byways and intellectual traps of contemporary literary life to arrive where I should have begun—and that is by coming on with every ounce of everything you've got—but I hope to put the experience of this nightmarish pilgrimage into my work. Not hope to. I have to (and since it is now part of me it will come out regardless) for my mess was not unique and is almost a typical blood-specimen of what the majority of us late 30ish, serious and intense artist-types have gone through in an effort to define ourselves and our way.

Let me start at the beginning. I had always wanted to write ever since the age of 13 and followed the usual pattern gone through by a dozen of my friends in the same line. Namely writing for the highschool magazine (in my case the DeWitt Clinton *Magpie* up in the Bronx), co-editing a mimeographed literary sheet called *expression* (man, were we swingingly lowercase back in 1939!) because of the kid-stuff in the official one and getting temporarily kicked out of highschool for selling it in the john, then going on to college (I deliberately followed Thomas Wolfe's big romantic boots to the University of North Carolina) and writing for the magazine there. Then after quitting college I returned to New York and had the usual erratic round of uptown editorial jobs: editing a Western pulp magazine, working as a snotty silly kid reporter on *The New Yorker*, ducking the war in the OWI writing publicity for Paramount

Pictures,[1] writing the commentary for a newsreel (a job handed to me by the stylish poet-painter Weldon Kees who is presumed to have committed suicide in San Francisco several years ago although his body was never recovered from the Bay) and living off the advance for a novel that I never finished in the posh 1947 days when Don Congdon was giving away Simon & Schuster's money to young writers. He had come over from *Collier's* as their whizbang boy editor and I plus a few of my friends managed to get in line for the $1200 advance-money handout.

In case you know little or nothing about how American writers live (which includes the various art-sanitariums or retreats like Yaddo and the Huntington Hartford Foundation where I and my brother pack of hungry art-wolves made the free scene for wasted months at a time) the above is average until the writer unwinds and starts turning out the novels and stories that he presumably wants to. But I never unwound. I had natural sock as a storyteller and was precociously good at description, dialogue and most of the other staples of the fiction-writer's trade, but I was bugged by a mammoth complex of thoughts and feelings that prevented me from doing more than just diddling the surface of sustained fiction-writing. Much of this was personal; some of it was due to the highly critical (how can you write when you haven't read *Bartleby the Scrivener?* etc.) period I came of age in; and some of it was due to grave troubled doubts I had that the novel as a form had outlived its vital meaning and was being perpetuated by the dishonesty and lack of imagination of its practitioners. Taken together all these facts threw me off the narrowly uncertain balance I had to begin with and sent me shuddering down the tunnels of introspection and cosmic-type thought that more or less paralyzed me for a decade; until I finally vomited up my wretched life and found myself no longer even an amateur writer but a bona fide all-American-1-out-of-every-16 psychotic.

During this period of so-called paralysis—for it was that as far as the no-crapping-around, basic, definite creative birth of an *object* was concerned—I sought out the best intellectual minds I knew and absorbed, absorbed, argued, learned, was criticized, and finally found myself

---

1. OWI is the Office of War Information.

turning to literary criticism as a way of writing and thinking. Behind this choice-necessity (for I desperately needed some way to express even a little of myself and with it a mental center from which to operate) lay my painstaking conscious effort to think through literary problems that before I had instinctively sensed. But by now my self-conscious intellectual glands had become immensely swollen as a result of the people I hung around with and at the age of 28 or so I could no more go back to my former glorious naïve conception of "the writer" than to knickers.

My most articulate friends were Jewish intellectuals (I'm Jewish but not a card-carrying intellectual) and they made me toe the ideational line like a spinster aunt going over her maid's cleaning with a white glove poised for dust. I was not permitted the excesses or romanticism I had kidded myself with before and if life were eternal this education would be recommended by me as a must for any kind of mature achievement. But life is lived in time, time is short and the burden of mortality is heavy, and a writer has only so much to say and should get to it without wasting his precious (to him) hours with scanning the heavens when his fly needs buttoning.

I didn't know this during those days in the Village in the early 1940s when I was part of a highly intellectual but not necessarily artistic group of brilliant minds which roved with barely believable and almost illegal freedom over the entire domain of the thinkable and utterable. Some of these minds—like Isaac Rosenfeld, Dave Bazelon, Manny Farber, Weldon Kees, Willie Poster, Chandler Brossard, Anatole Broyard (plus the occasional appearances of Saul Bellow, Delmore Schwartz, Alfred Kazin, James Agee) and the inimitable Milton Klonsky—were in literature partially or completely; some—like Will Barrett, Herb Poster, Clem Greenberg—were more interested in "ideas" than expression. All of us were broadly part of the *Partisan Review* and *Commentary* worlds where ex-Trotskyites, ex-anarchists, ex-Stalinists (everybody seemed to be an "ex" something) mingled with fancy Ph.D.s and metaphysical poets to produce that modern eclectic monster who is as much at home with surrealist poetry as British radical politics, with baseball and boxing (the big sport for intellectuals then) as the foolproof technique for banging a girl. There was a tremendous charge in all this to me when I was accepted into the group and soon I was trying to graft this interstellar burst of new ideas onto the emotional-instinctual drive of my being that had originally led me to want to be a writer.

Ideas are wonderfully fecund but they can be bait for ruin and the most miserable self-deception unless the party involved is modest and selective; I was neither; I wanted to swallow the entire fucking world and spit it out again not merely as an artist but as some kind of literary-human-intellectual God. What had happened was that my imagination, which coupled with experience is the source of fiction, took the implications of these (to me) new ideas and lifted them within my mind to extravagant heights buoyed up by the very helium of fantasy and inventiveness which—if channeled differently—could have made a modest career for itself writing novels. I had come from an entirely different background and self-taught tradition when I got my intellectual initiation in the early 40s; I was intelligent enough but my touchstones until then had been strictly literature and, humanly enough, American literature (because that was what I wanted to write).

But overnight it seems I became internationalized. I saw how parochial my small Hemingway-Wolfe-Dreiser-Faulkner standards were in the midst of these swinging world-dominating intellects and I was put in the impossible position of trying to write a piece of emotionally real description about some homely thing that happened to me and relate it to the interplanetary discussion I'd had the night before (tea-high, shouting, yelling, laughing, ideas zooming, then falling into Ratner's at 3 A.M. for chopped eggs-and-onions) on Joyce, Trotsky and (yeah my dear Klonsky!) the poetry of Marvell. This contradiction between my own small hut of experience and the skyscrapers of new thought obviously cut deeper than just literature. Soon I was spinning like a human top as a result of this fantastic dazzle of diamond-bright gab and revelation and almost every standard I had previously thought was impregnable began to crumble the longer I looked at it. I didn't know then that this is the fascinating, tempting, delusory (I'm learning! I'm growing! I'm developing!) thruway to nowhere and that self-providential man was made to draw the line when common sense flashes its light.

Some of this interpenetration of ideas into literature now seems to me inevitable in this high-questioning time of ours but its accommodation in the mind and the relating of its parts will faze even the most selective intellects, let alone untrained ones like mine was; it is inhumanly tough to think your way through the skein of the world today; but what I didn't know in the early 1940s is that nothing valid or true is ever cancelled out—you can add to it or increase its significance with resonant symbolism if you know exactly what you're doing, but even the most peasantlike or humble truth remains a grain of gold and therefore a plus factor in the world. I had stubbornly hung onto my faith in basic truths all through this tour of the upper atmosphere but I recognized many new truths as well that had been offered me through electric interchange with more refined and knowing minds, and the tragedy as I see it was that I was helpless to put them together and too proud to do the menial work I was sure of until I realistically outgrew it.

2

The phantom of great European-inspired ambition drove all of us in my group to the most miserable heights and voids of despair, like Hitlers in our own mad little Berchtesgadens; the reader shouldn't forget that the casual small talk of the people I greedily learned from was Kierkegaard, Kafka, Melville, Blake, Lawrence (Joyce was considered a misguided second-rater) and with such standards running wild and demonic in our lusting heads there can be little wonder that some of us cracked under the intense pressure we placed on ourselves or died (perhaps there is no direct provable connection but the deaths included Isaac Rosenfeld, the very well-thought-of Bob Warshow, my editor at *Commentary*, James Agee, Kees's and just recently his good friend Willie Poster's suicide) or sucked nightly on Christ's vinegar sponge because we could never attain the impossible.

Driven by this illusion of great power and omniscience—getting daily more intoxicated by handling the tools of thought which made mincemeat out of famous names admired by the square public—I aggressively moved over the line into book reviewing. Marjorie Farber, a peripheral member of our group and then an assistant editor of the *New York Times Book Review,* eased me into the Sunday section in 1947 and I showed off in print like a cramped colt led out onto a fast track. I was never completely at home in book reviewing and literary criticism during my 12 years doing this kind of writing (although I think I brought to certain novelists the insight that could only have come from a constipated brother) but it became an ego-habit. Having tasted the blood of print I couldn't stop; criticism was very much in the air, was hip, impressive, the sign of rank, fiction was for brainless impressionists (thus ran my snobbery), and even though I felt split about reviewing from the start and kept telling myself it was only a temporary filler the drug of seeing my glistening thoughts in print hooked me and I didn't have the courage to stop.

I felt I had to keep writing for publication (you've got to be printed no matter what or howl—young writers will recognize that junkie urgency) while I sweated out the private war of trying to reach a unity between my experience and the murderously suggestive new ideas that were being fired at me and even beginning to shoot up of their own accord in my head. My dream was to make a peace finally between my imagination-experience and these foaming ideas and out of this come forth with a high art of my own making which would combine the sensuousness of great literary style with the startlingness of an unprecedented approach. It would come, it would come—I *knew* it (in my blindness). Meanwhile reviewing was the only way I could almost consistently get printed although later on I was to experience, along with others, the regarding of a book review as a finely wrought poem by neurotic and snob-conscious editors: this made and makes reviewers overwrite and overstate their case to glitter more flashily than the competition and I too was to be such a shameless shimmy-dancer after suffering my share of rejections.

But at this point I moved on to *Commonweal* because they then had a tolerant and sympathetic book editor named Bill Clancy, who sensed I was not a native or orthodox critic but nevertheless brought out of me some of the best I could do because he had a taste for fullness of expression rather than the narrower, stricter conception of criticism then at its height (more or less going back to T. S. Eliot and made into a very subtle instrument by the scholarly Blackmurs, Tates, Ransom, Trilling, so forth). Along with *Commonweal* I began to hit *Commentary* and had one small piece in *Partisan Review*—both places then giving the avant young writer the most superior feelings of having made it for keeps when actually he was copying his elders' manner in most cases and being dishonest to himself and his own generation in the way he expressed himself.

I was never comfortable at *Commentary,* which I felt then and feel today can be no true ally of literature because it has to watch its step like a nearsighted cripple with asthma, as far as what it publishes; it is sponsored by and beholden to the American Jewish Committee and tries to navigate a course between the impossibles of freedom and a cautious, worrying, ingroupy conception of "responsibility" (translation: the current line of the New York radical-highbrow corporation which loves to be sentimentally eloquent about avantgarde heroes after they're dead and helps freeze them out when alive because their black charm never fits the latest abstract recipe for profundity). Even writing for a Roman Catholic magazine like *Commonweal* I literally had much more freedom of expression than in *Commentary,* where I and a number of writers I know have had their most felt thoughts squeezed into grey lines of qualification, humorlessness, overediting, unoriginality, by the staff's tiptoeing fear of making a booboo. It took the *life* out of a young American-Jewish writer to do a piece for them—the ton of worry that preyed on you when you sat down to the machine made sunny days automatically gloom-ridden—and the eventual non-you solidity that could ultimately be wrung out (after 6 rewritings) by knowing their Teutonic idea of a distinguished piece of work was not compensated for by the crucifixion of self and the joylessness of the writing. It was truly immoral to the whole act of writing. *Commentary,* taking its cues from the universities and the various respectable academic and/or ex-radical pros like Richard Chase, the Trillings, William Phillips, Leslie Fiedler, Dwight Macdonald, became a suburb of *PR* in literary evaluation and both magazines were sewed up with *reactionary* what-will-T. S. Eliot-or-Martin Buber-think timidity as far as the natural roaring young independent went. I feel sorry (premature as it may read to some who feel only the competitive sweat and panting breath of the race) for the hotshot young critics today like my friend Podhoretz, Steven Marcus, the various smoothie sons of the older literary generation who were taken or foolishly slicked their way into the smart-money fold. Unless they chafe now and discover their own style, thoughts, even magazines, they will not speak to me or for me in the wideopen days of the future that lie ahead. And it will be our mutual loss for we are of the same generation and face the same problems, as their benefactors do not.

As for the influence of *Partisan Review* on American writing during this time in which I was trying to establish myself assbackwards I will say nothing: it has lost its impact today for the whole beat shocktroop of young expressors, as historically it had to and humanly it was fated to, and tried to span the world at the dreadful cost of patronizing (not caring enough, being too snob-clannish, overcerebral, Europeanish, sterilely citified, pretentiously alienated) its own country and the terrific reality of our life here. Factually it led writers to more disappointment—overevaluation of themselves, illusion, smugness, fancying they were extraordinary philosophers or prophets when they were just ultra-sensitive Americans who didn't always write well in their own language—than it ever saved or gave a point of view to. But it was the creation of a monstrously inflated period wherein it thought it had to synthesize literature and politics and avantgarde art of every kind, with its writers insanely trying to outdo each other in Spenglerian inclusiveness of vision. Yet it obviously printed many significant things and there was no place quite like it; and in my circle it was a hip badge of prestige and real in-ness to appear in its elephantinely big-gun pages. For people of my age and bent however the whole *PR* phenomenon along with the *Kenyon Review,* the *Sewanee,* the *Hudson Review* (to be discussed more closely) and all the others unfertilized into being by the Anglo-Protestant New Critical chill was a very bad, inhibiting, distorting, freakish influence. It made us ashamed to be what we were and the cruel acid of its standards tore through our writing and scarred our lives as well; in our prose we had to put on Englishy airs, affect all sorts of impressive scholarship and social-register unnaturalness and in general contort ourselves into literary pretzels in order to slip through their narrow transoms and get into their pages. Sometimes I got the impression that the editors of these magazines wanted to relax the entire torture-chamber that literature had become but didn't know where to begin. Whether I was right or wrong this masquerade obviously prevented direct writing for most of the perspiringly overwrought contributors and became a weighty, suspicious bore for the normally intelligent reader who couldn't rationalize it the way the insiders did.

By now as far as my so-called career was going in my late 20s and early 30s I was publishing an occasional short story and gaining a small steady reputation as a good critic—not a brilliant textual beagle or a conceptual Coleridgeian literature-shaker but unanonymous enough for a few party-met strangers to know my name and work. In spite of the kick of this I hated the critical reputation (a kid in the White Horse Tavern one night shouted out in a beer-voice that "Krim is one of the best critics in America!" and even though I knew this was a tight-type exaggeration meant to please me I suddenly felt that my very being was a sham) because I knew it was horribly unfair to my truer, realer imaginative bounce as a writer; what I didn't know was that each time I dug into myself to try and write an "important" piece of criticism—and even succeeded to some extent in pieces on Wolfe, Dreiser, Hemingway, Edmund Wilson, Whitman, etc.—I was committing myself to impossibly high standards that made me feel less like giving out with my own untested jazz than ever. I was weekly and monthly killing the best part of myself; setting up endless self-defeating dialogues and fancy but illogical rationalizations within; squirming always in the pain and defensiveness that goes with cheating the self of what it really wants and all for the perverted boot of being a small Name on the scene and keeping your hand in the pussy of even petty success, no matter what. Seen coolly it was disgusting self-murder but there was no one to tell me this because almost all of my friends were caught up in the same narrow pocket, becoming increasingly more exacting, fussy, competitive, fanatical, less human in their writing and standards.

3

I should have gotten out of criticism, said to hell with it, but one turned scared at the thought because where could you go? Until the beats came along and revived through mere power and abandonment and the unwillingness to commit death in life some idea of a decent equivalent between verbal expression and actual experience, the "serious" New York literary scene was becoming a prison, to the point of shutting off the real, gamey, lowdown communication that must go into writing if it's to have even as much meaning as the telephone. But such obvious realism was of no interest to me then. I was hooked in the life, as hustlers say, and even though I knew it was fundamentally wrong for me I felt I had to follow through until my creative work "matured" (illusion! perfumed bullshit!) and swept me off the bed of nails that criticism had become.

I was afraid to quit because then I would have nothing except the crumbs of the very few short stories I had managed to grind out. Thus I graduated to the *Hudson Review,* the very latest and coolest and most technical of the swank highbrow quarterlies. My editor was Fred Morgan, Park Avenue and Princeton, and even though the money-family thing is not one of my comes I strutted a little within to find myself in such Fortune-acknowledged (the name, the loot, the leather-binding-mono-grammed-cocktail-glass-old-print montage) company and able to hold my own. On the cover of the *Hudson Review* were the names that impressed all of us (Yvor Winters, R. P. Blackmur, Ezra Pound, Robert Graves, Wallace Stevens) and I was now to be among them. So I punished myself to produce a couple of critiques that whatever their merit had no relationship in the pain of composition to what I could have said given the encouragement to loosen up, be real, fail richly rather than succeed as a miser and a tightrope-walker. I succeeded and became one of the *Hudson's* second-string boys until I lost favor, but in so doing I again made a cramped miniature of my spirit, chorus-lined my self-respect, tidied up my originality, emasculated my real iconoclasm. I was sucking the sugar-tit of local snob success and didn't want to let go for nothin, momma, not even the cry of perplexity and sadness that came up from the being of the man who had once wanted to be a big stubborn writer in the grand tradition that laid waste to crap and lying everywhere.

Fred Morgan, co-founder and editor of the *Hudson Review,* was and is a formal decent guy (approximately my age), particularly so in view of the heavy-moneyed life he had to duel with to find a way of his own; but his allegiance to his near literary fathers—Blackmur, John Crowe Ransom, Eliot, Pound, the whole over-studied list of recent saints who are not guides for *today* and should never have been sanctified since literature is no church—made him uneasy among the very equals in age and experience whom he should have embraced. The young need the young more than they need the old and honored; great writers take care of themselves and don't need monuments and schools since their influence is always present;

but the brilliant kid writer can be crushed or turned into a foolish acrobat unless he gets an enthusiastic response from his own contemporaries, not elders whom he has sensible mixed feelings about no matter how concerned they are. Love your own kind and the love and faith of even your enemies will eventually come to you! But if you choose instead to rely on the judgment and values of another generation as I think Morgan did—out of caution and over-respect and measuring his qualities against theirs as if they were the standard—you will inhibit your most vital contemporaries and get their most studied showoff writing, not their best. An editor's spiritual job (and I have had two excellent ones, Bill Clancy and Jerry Tallmer of the *Village Voice*) is to inspire the writer to top himself with each new effort and this is done by the writer's knowing the editor has complete confidence in him. An editor who has no confidence in a writer should tell him so very early in the relationship so that both can relax. Tact in this very close business is much less important than faith and eventually degenerates into hostility and an insecurity that ruins the writer's relationship to his work: show the writer you are completely behind him or very early in this tight intimacy have the courage to be frank. But all of this implies a security of belief and a personal four-squareness (or four-hipness) which in this time of upset and fear and daily reversals of personality is uncommon.

In this way did I fitfully work, masochistically and unjustly spending whatever was precious within me on criticism—I'll show these intellectual pace-setters I can lick them at their own game!—when I wanted desperately to return to the blast-furnace of open creativity. But, went my inner monologue, what *is* creativity in this time? Semantically the word means "to bring into being, to cause to exist." Didn't an insight—ah how we loved insights and illuminations in my old gang!—bring a new thought into being, wasn't a thought a window into reality, and didn't ever new truths about this vast clutch called existence mean that you were doing the holiest work you could? It was not only rationalizations like that which kept me and mine ("I write criticism like hammered steel," one poet who wrote comparatively little poetry told me proudly) chained to critical-analytical prose; it was basically a passionate sense of *intellectual superiority,* a fanatical personal pride that used the mind and its accomplishments as the test for true aristocracy in the modern world. I formerly had believed in the aristocracy of the novel; but in this community of hip intellectuals I was justly in their eyes a *naïf.* I reformed to my ultimate personal unhappiness. I fell in stride, saw or tried mightily to see a more subtle and extensive creativity in criticism, shaped and directed my protesting mind into abstract ideas and became another of the young avantgarde gigolos who moved with patent-leather nonchalance from French symbolist poetry to philosophy to psychiatry to—you name it.

I had become a contemporary intellectual in the eyes of my pleased older friends, which meant in the scheme of values implicitly held by us a suave masterspeaker (and theoretically thinker) in practically all literary and ideological fields. In simple actuality I didn't have the formal training for this glib seasoned role nor could any of my friends have had as much background as they would have needed; yet when we picked up a copy of *PR* and saw (or wrote!) an essay on Toynbee next to one on Wallace Stevens, followed by one of Robert Lowell's obscure early poems, it was necessary to keep up both to oneself and the killing standards of the superintellectual community by patiently tackling and understanding each of these works. I drove my mind to *inhuman lengths* to absorb and make mine each of these different offerings until I later sounded and sometimes wrote like a bastard encyclopedia. In the meantime my brain had the impossible task of trying to integrate this deluge of suggestive, often profound thought with my personal experience and the vivid fantasy-life of the potential novelist; because I was stubborn I kept adding the one on top of the other without restraint until I too thought I carried the entire world in my head and felt that I was the living embodiment of the modern god-writer, the omniscient one, the heir of all the ages and the true king of the present— out of my way slobs!

I now come to an unpopular topic but one that has to be opened up. Most of my friends and I were Jewish; we were also literary; the combination of the Jewish intellectual tradition and the sensibility needed to be a writer created in my circle the most potent and incredible intellectual-literary ambition I have ever seen. Within themselves, just as people, my friends were often tortured and unappeasably bitter about being the offspring of this unhappily unique-ingrown-screwed-up breed; their reading and thinking gave extension to their normal blushes about appearing "Jewish" in subway, bus, race track, movie house, any of the public places that used to make the New York Jew of my generation self-conscious (heavy thinkers walking across 7th Avenue without their glasses on, willing to dare the trucks as long as they didn't look like the caricature of the Yiddish intellectual); thus the simple fact of being Jewish when fused to the literary imagination gave a height and fantastic urge to our minds which outran reason. I may be reducing the many causes for the terrible display of intellectual egomania to a too-simple basic source—for surely the over-worshipped genius-standards of the literary climate as a whole goosed the entire phenomenon—but if I can generalize on the basis of my own experience it was the ceaseless knowledge of knowing you could never erase this brand of being that drove us mentally upward without rest.

We were Americans who loved our country and its experience (being writers who thrive off the real) but we were also Jews who because of Christian society's traditional suspicion and our own heartbreaking self-awareness became almost fanatical within ourselves to try and triumph over this blotch of birth by transcending it in brilliant individualism. It was an immodesty born of existential necessity and it was reinforced (as I've said) by the constant references in the conversation of my group, in *PR*, in *Commentary* and the other reviews, to none but the highest figures in Western literature-art-thought. When I relive it in my mind now it seems like a hallucination but it was a specifically real personal and cultural fact; and it is being carried on to this very day in determinedly intellectual New York quarters that seem ultra-responsible from the outside but in fact are crippling natural genuine expression by their cruelly ambitious standards—born in this case out of the soul-pain of a hooked beak and a dead uncaring Jewish God who left the mess stamped on our faces and beings, and neurotically spread from there into a grim literary puritanism that uses the name of reason but not its pure spirit.

4

It is ironic that what was once an unquestioned good—such as the high-brow magazines printing nothing but the best, most honest, most imaginative non-commercial literature and criticism—became a 90 percent

disaster. It encouraged, not fulfillment of writing ability on the just level
that the guy had in him, but a competition with the heroes of the past and
present that placed inhuman pressure on the vulnerable young writer. If
he couldn't be "great" in the sense of the over-reverenced Eliots, Yeatses,
Prousts, Joyces, Kafkas (the chief figure in my group) he felt like a failure in the airless climate in which we all sweated. I knew gifted, fresh,
swinging writers who told me in moments of confidence that they knew
they weren't "great" or "major" and their voices were futile with flat tone
when they confessed this supposed weakness: as if the personal horn each
could blow was meaningless because history wasn't going to faint over
them. History, the god of my grotesque period, the pursued phantom, the
ruby-circled mirror of our me-worshipping egos which made monoma-
niacal fanatics out of potentially decent men! I found in my group that
this sense of measuring yourself against history prevented the best talents
from opening up and developing as only the practicing writer can—by
publishing and exposing his work to other human beings, the public so-
called. The self-deceiving chic snobgod of genius—reinforced as I've said
by obsessive references to only the giants of literature and thought—grew
like a tumor in the minds of myself and my friends and infected us in a
sterile self-deifying way. In many cases including my own it prevented the
writer from penetrating his own special vein of material, developing his
own point of view, becoming adult and realistic about the tangible earthly
tricks of his craft. Much of this fundamental understructure was snottily
put down and dismissed next to the tremendous ego-thrilling zoom of
loading one's work with "great" or hidden meaning. Atlas-like trying to lift
the most commonplace material to an almost religious or epical height.

I can't stress strongly enough the insecurity that was put *into* the
naturally talented writer with a feeling for people and story and good
dialogue by such a Kafka (scripture)-quoting, perfectionist environment
as the one I both wrote for and lived in. To be profound was not only a
value in this world, it was almost a necessary card of admission; it was
as if a person who had the wit to be intelligent should realize that the
age demanded nothing less than genius as the bare minimum, and good
taste itself required at least brilliance. As I look back on it now from the
vantage-point of what I have been through it seems that our demands on

life itself had gotten dementedly out of hand, for even a half-dozen of the most original works of the century—which my group did not and will not produce—could not have justified the height of our arrogance or the depth of our frustration which was caused by this sleepless mental anguish (like a drill on a New York street) to produce works that would shake the world and crown ourselves. The conceit of man, I have reason to know, is boundless. A naïvete about the limits of human nature plus a riotous intellectual ambition—encouraged by the top-heavy literary reviews who with each issue salted the bitter wound that Man wasn't yet God, what a drag!—helped cook more lives and work during this period than it ever aided or inspired. In fact it uninspired, depleted, broke down, de-balled the very work it was theoretically supposed to encourage.

Concentratedly put, what had happened was that each outstanding single achievement of the recent past—by a D. H. Lawrence, Picasso, Stravinsky, Gerard Manley Hopkins, Melville—was linked with the other to create a vocabulary of modernity; familiarity with great work was as casually expected of a person as familiarity with the daily paper; combined this stitching-together of extraordinary achievement provided the background for all conversation, friendships, feuds, affairs, and such things as status in a livingroom or victory in argument were dependent on one's knowledge of the new Hip Bible of greatness. In other words, this acquaintance with greatness was turned into serviceability; and this serviceability took the form of coming out of the mouth at gatherings where it was used as a weapon for personal advantage by highly articulate and severely critical intellectuals. And in this arena I nursed my private dreams of writing—not talking. Yet verbal aggressiveness, mental agility in conversation, knowledge and insight as shown by the deftness with which they sprang to the lips, were actually much more valued among my friends than literary originality, which took grubby hard work and had to be done without glitter in private. The stuttering crudenik who couldn't come on in public and didn't understand or like Kafka—but who had a small, hard, true American imagination of his own sans the big-city vocabulary of genius—would have been slaughtered if he stuck his head in a jumping livingroom where my teachers and I mapped and remapped the world by the second.

To make an enormously charged, complicated, dizzying long story short, mine was as severe a critical-intellectual environment as can be imagined and being without true shape or definition as a writer (except for my stubborn urge to weave a unity between my actual experience and these new dimensions of abstract thought) I was strongly influenced by my friends. I put aside and did not develop my storytelling abilities—in fact they began to seem as I've said simple-minded to me—and got in ever deeper into the speculative manipulation of ideas. In the meantime, in the hours before sleeping so to speak, I would torment myself with those vain attempts to make a bridge between my newly found critical hipness and the emotional-experiential material that was begging for release and could only get out by working its way into my criticism—sometimes rawly. If I had been more restrained in my own ambition and more sure of the worth of what I had to communicate as a mere human-type writer, I would have been less knotted and uncertain about what to do. But all of the minds I most respected were almost without exception (one was the writer Michael Seide, not a member of my "group") as omnivorous in their intellectual greed and *not one* ever bothered to take me aside and say: "Why not be truly original Krim by cultivating your own natural garden and doing some accurate limited work that is right under your nose."

It wasn't until I was 33 and had to scream my way to the inevitable climax of all the foregoing inner-wrestling, doubt, confusion, backtracking, fantastic imprisonment, the me-self dying for release—not until I spewed up every hunk of undigested matter in my psyche and bloodily broke through to my own raw meat via the whistling rocket-ride of what is called insanity—that I began to think for myself because I had to. Man, this wasn't any bullshit about beautiful words and dream-masterpieces anymore—this was life and death and all that cellar-deep jazz! It was difficult to swallow the fact that I probably would not be a great writer because not only had I envisioned (in fact known!) that this would eventually come true, a few people had even used the magic word during my 20's and I graciously took it in stride. It was just a question of time I then thought, and in the meantime Time was ticking away and I was caught in the same vapor of twists and doubts that I'd been in since my early 20's: imagining a revolutionary prose in my mind while doing criticism for my ego's bread. But when I almost threw the switch during the sui-cidal depression that followed the revolt against my frustrations—then pulled myself out of it—it seemed stupid from that time onward to revert to such hypocrisy as keeping up an act as far as writing went. The criti-cism I did after this was much more straight and finally led to the series of controversial but definitely more initiative-taking articles which I did for the *Village Voice* (1957–1959) and *Exodus* (1959–1960). The cover-up of a stilted conception of writing always rips under the unshavable hairs on the dogged face of life.

5

I stand now at the end of any pretense with formal literary criticism (even if busted in pocket and adulation and blocked on my own road) but I will carry with me always the infection with ideas that no one in my environ-ment escaped. When today I feel overextended and almost drowning in the sea of speculative thought—hangover from endless nights spinning the world with my brother-gods in the most brilliant untaped talk of the cen-tury—and know I must call a halt for my own preservation, then does the commonsense of Gertrude Stein's shrewd remark strike home every time:

> I know that one of the most profoundly exciting moments of my life was when at about 16 I suddenly concluded that I would not make all knowl-edge my province.

But this kind of focused chastity can only be a pastoral memory for me and mine—the seeds of oceanic thought were sown too beautifully in the ripest season and we must struggle with the bastard harvest in our heads. It is too late to duck the responsibility for what we so super-humanly craved; to wipe out the engrams grooved in our brains would need a Frankenstein-type operation. We became what we admired, in that joke of jokes always heaped on sinners who now pray for a leaner diet. Yet should such a communication as this be dug up in a future period I would insist that the reader try and appreciate how extravagant the whole con-ception of making volume-long outsmarting footnotes to the writings of others became, how superior to the unclothed novelist or poet the shrewd parasitic critic normally felt because of his safe armchair perspective (*sub specie aeternitatis* my ass—he was wielding power and making the law!). It was a period and still is in some dated quarters where the display of Mind—disembodied from its blistered feet, overloaded, speaking a language unlike the language of regular life—snubbed the value of imagination and offbeatness and found it juvenile or irrational because it met no preconceptions. The haughtily articulate became a hard iron criterion to hang onto because of the threat of the unknown in a time that was subterraneanly groaning in labor; university-groomed fraidycats clutched this rehearsed script with fear or at least insecurity and defensively called it Reason; and those of us who finally rebelled and refused to punish our beings any longer in imitation of this perversion of truth became ultimately what we had always secretly wanted to be—individuals thrown back on our own clumsy resources, free to err, live, die, speak the truth or a half-truth or a lie, but free baby free!

In the world I lived in the greatest applause went to those critical writers who traced out what were called original ideas; the entire notion of originality was drained out of explicitly creative writing and put into under-glass exegesis, where the critic could fly to the moon without risk or croon masturbatorily over the courage and demonism of a Dostoevsky but jump five feet if he met it in present-day life. (It was peculiar but sad: originality was the big kick, it was worshipped because of the gallery of approved modern heroes and the critics tried to duplicate it in the realm of ideas, but it was feared and dismissed close up if it was *unfamiliar* as it had to be.) Meanwhile in this artificial reality-denying paradise mere Somerset Maughamish competence in writing was looked down upon as a value crappily pedestrian and unchic. Mediocrity became the most disgusting enemy of this highly cerebral avantgarde *in theory,* with few realizing that they were installing a gorgeous new mediocrity (or orthodoxy) of the so-called alienated modern saints which inhibited and killed the genuine if crude life-reaching around them.

My style as man and writer was shaped by the prevailing superior tone of this straining decade and even the swinging creative work that I hope to do will never entirely shake off the odor of condescension and literary verbalism that was the norm in my circle. It is a fairly subtle distinction that I would like to make here—but the fact is that even if one of us self-chosen brillianteers wasn't natively the most gifted mind or writer ever to land on earth the *style* we expressed ourselves in *had* to be extraordinarily intelligent-sounding as a matter of duty. If you see it through my eyes for a moment you will realize that this injunction to be brilliant meant that natural flashes of illumination had to be hardened, that the posture of abnormally high intelligence had to be maintained at all cost if you were to hold your head high to self or others.

But what ultimately happened was that this emphasis on rare theoretical intelligence lost its value under the impact of life itself. Men and women who had trained themselves to be profound found in later years that they did this at the sacrifice of their total personalities and had repressed certain urges and over-evaluated others to their final literary frustration and personal unhappiness. Real life as it is lived in this time must inevitably influence those who would shut it out and *all of us* from my group have been justly lowered in our appreciation of ourselves and—if my experience is any judge—more respectful of the power of brute 1960 human reality than in its fancy intellectual transcendence. If extreme cerebration was part of the mental manners of my period, one shouldn't forget that a needy and sometimes adolescent romanticism was hidden beneath this fascinating agility with ideas; the desperate and often simple needs of the soul went on as they always do, under and quite disproportionate to the big ideas that were borne aloft on the fuel of fanatical ambition. I found in myself that I gave mental size to emotions that in themselves weren't worth it out of a need and desire to impress my Village scene with the image of my worth—converting bits of trivia into big-sounding phrases that used our mutual vocabulary and hence were kosher, no matter how intrinsically minor or childish the emotion was in itself. I'm sure my friends were guilty of the same distortion to some extent.

The path ahead is hardly an easy one for me now. Nor would it be for anyone who came from the intellectual-literary electric chair that high-voltaged me or had for years (as I did) judged and fantasied himself in the platinum currency of literary greatness that was tossed around like pennies by my friends and the magazines we wrote for. In a real way—assuming I had the choice which I don't—it is not greatness that I want now; my heart and mind are tired of the inhuman selfishness and egomania that I associated with its self-conscious quest. In itself it has lost its value for me, completely unlike what I would have imagined 10 or even 5 years ago. I realize of course that the choice is ultimately nature's and not one's own but having lived among superlatives for so long I am weary of pursuing what is not necessary. The talking and thinking in nothing but extraordinary, grand, complex and mentally suffocating terms for so many years has taken away my appetite for self-willed genius and made me doubt the value of the entire genius-concept for this time—which reeks with such self-idealization because of *personal identification* with the stars who make up the avantgarde constellation. I can never forget that so much of the pompous inflation of myself and my literary buddies came from just this injustice to the present by injecting the most pretentious traditions of the past onto a scene that is made on a different scale and should have been treated in a more direct, informal, speedy way, without the stiffness and Europeanisms that exaggerated the self-evident and prevented sexy vital American pace from busting out. (Nothing can speak for itself like what is, with the exactness, punch and accent that an unbugged, unproving-anything natural writer can lay down.)

The writing I want to do now is inspired by the pertinent, the immediate, the actual of this very minute; that would be sufficient greatness for me if I can give it full voice. My longtime secret dream of a consciously heroic style and attitude toward American experience which I envisioned as being legendarily all-inclusive and Proustian-Whitmanesque (a conception of mine for one monumental-type grand work which I lovingly nursed through the years) has been ground down by the steel heel of present-day necessity into a keener point and I am grateful now to be given a second chance to gun out some leveler messages about reality. It's the old story: the overthrow of unattainable or perfectionist ambition is the most freeing thing that can happen to a writer for it unlatches him to write what he believes in without strain and with humming conviction.

I believe my imagination is still my most unique possession as a writer and I want to use it to its uttermost to make such creations out of the life of my time as I am particularly geared to do. The critical form which I forced myself to approximate over the years has left its cast on my mind for good, but I have learned or am learning how to cut its magisterial bondage to "judiciousness" and "responsibility"—believe me there is deeper responsibility in the human soul than playing supreme court justice and that is to make the things that others can judge!—and use whatever organizational, reasonable, analytical powers it brought out as the mere mucilage to hold living thoughts together. I remember the ironic inner laugh I had recently when a good but literarily unsophisticated friend defined me to my face as a "Jewish intellectual" rather than a Jewish *writer*—ay, the stamp has probably taken permanently despite all of my protests and the attempt I have made here to show the way in which my innocence was raped (willingly) by the obviousness of intellect instead of the subtlety of soul. We violate ourselves ultimately and much as I can point factually to the historical period that over-evaluated abstract articulateness and lured me into imitating its way (thank stubbornness my voice had its own concrete human sound at times) it was the mush of my own being that permitted this plastic surgery in the image of what was outwardly impressive.

I can only trust now to remake myself as a writer in the light of the truths that I can clearly see are *mine,* won by experience and temperament and personal vision, without forcing myself to engorge the thoughts of a thousand other minds or mind-binding myself in the suicide of absolute perfection. There has always been a place in writing for candor and frankness, for real personal honesty, which I would like to extend with my actual American experience (Whitman, Dreiser, James T. Farrell and Henry Miller have already hewed this most marvelous trail over here but it can be taken into exciting new country) and a higher one for the imaginative emancipation of life based on this same ruthless love for what is. I am now committed to trying to combine the two, to creating a reader-participating living experience about our mutual days with my certainty that the foundation is real because I have lived it, not merely thought it.

All this assumes there is time. And yet time is just what I don't have, what is an uncertainty, what becomes more uncertain with each day. The years that have been wasted in living for the future when the great work would come and one would just have to transcribe it are never to be recovered; it is a bitter thought but one that I and my equally grandiose friends will pay for with increasing remorse as "The September Song" plays on the juke in the background. The trivial literary deeds (shreds of stories, memoir, unsatisfying critiques, a miserable few over-elaborate poems) that were to be a prelude to chords unheard on earth before may be all that many of us will have to show when the time comes for us to justify our presumption. My tears (both for myself and my brilliant friends) must turn to ice however when I consider our ease of opportunity as contrasted with the struggles of the men we quoted and the oceans of spirit we squandered in vanity that called itself by other names: exploration, speculation, experimentation, High Art, etc. That time is dead! We killed it! It can only return in the immense concentration of all this lost mortality that one of us can get into his work and unlike what I once would have proudly hissed out, that person is not likely to be myself; and even if this past is recaptured in words of eternal life can they compensate for the waste that the rest of us squatted in while competing with God? I saw what I used to think was the cream of a generation get increasingly sour because it talked more than it worked, criticized more than it praised, and not only demanded but accused life for not giving it the key to the universe—with the tacit encouragement of their unrealistic, too-haughty elders who flicked off a Thomas Wolfe for being a greedy romantic and could tell you in a flash what *hubris* meant but sinned quite as much as Wolfe. Not in the bad-boy area of sensuous excess but in the much more arrogant and sinister and fatal realm of mind, where vices are perpetrated that make those of the flesh mere child's play.

I must end this introduction to my first somewhat bloodstained collection (and it is curiously remarkable to me that in the middle of the weirdness that frankly describes my apprenticeship into the hip modern writing life I got this work done) with some simple logic. The world and living are obviously much more difficult than they appear and ask by their very nature for our fighting intelligence and full humanity; if we don't give proper moral payment the just angels of retribution squeeze it out of us when we are begging on our knees and all the literature we mouthed so fancily degenerates into a few humble words. What I am trying to say is that my period and its spokesmen used too many words to say too few things that matter today to young life-bombed kids; theirs was the elaborate rhetoric of ideas but when in time of crisis one went to grasp them for human use there was nothing specific and tangible which you could hold onto. I resent as a person as well as a writer having been misled by such a self-congratulating, aloof intellectual bazaar that failed to direct its statements to each very real individual who comprised its audience. Or as Tolstoy might have said with the simple nerve of greatness, what good was it? It is no longer enough in my opinion to deal in truths that are not directly related to the people who eagerly read you and take seriously what you say. Published writing is becoming increasingly a crucial public act in our stripped-down pressurized environment and its immediate goal should be to penetrate like a bullet the mind and emotions of each contemporary who reads it. This is basic in a time when people are hungry and desperate for straightforward communication about the life we are *all leading in common;* inflated or overwrought theory becomes an almost self-indulgent luxury—perhaps even a crime—under the hammer of the world we live in.

I was confused and torn apart by the amount of material I was expected to absorb reading the more abstruse literary quarterlies, I who wrote for them, and if this was true for a "professional" avantgarde writer like myself what can one say about (1) the bewilderment (2) the lack of human time to pit against the obscurity of much of the work (was it worth it in the mortal countdown?) (3) the lack of everyday experiential clues (4) the feeling of being a thick failure unto self of the unprofessional intelligent reader who wanted to know and experience this "apex" of modern writing but most often felt ironly left out in the cold? Literature is not worth the suffocation of life and the unnecessary alienation of your public if you have any respect for being alive yourself; it can't possibly be superior to existence and yet we often wrote about it as if it were separate from its living source. No single person can waft aside the chain of history and what I have described in these pages is now a historical accomplishment, with the overtones of the highbrow era having been filtered down to thousands of college students throughout the U.S. who read the magazines I used to write for and who will soon begin the same tortuous journey as myself if they want to be serious writers or even serious humans. I pity them. No, we cannot dispose of history; but we can change it by a recognition of where it has led us. In fact change only occurs I believe when we stand against the ultimate wall and realize that there is no place else to go except in a totally different direction. By the value of one man's life to himself and his conviction that others must feel comparably he has said goodbye don't bother getting up I can find the gate myself. I'm going out!

Milton Klonsky,
My Favorite Intellectual

The frustration, irritation, and anger Krim directed at intellectuals were soothed by Milton Klonsky. Here was an intellectual poet that knew "the most formidable of the contemporary headache-makers," such as Kafka, T. S. Eliot, and Ezra Pound. His mind held "the entire hip literary-intellectual university." But he also, as depicted in the Off-Broadway play Klonsky and Schwartz, *knew his way around. As a* New York Times *review of the play noted, Klonsky's passions were "art, blondes, horses, baseball" (2005, E10). Krim loved this about Klonsky and celebrates him here as one of the first postwar Jewish intellectuals to integrate "the once-opposites of toughness vs. literacy, snarl vs. beauty." It was also what the legendary* Commentary *editor Elliot Cohen was doing at the same time in the early 1950s, jumping in conversation from "literary criticism to politics, from politics to Jewish scholarship, from Jewish scholarship to the movies, from the movies to sports" (Podhoretz 1967, 100). This yoking of opposites appeals to every bookish type who ever yearned to create the perfect life cocktail by mixing one part mind with two parts body. Such readers will grin with deep appreciation as Krim recalls dinners at Klonsky's "one-room-and-kitchenette oasis" in Greenwich Village where Klonsky's wife "would cook a knocked-out Yiddish meal for us all and then Milt would get the pot and Zigzag papers out and roll those marvelous tight joints with his meticulous alchemist's attention to every grain of gage." This new Jewish style of hip beckoned to Krim like a true north of the spirit. But in the end Krim sees Klonsky as another victim of the intellectual world's terrifying standards, which made writers shiver.*

first met Milton Klonsky in probably the early spring of 1945. I had inherited a (to me) charming small apartment at 224 Sullivan St. from a girl I had been dating who suddenly winked at me in bed one morning and said with a smile that she was getting married. She had realistically been cheating on my remarkable self-conceit that I was irresistible and had nabbed herself, while I was absorbed in making love to me, a guy much more of this world and less mirror-riveted than yours truly. So she moved out in a bridal rush and I moved into this clean swinging little hideaway with a feeling of delight (once I told my bruised ego it had no case). What the hell, women were replaceable but groovy apartments were something else!

I didn't know then as they say in the old stories that my 2 to 3 years at 224 Sullivan were going to radically change my formless young life, but they did. I was wide-open for it though. Full of bounce, full of fanatical seriousness about writing and ready and willing for every mother-loving experience—"black, white, a zebra or anything new they can invent!" as a laughing call-girl once nailed it to the door—I was able to overcome my native shyness and redhot anxieties and blossom to the point where my clean little pad became a nest for Vassar–Bryn Mawr chicks to make fairly happy weekends for me. I got mostly literary types when secretly I thirsted for expensive, well-stacked, fine-assed royalty, but I had no kicks coming since I knew how half-man I was in the deep dark cellar of psychic me. Not that I was queer, baby, but that I often felt as unreal as Kafka and neurotic as Proust and shaky as a leaf in the privacy of my own head. I take little pride in spelling it out but I was bugged, fearful, "sensitive as a baby's ass" (as Klonsky once described me with that fearlessness of intellect that could allow you to take a personal insult and not flip because you saw the truth-clicking mind behind the words) and at the mercy of a fireworks-livid imagination; but the big thing was that I was a kid, 23, and in spite of everything, the world and Eternity were just ripe dandelions waiting for me to pluck. Everything lay before me, I felt (what 23-year-old globe-eater hasn't?) and now that I was out of the rooming-houses and chance 3-week flops in friends' apartments and the whole general weirdness of living that made the war years over here a night-and-day rollercoaster I was feeling feisty and ready to ride herd on everything that plagued me. Man, the world was going to part and bow low for me! Neuroses look out, cause Krim's gonna boot you puny little assassinators right out of his life! I had never really had my own adult-decent place before and I took tremendous pride in keeping it shining and kept clapping myself on the forehead, in effect, and saying over and over to myself, "You don't believe it but it's yours, yours!"

Billie Holiday blew her blues from my new record player (I took over my ex-girlfriend's first-rate modern furniture and equipment, too, when I moved in and still owe her $48 on the deal although I haven't seen her in 15 years), Miro prints danced on the wall, a lovely pungent undefinable furniture-and-straw-rug odor smelled through the place, and the optimistic merriment of having this nice new apartment really picked me up high. I had made the Village scene 2 years before, but in a much more squalid depressing way. I had lived with the first important girl in my life, Connie S—— (now just out of a midwestern brain-lockup, as I served my time in a Manhattan one, having gone back out of awful need to a convent-girl brand of Roman Catholicism and following priestly bluntness after being one of the Village's most wide-open soul-sisters) in a lousy one-room bohemian fantasy on Cornelia Street. I had felt excited about it all when we took the place because Jim Agee had lived on Cornelia when I first visited him while in highschool (he was now down on King Street), and I was a book-hugging literary romantic who got high inside identifying with my crushes, but Connie's and my little stint on Cornelia was a savage bust. Nothing worked for us. I was scared of the Italian street-threat that used to psychically de-ball all us violin-souled Jewish boys who had fled downtown, I was wildly insecure and neurotic as was Connie, and together we managed to stagger through an unreal man-wife life for about a year before it became a comic tearful enraged nightmare and she pulled out (for she had personal integrity, God bless her).

But here I was now in my new Village cozy-pad on the second floor of F Building overlooking the clean-swept courtyard—there were and are 5 small buildings built around a courtyard sporting a concrete goldfish tureen in the center and the whole scheme is protected in a Shangri-La kind of way by a big gate which locks out the Sullivan Street strongarm locals—and it was a pleasure to get up in the morning these days, leg-tangled or alone. I was pulling down nearly $85 per week at the OWI writing war news, going dutifully to an analyst with the usual boy-scout dreams of solving all my "problems" (the echo of Klonsky's chanting quotation of Blake's "O why was I born with a different face? Why was I not born like the rest of my race?" coming back to me as I write this, for he had a profound sense of tragedy and wasn't snowed by pleasant theories of mortal amelioration) and I was full of the immense future-kissing conviction of glory that your average U.S. writing nut of 23 usually glows with.

Going in and out of this lovely courtyard I used to see with increasing regularity—since I had my eyes peeled for it by now, especially when I was wearing my glasses (for I used to wear them and not wear them in the usual near-sighted hangup that is almost a universal small symbol of uncertainty and shame among the boys and girls of my generation)—a strange shortish lithe dark-looking cat who would brush by me at the entrance with brusqueness and what seemed like hostility, but also looking me over in a grudging way. There was an under-the-rock air of furtiveness, reptilianism, about the guy; his eyes would never meet mine, never signal hello, but out of their squinting holes they'd flick off my buttons so to speak in one razor-swipe and then stare stonily beyond. Frankly, I'd feel like melting sheet every time I ran into this dark trigger-man and it jarred me—me, brilliant, handsome, proud, a Beethovian earth-shaker missing heart-beats because some dark snot didn't know who I was and stared through me! I resented this creep and steeled myself when I had to walk past the inhuman guns of his eyes, but even then—in spite of myself and my pride—I thought they were great eyes, green-grey, cat-like, opaque, the possessors of some secret knowledge of mystery which later reminded me almost exactly of the hypnotizing eyes we see in photographs of Rimbaud.

This was Milt Klonsky, although I didn't know his name at the time. I also didn't know that part of the deadly looks he'd shoot me there in the courtyard-entrance was due to his own myopia and the accompanying bitching pressure of having to squint and almost bore holes in the air in order to see clearly—or else be forced to wear the anti-heroic, anti-moviestar, anti-chick glass over his unusual eyes. (He was and is less nearsighted than myself and has never fully resolved the problem downward as I have had to do because I was fingered by that dear old maniac, Mother Nature, as Dr. Chandler Brossard once dubbed her.) I knew nothing about Klonsky except that I was scared of him, aware of him, the cat was creepy—where did he get off acting so stony, rude, the hard-guy? I was mattressed sweet right then in my own terrifically self-important world—new pad, fears held at bay, fawncy-voiced eastern college pusserino tumbling (some), me not getting killed in the war and also living out an old newspaperman-dream via my OWI trick, some prose steaming in the Remington Portable at home and great-writer fantasies gassing me even as I shaved in my new hospital-slick john—and I didn't want some alley-hustler off the streets, some foreign-looking Mafia slitter, threatening my ego this way goddamnit!

There was no doubt after a couple of weeks of these minor eye-crises at the doorway to 224 that the two of us had sniffed each other out, the way hipsters or Beards or Negro chicks who refuse to get their hair conked will get animal-feelers toward a member of the same club walking down the block. We knew, baby! I don't remember exactly how it happened, whether it was a muttered defensive word (both of us shy) exchanged near the mailbox or a mutual friend like the now-gone Isaac Rosenfeld who placed a hand on both our shoulders and drew us together (although I doubt it), but soon, unexpectedly, easily, we were speaking and digging each other. Even though he was only about a half year older than myself, Klonsky immediately (the classic take-over guy) buttoned up the role of older brother and with good reason: he was wiser in the ways of the world—although a consummate practical fuck-up like myself—wiser about women (he was then in the process of teetering on the brink with Rhoda Jaffe Klonsky, his first wife who has long since split with him and remarried), wiser, in fact, period. Once I was able to penetrate the hard shell he grew for the world and swing with him I confirmed that there was nothing a hair's-width false in this wisdom except for the occasional high parabolas of thought, as in all under-30 visionaries, not backed up by enough experience to give them the body needed to support such rarity. Other than that the man was a masked literary marvel. He had matured much earlier than myself, especially in the minds he had trained with—difficult English poets like Donne, Marvell, Christopher Smart, his much-quoted Blake, the French Symbolists, Rimbaud, Baudelaire, Valéry, Laforgue, all the way up to Michaux; plus the most formidable of the contemporary headache-makers like Kafka, Eliot, Pound, Auden, Joyce, Yeats, Stevens and critics like Coleridge, Blackmur, Tate, I. A. Richards (with a Trilling read for mere entertainment like a mystery). Klonsky's mind seemed to contain the entire hip literary-intellectual university and closely grasped with an IQ that could stutter your butter too. When we got more relaxed and informal with each other after the initial feeling-out sparring—"Whodya like in prose right now? Chicks: Bennington or spade? Dig a tenor or a trumpet? You a Giant fan? What about Matisse?"—I got the downhome goose-flesh warning that I was on the way in for the most significant human and intellectual experience of my life up to then.

I wasn't wrong. Klonsky's personality was a subtle, forceful and, later I was to recognize, deeply profound one and it entered my being—tore through it actually—like a torpedo into the unguarded gut of a battle-innocent smug cruiser. I had never met anyone even remotely like him nor could I have conceived him in my imagination. Instead of being direct (my holy-grail kick at that time, encouraged by the prose of Hemingway, Eliot, Pound, which made a glistening literary virtue of straightforwardness and which I translated into an ethical ideal—even then trying to convert beauty into life-action!) he was indirect, elusive, paradoxical, frowning, iceberg-cheerless often. And yet one always had the impression, felt the impression I should really say, of a fine and deep mind that was fixed like a rule beyond every flare of mood, behind his furrowed swarthy face (now Roman-looking, now Jewish, now Spanish) and in back of those special catlike eyes. The guy's strangeness, uniqueness, was heaped further on my barometric apparatus by his style: although quotations from Blake or Hart Crane or Wordsworth—in fact most of the whole noble repertoire of English-speaking verse—sprang to his dark purplish cracked lips at appropriate moments, he electrically bit out the language of the ballpark and streets too. The combination was fascinating to me, jazzing my ear and mind with such new contrasts and perspectives on reality that I felt my simple-minded conceits blushing out of embarrassment. When I later found out that Klonsky was a hard-driving stud also, a refined digger of modern painting, a rigorous ace at mathematics and logical thinking (I know this sounds too good to be true but it was greased perfection), I willingly doffed my inner fedora all the way. I had never met anyone my own age before Milt who I didn't think I could top as a writer and ultimately as a man—a psychotic piece of egomania (shared by you too, my self-worshipping pals!) to set down yet true; but with Klonsky I had more than met my match and although I felt that hard lump of frustration at his being better and righter about so many things, something I was to feel at different times angrily or casually over the next 15 years, I was able to leash in my envy at his more perfect image and become a happy sidekick and admirer.

2

I've got to explain this. I'm afraid (pretty damn sure, in fact) I early wove a passive style out of a fear of being ego-licked in competition, a female (yes, say the hurting word shmuck!) containing absorbing quality which lived side-by-side with my "manly" or active self; it almost asked I be exploited, yet permitted me to suck life in like a plant does water, to be stationary and easy and gentle and quiet in a huge bid for harmony and peace after the violence of my growing-up years; I also have a strong dynamic charge which exists in opposition to this controlled homemade Buddhism and chances are that in spite of my life-long wrestling I'll never make groan-less harmony between the two. In Milt's case my sense of reality told me with no tinted lights that here was a man better than myself—how we U.S. obsessionists measure ourselves tirelessly against the surrounding flesh, no?—and that it was a testimony to my own manhood to acknowledge this fact instead of taking refuge in the sealed tower of would-be great-ness which I had built up in my head. So he became my great pal, I his more youthful greener gunsel, but my boy was always the leader in either the itching hunt for pleasure (meeting new chicks, going down to Bleecker St. to slurp up cool clams and hot sauce, getting high and taking a double-decker 5th Ave. joyride up to the Modern Museum to dig the new shows) or in literary-intellectual discussions where the bastard invariably knew more than I did and could lucidly back it up down to the final comma. But being a superconscious writer-type—being always first a writer-man, a coldblooded Associated Press eyewitness of the reality around me—I could tolerate this superiority of his because I was always trying to learn more about life and transform it in my mind into miles of literature. A defeat, a put-down, another person's being sharper than myself was usually redeemed by me into a triumph for knowledge about existence (the human is a great and devious animal, daddy!) and in those days when I hung as closely with Milt as man and his shadow I felt I was living within at the top of my speed. I was swinging inside, learning, absorbing the brilliant angles of thought that K.'s mind created as naturally as most East Side tenement-hipsters scratch. There was nothing second-rate about my role to me, I was getting more out of it than when I'd been the power-boy in other relationships.

Klonsky at this time was finishing up his master's thesis on Metaphor at Columbia (a paper I understand that is still used as a model in the English graduate department) and ready to tear the last remaining fabric of his marriage with Rhoda. He had been catting around with various stuff as the marriage rocked on its last legs and now when I often came up to his little pad diagonally across from mine—across the courtyard in A Building—he and Rhoda would be in the midst of some shrill argument over his passion for stray pretty nooky. He wasn't like me in this very important, as-long-as-you-live hard-on of male being. I had kidded myself along, brought myself up with the typical (every young guy's autobiographical novel up to World War II) ultrasensitive, unaggressive, slightly-trembling over-romanticized attitude toward girls that I hoped could make it as a style because I was a spiritually "noble" literary type. But Klonsky, and I admired him for it, was much more of a tricky swinging operator with women and moved right in with dark cocky evil; he had his blushing hangups too (after all he was a poet and he knew the deep freezes of outer space, I had seen it in his eyes) but he would corner a chick the way a cat does a mouse and at a party it always gave me a feeling of reassurance, of the world spinning right, when I looked over my shoulder and saw Milt stroking a soft palm and purring out his line of mesmerizing jive. There was no nineteenth-century poeticizing for him as far as yon fair skirts went, at least nothing like my tense and elaborate literary-man come-on. I got my share of the good cush of course—and I always loved sex like a monster, which made my "gentle" approach that much more of a lie to myself when I really laid it on the line to the naked me—but it always seemed to me that I play-acted and almost stood on my head to get it, unlike Milt, and slowly I borrowed as much of his thrust and deviltry with pussy as I could to charge up my own style.

At any rate, I would go up to Klonsky's little one-room-and-kitchenette oasis and Rhoda would cook a knocked-out Yiddish meal for us all and then Milt would get the pot and Zigzag papers out and roll those marvelous tight joints with his meticulous alchemist's attention to every grain of gage (always rolling sticks over a white piece of typing paper and then carefully hand-sweeping the leftover grains back into an envelope or a tiny pill bottle—a pleasure for me to watch because of his absorbed concern with each microscopic detail) and soon we would all get easily, nicely, groovily high. This was our Hip Century after-dinner brandy and it warmed our modernistic freakish heads the way juice once carved slight heaven in an English lord's belly—just the same, kicks won and scooped off the knifeblade of being alive. These were wonderful moments for me up there in Milton's pad, no matter how commonplace they seem to any brother-sister hipster who is high right now while his-her eye snags these words. I had never had a true family scene (pop died when I was 8 and my mother killed herself roof-wise just before I turned 10 and at this time— The Time of Milt—I didn't have the security or ability to make a family-type situation for myself). But these dinners up at Milt and Rhoda's had for me all the warmth, goodwill, informality—since by now I was completely accepted by both of them as a kind of naive lovable shnook—of the most swinging kind of family setup,[1] the kind where you really enjoy your own flesh-and-blood and share your precious mortal breath and laughter with them. Oh what a lovely, unplanned-for, forever-stamped gas it can be when it happens!

After dinner with the lights low, the food warming the gut, the pot working, the pad cozy, we would stretch out on the floor or bed and give laughing play to whatever came into our minds. Milt was always the leader in the thoughts we gave expression to while Rhoda and I chimed in at appropriate moments with our own giggling two-cents' worth. But

---

1. *Shnook* is Yiddish for a gullible innocent, a fool.

even while I was stoned, jelly-relaxed and happy, I could never get over how unself-conscious Klonsky was in expressing himself; even while high and floating (probably even more keenly then) I could appreciate more than ever the lack of decoration in his thinking, the pointedness, the quick catlike way his brain would leap from silence and meditation into some clearly conceived picture or thought that had taken invisible birth within his mind. It hit me at these moments that this was truly what was meant by creativity, the ability to conjure up out of nothingness a pearl of thought that no one else could conceive. It was magic, man, and at the same time—as with all of Klonsky's far-out imaginings—there was nothing whimsical, cute, one-legged about it (as every pot-smoker knows imaginative types try to vie with each other when high to see who can cap who with new visions and often slay themselves with the novelty of their thoughts instead of the devastating beams of reality); Milt's ideas even when high could stand up under M.I.T. scrutiny and if I had tape-recorded them (what an all-time goof that I didn't) they would have rung every bell even in the unwashed-dishes sobriety of the next morning.

We had wonderful fun on those strictly ad lib nights—ideas and warm love commingling in that tiny box over at 224 Sullivan, with the dangerous black night shut out and a million miles away—and I will never be able to forget them. As you can see Klonsky had already become my hero, the person I would think about when I couldn't sleep (his fantastically dominating image once rose up in my brain while I was in the saddle and I began worrying how he'd go about getting further mileage out of the party I was balling—and I'd been content as hell until that black presence of his scorned my easy unimaginative ride and burnt away my paradise!), the person I measured myself against in every way: measured my reading, my writing, my thinking, my style as a human being. No doubt he torpedoed into my life with such great power because I still had a kiddy-car need for hero-worship, was more deeply uncertain about life than I would admit to myself, was coltish and goggle-eyed and impressionable as wet cement—at least that's what my analytical sense tells me and the beautiful irony is that it was from Klonsky that I learned to wield natural unsparing analysis, so even this explanation of his effect on my being owes itself to him.

I had almost willfully avoided cold and unpretty analysis before he pried his ideas into my head by sheer steel of logic. Certainly I was capable of spotting faults and holes in things, people, ideas, but my deepest feeling was in giving life an upward lift instead of reducing it because my fantastic ego-hopes couldn't bear shrinkage of any kind. I identified my own future so completely with the life around me, saw the world as the mirror of myself, that any acid undercutting of even the outer scene toppled my happiness-craving heart within myself. To be honest, I was a tremendous self-intoxicated idealist who often perfumed the reality around me as an extension of my own inner needs (fears!), who shaped and reshaped the girders of actuality to fit my hungry dream, and now Klonsky moved into this myth-building factory of mine carrying the hard club of impersonal truth. It smashed without meaning to—his sense of its weight was not mine, my universe quivered under its most casual swish—and bang! a vase of my most hoarded moonshine would topple to the floor and spill sadly, floodingly, over my entire being. But it was then, on my mental hands and knees picking up fragments, that I began the long arduous work of trying to integrate my spirit with the heartless real world, it was then and through Klonsky that I ultimately realized I had been living in a self-made diving bell where everything was just the way I wanted it instead of the way it more truly, cruelly was.

Milt was to drum away at me all through our friendship that I was an enthusiast, a rhapsodist, a jazzer-upper of reality and the constancy of this anti-lyrical vigilance of his beat so put-downishly into my mind that I became five-headedly aware of each exuberant yelp I uttered or even thought. What is fascinating is that Klonsky, schooled and fashioned by anti-Romantic verse from Marvell to Marianne Moore, became the living embodiment of poetic reason while I, identified in my heart with modern American prose literature which is both romantic and lyrical from Dreiser to Kerouac, was the opposite embodiment of vitality and excess. But just as I thought that poetry was a higher form of expression than prose—because I could never enjoy or want to understand it in school (it seemed like punishment compared to the groove of prose) and admired those who could—so I thought without a hair of doubt that Milt's judgment was superior to mine and I strove mightily to sculpt those raw "distortions" in my own makeup so they could live up to the more authoritarian standard he set. It was a strange war I was living out in myself after I began digging Klonsky's ideas, a war between my powerful instincts which led in many directions and his even more powerful reasoning abilities which compressed the world to the space between his hairline and the bridge of his nose. Here was a man and a mind I admired unqualifiedly and from whom I learned with the greed of a saved-up lifetime of unanswered questions, whom I loved, who I knew was more profound and valuable than myself under the eye of God—so I tried like a fiend to lace my molten wildness into the forms he upheld. This was not only so I could know and be "the truth" as a writing-man who had a massive hunger for a giant ultimate greatness (I turned the face of Ambition white so murderous was my lust!), but also—down deep in the most human cry of my machine—so I could, by virtue of the holy mathematics I thought Klonsky would provide me with, cut in half or to zero my perpetual inner suffering, hurts, confusion, the dreadful globe of consciousness I wore on top of my neck. In other words: "You shall know the truth and it will set you free," and K. was and spoke more truth than I had ever heard before, so I tried to heave the most fundamental baggage of me off my shoulders and open-armed embrace the very Christ of Truth I believed my friend stood for. It was—this need and effort of mine—ultimately to be against the character, the reason-for-being, of my particular self but I tried, I tried, I tried, and so grateful and romantic and tearfully kidlike was I in my fantasies that I used to imagine a showdown scene of some sort in which I dedicatedly gave up my life for my friend. And, dig, I was already then a published writer, not a nut, and yet so powerful was my need of finding and being "truth" and being made whole through Klonsky's teaching that it took precedence over everything. Religion, the spirit of life and not the sensations which up to then had ecstatically gassed me and (in the guise of "style" and "beauty," especially in words) been my substitute for the less obvious lightning which underscores all of human life, had been shown to me by a buddy who was also the closest thing to a model of mortality that my raw heart and brain had ever had the mixed luck to mold itself on.

3

I can back up Klonsky's objective weight and influence on the New York literary scene by pointing out that at the time I first knew him I wasn't alone in being literally soul-struck by his rare qualities. Others who also used him as a standard of excellence included his old friend from Brooklyn, the writer Anatole Broyard, my ex-girlfriend Connie (who would beard people in the Village, including the present *New Yorker* poet-poetry editor Howard Moss, and back them against Whelan's as she preached Klonsky's "genius") and even the much older poet-critic Allen Tate, who told me in the summer of 1959 on Cape Cod that Milt had left a lasting impression on him after a brief two months they spent together at the writer's colony in Cummington, Massachusetts, in 1942 when K. was a bare nineteen-and-a-half. Cocktail glass in hand while the breeze blew off the pond in Wellfleet at an outdoor party at the summer home of historian Arthur Schlesinger, Jr., Tate kept asking me questions about what Klonsky was up to. Tate's questions were strong, direct, wanting answers, and he wouldn't let up as I tried to duck the issue with a ginny, let's-have-a-good-time grin on my face. The reason I dodged giving full value to Tate's questions was that I was peeved, as I always was after I had become a fairly "known" writer, to have Klonsky the magnet of conversation instead of myself, but underneath the momentary bite of jealousy and the goofy gin-grin I was gratified that without realizing it Tate was reinforcing what I had always felt about my extraordinary friend—and Tate both thirty years older than Klonsky and myself and also, as you'll remember, the great ex-pal and critical explainer of our most brilliant modern American poet, Hart Crane: additional proof to me that he was an A-1 spotter of poetic horseflesh and knew as I knew that Milt belonged in the very first brigade. It was a vindication from an unexpected source in an unexpected place—the boozy giggles of women sexing the air, the sun darkening over Slough Pond and the twilight breeze swirling Tate's thin hair as he sharply spoke of Klonsky's analysis of Marvell's "The Garden" above the drone of sixty summer-hedonists—if any vindication was needed of what I always knew to be true of Klonsky and an answer to the skeptical or jealous cracks that I sometimes heard about Milt in the angry boil of New York intellectual-literary life.

As I got to know Klonsky better in the beginning 1945–1947 period—and don't forget the relationship has gone on for fifteen years—certain things I had barely sensed at the start became more pronounced. He was much hipper than I was, a word and attitude just feeling its way toward the light at that time but true just the same. From the age of fourteen on he had known pot-smokers, painters, swinging young musicians, fast-moving operators of one kind or another, and they helped leather his young skin and sleek his ideas. I saw that Milt combined the outward toughness of the streets—specifically, the teeming unprivate be-quick-witted-or-be-suckered streets of the Bronx and later Brooklyn—with a fine, mystical, extraordinarily sophisticated mind. Pure as a star fathoms deep inside his wickedly complex mental machinery, he came on with a veteran's knowingness, the bite to his thoughts was as stinging as iodine, he had been taught and schooled and skilled in New York's ultramodern lifeshop and the techniques of irony, double-meaning, deception, feint, twist, turn, were as native to him as the alleys he had dodged down as a metropolitan kid. Klonsky was ancient stuff in comparison to my Tom Wolfean [the author of *Look Homeward, Angel*] green exuberance and naïveté; not only had the concrete streets and the tricky heels that scarred them toughened and compressed my friend's outlook—and these streets, these New York forms were long to glow in Klonsky's mind as materials for a brilliant poetic vision—but his mind had also been sharpened and seasoned by personal acquaintance at a very early age with extremely brainy Jewish radical-intellectuals (one or both of his parents was socialist) and later on with such avantgarde wheels as W.H. Auden, Tate, Delmore Schwartz, Marianne Moore, etc. All of this plus his reading (the Bible, Milton, Shakespeare, in addition to the contemporary mind-punishers I listed before, literally every literary landmark you can think of plus the most difficult philosophers with special loving attention to metaphysicians) had submerged him much more deeply and gravely into adult life than myself. Recognition of this soon overwhelmed me, I was diminished intellectually to the size of a dime, and naturally I got on board this new brain-train as soon as I could and forced myself to read many of the same books—even though they didn't particularly rock me in many cases—and tried to expand my own broad but essentially nearby tastes.

You see, I had always thought I was going to be a novelist (from about fifteen on), not a philosopher, not a poet, not an omniscient intellectual type who does graduate work here and Marxes it up there and Freuds everywhere and achieves passing livingroom glory while making his genuine bread working for some committee. My interest was keen and insatiable for modern narrative of all kinds and I particularly dug the American scene (my scene!) and gobbled up novels by the shelf-full from Dreiser and Edith Wharton to the present. I was and still am in love with the American experience, which I identified with myself, my life, and Klonsky's more exquisite kicks with the English metaphysical and French symbolist poets was at first totally alien to me—impressive but distant. But I plugged through the new books and new thoughts with Milt as my grudging guide and tightlipped teacher (he was more consumed by his own vision than in wanting the ego-boost of imposing his thoughts on me, it was I who plucked this whole self-educational scheme out of him), always trying to relate this new dimension of literary experience to my maddened interest in the naturalistic, seeable, graspable, "real" contemporary U.S. world that excited all the glands within me. Even at the time that my idolatry of Milt was at its highest I never had any doubt about giving up my own way of writing or trying to become a poet, or doing anything to resist the savage thrills that only the present-tense U.S. scene was able to give me as writer and person. I was pliable and appreciative of ways of looking at life other than my own but central to my being was my own destiny as a writer, even at the cost of the pain I once thought I could shed with Milt's mighty formula; Klonsky understood and had faith in this daemon of my own and so was able to give me with unaccustomed straightforwardness the overflow of his closely-guarded inner thoughts. Without a doubt he thought I often suffered from what skin-divers call "rhapsody of the deep" right here on land, but he respected this drive and need of my own, I could tell this with certainty from the beginning.

By asking many questions—the ancient device of the novelist-type, who is usually bugged as sheer human with a mammoth curiosity—I sucked in and pieced together the background of Milt's life for very personal basic reasons. Primary was the whole Jewish problem which used to murder me blind both as man and writer; I know from experience that my swinging non-Jewish friends, occasional girlfriends, even detractors, feel this whole Jew business comes out of left field, is a private obsession, in today's new interscrewing world where the name and rank you carry means nothing compared to what you can lay down. But I would lie to myself and to you if I said that my life has not been conditioned by my enormous wrestling with this historical mountain on my back; by this I simply mean that when I set out to hurl myself into the America I loved through my imagination, as a would-be novelist, it would always come to me in the black of the soul that perhaps I was trying to run out on my fate or responsibility as a Juden, that maybe I was trying to embrace so fully the American cosmos in order to wipe out the "Oy vey" self-sneer-ingness, awfulness, shameness, strangeness, which had vomited all over my psyche after I got my first dose of lipsmacking anti-kike contempt. I only knew the curse of the Yiddish tag not the joy (if any exists—O send me the word, Lord!), because having been orphaned, bounced from home to home, taught no heritage except what I learned in newspapers, Hitler-raving newsreels, tough-guy U.S. fiction and chalk-scrawls in the street I couldn't imagine any balm for this filthy trick played on me. I had only crawling shame and no pride whatsoever in being Jewish, had my beak clipped at age seventeen (a pioneering practice then among Jews with loot and now a widespread staple in every self-respecting, face-hating Jewish suburb), had turned my back and ear on the Yiddish spoken at my Grand-ma's, refused a bar mitzvah out of contempt, bawled my eyes red a 100 times for having been "chosen"—you can have it, baby, yes you Liz Tay-lor and you Sammy Davis!—and during the age seventeen to twenty-one period had more than once pretended I was a clean-cut (you should see the way even mature Jews admire that word, you justly peed-off ex–White Protestant dissenters!) gentile boy. I know I was driven into psychiatry like so many young American Jews by my inability to handle this hell-coal of identity, but I found—or was in the process of finding out during this time when I met Klonsky—that psychiatry could not magically change who you were or at least who I was. What almost sobbed in me was the obses-sive thought that I would never be able to participate completely, unself-consciously, naturally, in this great expanse of land and myth over here, that the unwanted Yiddle brand would label me forever a lousy outsider in the eyes of my countrymen, that I who loved America would be prevented always from truly knowing my love and therefore being able to sing her tremendous raucous song with word-pictures I had been minting in my imagination since 1939. What many critics and readers have not yet understood is that the kid who wanted to be an American novelist in 1938 or 1939 wanted to be an explorer, his imagination had been whetted crazily by the explorations of Lewis, Dreiser, Wolfe, Faulkner, Anderson, Hemingway, Steinbeck into the experience of the vast land, the entire unconscious meaning and drive of the American novel at that time was that it was uncovering—writer by writer by writer—the pricelessly real human scene that lay buried to all but the new prose-men who were truly surveying the continent for the first time. You must be able to see how this could fire the particular kind of imagination it took to want to be one of the new American novelist-explorers, how the potential novelist was smitten with the argot, color, dynamism, pace, smell, big-truck feel of the continent— and how the young hebe who had drunk all of this starspangled juice into his veins and wanted to live it and be it would burn triply because he felt in moments of acutest doubt that he could never legitimately be of it. Here I was consumed by the voice and landscape and (be truthful!) romance of roaring-drunk modern America—and, believe me, this is what has motivated your major U.S. "realistic" novelists of our period, the fact that their imaginations or fantasy-lives saw actual beauty and meaning in the giant, seemingly meaningless, even ugly reality of our daily life here—and I felt that because I was that Christ-killing, communistic, hand-talking, loan-sharking, ikey-kikey walking toilet known as Jew (the cultural reasons for this hatred and contempt were unimportant: bigotry, shmigotry, who cared what the thousand traceable causes were when the less-than-human reality was all that counted!), I would be forever shut out of this violent paradise. I got down in my psyche and impotently prayed to be different, I cursed the walls of my flesh for freezing me into a living advertisement of what seemed to disgust the majority of Americans (yes, you ancient Jews forgive me and you 1960 U.S. umpires call it as you see it!) and worst of all I felt I had been kidding the heart out of myself in thinking I could justly write of the broad America. What real right did I have to sing its wop-lifted steel or paint its electric-eyed face or show the golden music in the fresh-corn voice of a mid-western drum major-ette as if I were a downhome Wolfe or Whitman or my beloved Dreiser? Wasn't I just another Walter Winchell–type Jew who wrapped himself in the flag precisely because he was shivering out in the fucking cold? These were awful question marks that perforated my being and I desperately suspended final answers as I writhed around hunting for ways out of my psychic trap.

Therefore when I met Milt, dug him, watched the way he handled his Jewishness it was as if I had a thousand eyes that literally ferreted into his being and background in order to try and pluck out his secret for myself. By this I mean that he didn't seem to operate under the sense of Yiddish shame and inferiority that crippled not only myself but so many of the middle-class Jewish kids who came from roughly my own uptown environment. I later found out that Klonsky was gravely concerned with his heritage, had backed it up and fortified it with his reading in the Bible and with the thoughts of innumerable Jewish mystics from antiquity to the present, but in the sheerly secular everyday world of street and eat and movie-going jazz-listening he was not bugged in the same way I was. He acted like a man, not someone castrated and squirming because of their racial unease, and the more I thought about the unconscious pride and soldierliness he showed in ordinary life the more I was disgusted by my own sliced roots. Each of us typified to me two different kinds of big-city Jewish boy. I noticed that Milt and several of the other Brooklyn (for that's where he spent most of his formative years) Jewish intellectuals on the Village scene were much more ballsy and less superficially "sensitive"—especially about the Yiddle theme—than the Central Park West Jewish boys in whose aura and style I was formed. This observation bit deep into my own personal hangup and I had to trace it out in my mind with almost fanatical exactitude in order to try and free myself of the knife of self-inflicted pain which I plunged repeatedly into my being.

In case you don't know the snob setup or social hierarchy of New York Jewish life it was always assumed in the environment that clamped its teeth into my youthful jelly that life-successful Jews would live comfort-ably in fashionable Manhattan (before the suburb kick became as signifi-cant as it is today) while their social and financial inferiors would crawl it out in the Bronx or Brooklyn. I had been money-sheltered before my parents died on me as a 10-year-old, had gone to the usual Indian-name summer camp in Maine and later to a Jewish prep school in Harrison, New York; and because of insulated experience I had always thought— like practically all the kids from my background, which in New York was the Central Park West–West End Avenue area from the 60's to the 90's but could just as well have been Jamaica Plain or Newton Center outside of Boston, or South Orange in New Jersey, or Squirrel Hill in Pittsburgh, any of the well-hedged Jewish communities strung throughout the country—that Bronx and Brooklyn Jews were dirty, loud, vulgar, mockyish, all the things their upper-middle-class brethren tried to put behind them. ("White Jews," I once heard a half-joking lady hipster who had nervoused her way out of the Lower East Side swarm say about my relatives when she met me in their West 86th St., 20-story fortress.) But I found when I hit the Village in the early 1940s—and had it pounded home to me in the case of Klonsky—that the young Jewish swingers who had gone to CCNY or Brooklyn College (where Milt went before doing graduate work at Columbia) were on the whole much smarter, shrewder, wiser-neurotic, startlingly at home with abstract thought—carrying the real nail-chewed freight of life, ye manicured Temple Emanu-El solace-salesmen!—than their crewcut counterparts who had made it at Princeton or Harvard or the University of Pennsylvania. Even as I write this I can remember as if a closet had burst open the innumerable college-type fantasies that held middle- and upper-middle-class Jewish teenagers in thrall during high-school, the Yale banners on the wall, the clothes selected with a serious *Esquire* eye, the fraternity dreams (passionately acted out in the mind), the whole hanging joy of "going to school out of town." You see we were Americanized first, we Jews with money, and everything American was greedily eaten into our lifestreams until we literally pissed style, detail, USA-knowhow—jesus, how we West 86th St. F. Seymour Fitzgeraldbergs modeled ourselves on the dukely gentiles who had set the cool out-of-town university style!

It came to me as I watched Klonsky and later a dozen more Brooklyn and Bronx hipsters dealing-and-wheeling their way to dominance on the Village scene—and I truly mean dominance, with ass, with prestige,

with man-to-man and man-to-chick superiority which spoke for itself—
that we who had come from all the uptowns and suburbs across the land
had originally weakened our manhood in order to "get in," to be white
Anglo-Saxon imitations, and we bled so much more easily and bitterly
than these mental street-fighters who had been nourished on drives more
exciting than getting into Yale. Compared to the J-boys my own age who
had Ivy Leagued-it or gone to any of the second-rate rich boy's schools out
of town—yes my old Pi Lambda Phi buddies! the football game and the
Saturday night big-name-band dance, the amateurish quarter-screw with
the New Rochelle import in the back seat of the Chrysler convertible, the
grotesque wasted dribble of Jack Daniels (at $7.30 a bottle!) along the white
oxford button-down shirt collar, the crushed orchid still pinned on the
shoulder of Miss Fay Noren (formerly Nussbaum)'s formal as she vomits
in the approved, glamorous, God-it-was-a-wild-weekend style—compared
to that frantic and nowhere ritual I found many more new ideas and much
more mental determination and stature in these Brooklyn-Bronx-Avenue
A cats who had slitted their contemptuous way past a cornball Exeter-
type smoothness to a real subway-grasp of contemporary reality. These
unashamed (because they couldn't help it), often bitterly slanted and
harsh-talking Jewish boys knew chicks without Cole Porter romanticization and could throw a mature lay in the sunlight as well as the Scotch-
dripping hi-fied dark—Klonsky himself made 16-year-old time under
the boardwalks of Coney Island and Brighton Beach—knew the tough
classics instead of the latest Salinger or Hemingway or Graham Greene
confection, knew the sharp outlines and brick anatomy of human life in
the twentieth (and last! it often seemed) century instead of some wistful-
schmaltzy sentimentalization of it. I found this observation to hold true
time and again as I struggled with my own Yiddish self-consciousness:
namely that I was more drawn mentally and emotionally to Jews with
poorish, boorish, crude, rude, radical, intellectually-sharpshooting backgrounds than to those custom-tailored kinsmen of mine who rumbaed
feverishly above the scene in some chic dream of "good living" on one
side of Central Park or the other.

Getting back to Milt he came from roughly the kind of environment I
once put down, growing up in the Brighton Beach section of Brooklyn, and

as I said looking on first glance to my uptown-snobbed eyes like a hood or con-man—and containing in that vault about his eyes what seemed to me practically the fucking scroll of English literature and the high peaks of Western thought. It was a fascinating, dangerous, aggressive combination of opposites back in medieval 1945 when I first fell in with Klonsky; having a precedent in certain modern Parisian poets fathered by Baudelaire and Rimbaud, although I didn't know it at the time, and now of course much more prevalent on the beat or hipster scene where you can't move 10 blocks in New York or Frisco or New Orleans without seeing rough hewn or furtive or unshaven guys (and girl equivalents) who will stun the pants off you by their hip immediacy of perception—"Lightning to read by, yeah!" a strange cat muttered to me at the corner of University and 9th Street three days ago while we were waiting for the traffic light to break and the summer sky rumbled forth a few choice flares—who will quote Melville out of the side of their lip-chewed mouths, smoke pot, dig Monk, get a genuine big charge out of de Kooning's paintings and the rest. Klonsky in other words was a New Style, a new type of literary-man to my square, collegiate, ultraromantic eyes when I first felt his hooded devil-gaze back there in the courtyard of 224 Sullivan Street, and even now in 1960 that the cut of his angle to life no longer draws so much blood from others and his counterparts stylistically speaking have popped up everywhere, I still see him as the integrator of the once-opposites of toughness vs. literacy, snarl vs. beauty, making-out vs. delicacy—use the entire churchly nineteenth-century vocabulary and reverse it and you'll understand me—but at a deeper level than when he first undermined my corny middle-class images of taste and heroism.

With time, these truly crazy last 15 years, this original fascination of mine with Klonsky's surface uniqueness slowly shed itself for the deeper qualities that resided within the man. Again and again—in his apartment on Sullivan Street, then Morton Street, now West 4th Street, or at a party or on the street or in a tense jam with any of the hotheaded intellectuals and hipsters or wild "Fuck you!"—screaming chicks whom we knew in common—I was struck by the man's Roman courage, independence and always that profound sense of measuring the worth of objects and words without being carried away or yet losing the jaguar-spring of his vitality. He was durable, I realized through that decade-and-a-half when we'd be grooving after a great pot night and join together like old buddies or then again when we'd be formal, icy and estranged because one had trod on the other's being. Yes durable, as well put together as the finest timepiece and mentally as lean and muscular as an athlete. But beyond his wiremesh diaphragm, that tight sifting brain that could weed out falsehood and rhetoric with the unerring instinct of a terrier and make him the equal of any scientist or businessman I had ever met in his sheer assessment of reality, lay that brilliant poetic instrument-panel of a mind which created before one's eyes idea-designs and thought-organizations that had no precedent. Klonsky, as I've said, was not a Romantic poet or man, his first true loves had been the metaphysical poet-hipsters of the seventeenth century like Donne and Marvell, and he scorned like a war veteran a lyricism that was not contained in an idea like tit in brassiere. But this very sense of control gave added thrust to his utterances, there was no waste, and when you were walking or jiving with him and heard him throw out this verbal steel that his mind manufactured in its cease-less Pittsburgh foundry you were aced, man, it went through you like a blade, its concentrated truth created a standard from which you could no more squirm or dodge than JC from his cross. "It is impossible to speak the truth so as to be understood without being believed," said Blake or Zola and it was true of Milt—by the route of his imagination he seized on the inevitable and it left your heart numb as he tore down the supports of the world and rebuilt it by the cunning and inspiration of his vision. I am ashamed now, in the hour of showdown, that I can remember few of his exact quotes, that the years and the electric shock treatments I had to be slugged with during my season of so-called flip have knocked out the lines that drilled me to the core, even if I can't produce exact evidence like a lawyer I know that the reality has to seep through to you, that I have grasped and will grasp enough high moments of the extraordinariness of Milt to build an arch of testimony if not the graven tablet of profundity that his contribution calls for.

Klonsky as I watched him through the years was a man who bore a heavy burden—heavier than mine and my friends. In the midst of the innumerable endless intellectual discussions, raving fights that all of us hip young New York writers would have either at Isaac Rosenfeld's pad or Herbie Poster's when he was living with the now-Evelyn Murray—the yelling, sharp, sometimes hysterical bomb-throwing that would put a livingroom on fire with the Russian-Yiddish intensity that flamed in each of our overbearing egos—Klonsky would always have the tragic forbearance of a wiseman at least 120 years older than the rest of us. The whole feeling was eerie because not only was he younger than the older writers who threw their whole weight of emotional knottedness into the fray, he was grooving, he was fucking more, he was in their eyes the jazzy kid with a chick under each arm, there was nothing in the slightest Lionel Trillingish about him, it didn't seem to fit that he could be a goddamn saint when he had all this going for him! And yet by precept, by example, by knowing when to button his lip and when to stiffen up like Little Caesar his invisible mental and spiritual metronome dominated those living rooms of 15 years ago and set the beat that got into the very balls of all of us who were on that scene. Why, this cool mother was effortlessly putting us down at our own great-writer-geniusy trade and reducing to mere cartoons our private dreams of storming the turf of Joyce and Yeats and all that jive, there was too much perfection even in his apt silences for the ambitious blood to tolerate! And yet I always thought as I made my way home after a night watching Milt in action and then watching him abruptly cut out of a smokefilled, Trotskyish-type livingroom for real action—while the rest of us brainy cripples sat on and on reshaping the world in words until the words became a meaningless sexless hum in our tired ears and on our aching mouths—that his friends and mine had no idea of the extent and depth at which he lived and which allowed him such wisdom, guts, nerve, such jet-flight above our shrinking little empires of personal ego and pride. If ever there was a cat alone, not melodramatically, sobbingly, literarily, showily, but ice-locked in a moonscape beyond our knowledge and performance it was Milt—I thought that and think it still. "I once thought I was the messiah," he told me half-ironically once in 1950 while we were walking around the Circle in Washington Square, and even though his voice had its special irony-dripping tone there was enough truth in it to bring one up short. Suppose it was true? I thought, suppose I was indeed hanging out and digging the new crop of Washington Square chicks with

the Son of God come down again and I was one of the new apostles? I got
the mortal shivers as I heard Milt bite out his words that day because I
knew how different he was from the other highbrow writers I shmoozed
with along the 8th Street route or at parties, there was an intangible and
humbling mystery about his goddamn perfection, he literally could be
a new swinging Christ whose holy knowledge was concealed by street-
crust because of blushing shame at his immortal responsibility. I realize
how nutty this can seem if I say it cold and factually now, and yet you must
understand that Klonsky's entire orientation was metaphysical, religious,
"the poet must think with nothing less than the mind of God" he once
told me, and all of this was handled by him without an ounce of personal
display or the gross egotism that would normally make you suspicious of
someone's coming on in a superpretentious way. Milt had this unswerv-
ing chastity or purity of intellect which always gave "soul" to his most
casual observations—gave character, actuality, reality, none of the wordy
bullshit that big-mouthed writers so easily fall into—and it always took
the edge off his metropolitan wiseguyism, even when the latter unwittingly burned its way into the blisters and soft spots that most of us were
helplessly studded with. Once you realized the atonal scale he played on
it came like the rush of the sun that there was no deceit in this strange
man. He never whored to an audience, chicks excepted, no matter what
the stakes or the occasion; never dimpled his speech, unbuttoned himself,
apologized, retreated, or dodged the implications of words or action. He
was not above lying with foxiness for a specific goal or remaining stonily silent. But when he spoke he said what he had to say with clarity and
economy, he shot down the target of his thought with the swiftness and
proportionateness of an arrow, not with sadism, psychological peculiari-
ties (saying one thing and meaning another) or any of the extracurricular
gimmicks that even the keenest people we know dress their talk with.
What it all boiled down to was that of all the writers of my own generation
whom I had the opportunity to meet, talk with, buddy with, clash with or
even just appreciate through their work—and this includes Mailer, Kerouac, Ginsberg, Bill Goyen, Broyard, Brossard, Jim Jones, Baldwin, all the
35-to-40 hotshots who are blowing my generation's sound in print—Milt
to me was always pre-eminent, the Number One boy countrywide, the

living, human, ultrahuman soul with by far the greatest potential and a man I loved in an unqualified and admiring sense until for the fulfillment of my own personality and "career" I had to assert my own independence and almost break with him along the way. But that comes later.

4

In the climate we all make it in, the age of suspicion, put-down, sneer, needle, it's almost inevitable that a swinging person is going to probe himself for the hidden motivations in the way he acts, makes his little scenes. Introspection is the private playground of every brain around, there's no escaping it, and especially in New York where psychiatry has gotten such an incredible play is there a used condom of doubt that drags down every full-hearted gesture into the subway mire of the psyche's triple-dealing. Face it, man—nothing is safe in our world from the meanest interpretation, nothing is pure or uncomplex, nothing but nothing escapes from the enlarged vocabulary of analysis that our quick and unhappy minds grind out for sheer dissonant sport. Therefore when I once spoke admiringly of Klonsky to an outspoken chick painter who was a friend of mine she said that it sounded like a "faggot scene" to her and rightly or wrongly I was thrown for a skipped-beat loss by this interpretation. I tried to explain to her that as a writer, a guy fanatically engrossed (at that time) and even dedicated to the entire literary pursuit, I was especially appreciative of Milt because his language and thought— his articulation of the very cosmos, as I heard it—were the rarest I had ever run into. She said this was a rationalization, that I loved the man himself in an under-the-sheets, fruity, cock-twining way and used the other as a covering for this love. I cut it off there in a fiery inner rage and didn't try to argue my way through her thorns and up the hill to the mountaintop I knew was there; but afterwards, when I was alone, I was obviously forced in the privacy of my mind to try and cope with this hurting surgery into my masculine pride and come up with an answer as tough as the truth. If it were genuine faggotry I would have to concede it because I turned myself inside out in those days in my slavery to truth, my pride was more invested in what I thought was reality than in stooping to save face. You must keep in mind that I had wanted to be a "great writer" and not a star in a Sutton Place living room—listen to the innocence of a young stud's choices!—and I would have defiantly confessed to murder let alone cocksucking if I truly thought that Ibsen and Tolstoy and the rest of the heavenly lions would approve. My moral snobbery was pinned high to courage and honesty, and even though I felt fear and shame at my weaknesses and vulnerabilities I would at that time hurl them into society itself, blurt them right out rather than hide them even though it meant sweating through the follow-up cycle of anxiety because I felt it was necessary to upholding the fearless hero-writer's role as I imagined it. But I realized when I came down and thought coolly that I wasn't alone in loving Klonsky, and this helped undo the faggot knot which this chick had glibly twisted around me. I had seen the same quality of love for Milt in Connie, in Anatole Broyard, in various girls whom Milt had been making it with, and I finally came to the conclusion that the human qualities which inspire love resided within him—quite apart from me. This was not physical love on my part (which I suppose is the way the defensive modern cat immediately thinks when someone calls him on his masculinity, so bugged are we by what bad or embarrassing thing of ours might be showing to the world). But if it were physical—and I've had only one actual, lowdown homosexual bout in a long if erratic apprenticeship to flesh—I would have felt forced, as I've said, to own up to it and pay my dues.

Yet this was not Klonsky's kick (so far as I had ever known) nor mine, and the love I and others had for him came in awed response to the unique and often seemingly divine beauty of his mind and soul. I began to understand the deeper I thought about it that Klonsky had become a sort of underground institution in Village and New York literary life and that my close relationship with him was only one of a number he had with other eager-beaver young strivers (guys and girls both) who came nuzzling close to the shrine to lap up this supernal insight that my friend effortlessly gave out. This realization in no way lessened my appreciation or made me jealous—and I wasn't above such emotions, like yourself—because I felt from the beginning with Milt that I was in the presence of a man who had really major gifts; comparable in potentiality to a Sigmund Freud or a Joyce or an Einstein and I'm not laying it on even a sixteenth-of-an-inch, and that these ultimately belonged to the world rather than to any single needy individual who latched close to him. Yet it's true that I thought of him as my special buddy and winced when his interest in me wasn't returned with the love and respect—or was it more truly naked selfishness, my brutal wanting to suck his brain dry?—that I poured onto him. (I remember once in 1955 how I fidgeted all afternoon waiting to get Milt's judgment on a book review of mine on Thomas Wolfe's letters that had been turned down by the *Hudson Review* and how when I came into his apartment on Morton Street to get the trusted come-at-4 P.M. word he was sitting with three high hipsters talking of nooky and had forgotten to read my piece and how I grabbed it with a frozen smile on my face and did the cold exit routine.) But even then, smarting from this indifference in my own thinskinned way, I knew in my core that Klonsky could belong to no one person, that it demeaned his being for me or anyone to try and play footsy with it in some trueblue boy-scout dream of blood-brother friendship, that he had to swing where all his engines took him and fly right through our hearts and love if need be because he was surveying one wild fucking blue. Or so I thought—and still think.

As I watched Milton closely during the years of our thickest friendship I saw him silently groaning under the blackest weights of anyone I knew. His loneliness had been trebled by his sense of responsibility, the heavyweight pillar of his imagination stood upright in a galactic night all its own without any of the consolations that lesser dreamers could comfort themselves with. As a man as well as a poet-mind Klonsky had privately dared, challenged and even whipped by the might of his ideas the best figures of his time—to hear him speak of Auden, Yeats, Joyce, Kafka, Beckett, was to hear an equal, a Shelley plain, and the maturity of his comments swept away the champagne bubbles of romance that I sprayed on literature and revealed the steel soul of the cat I championed in all its mortal gravity. There could be no way out for him except by doing work of the same acknowledged stature, he had committed himself by word and action to the league of the "immortals" and he was self-condemned to the isolation and only half-thereness that "immortality" demands of men and women who live in time. There was no childish competitiveness on the part of Klonsky vis-a-vis these stern figures, it was not to test himself in the ring of literature that he braved or broke the standards erected by these twentieth-century culture heroes (like my friend Mailer, who puts courage above reality) but rather it was because he had truly been born with a special line hooked into the inner switchboard of existence, was haunted by what he heard—"Time is a sin!" he once burst out to me in that extraordinary way that made abstract concepts real as your hand—like a religious Poe and possessed a spiritual life so grave and proportionate that only the superbest adult utterance could do it justice.

It was precisely by virtue of this deeper and finer insight that Milt was alone, untouchable after all was said or done, a hip Moses locked on his own Sinai who had to bring those commandments down to the terra (as the good Lord Buckley calls it) via his typewriter or the whole thing, life itself, his life in particular, all things that have meaning and value, would be just one big "hipe" (fake), to use a word he had picked up off the snarling cement of the big town. I saw him embattled in this way, quiet about the enormous confrontation that awaited him in literature, the sleek ships of thought gliding ceaselessly in his mind beneath the con-trolled surface he showed to the outside world. Those of us who loved and admired him—Anatole Broyard and myself, Delmore Schwartz before he went totally into his paranoid bag, to name only three among two dozen who had the literary sensitivity to appreciate what a great horseman into the unknown this dark villain could be—expected tremendous things of our boy and I'm sure he did of himself, very justly. But the pressure on the guy was fierce, always present though unspoken, and I in particular bugged him almost daily about what he was working on and always got an almost virginal, evasive answer—as if I were trying to rape him of his treasure. Unlike the rest of us self-infatuated literary giants on the downtown scene Milt never spoke about his work or inmost thoughts in public, would've bled internally rather than use the work-bit as a gambit at parties, didn't once spill his guts for a momentary psychological or cunt triumph (although it's conceivable and understandable to me that in the night-stillness of his apartment he used his literary weapon to awe down a skirt and get at the morsel). He carried the undissolvable lump of his being intact wherever he went, the boil never broke, he was never wet or rhetorical or easy in any way towards himself or others and I knew from the small-talk of mutual friends of ours that he excited the same sort of curiosity in others as to what he was carrying around in that locked safe-deposit box.

But he was in heavy trouble—had been since the day I first met him although I didn't know it until 10 years later—and it was this that he knew before the rest of us I am now convinced. Geared to poetry, having a potentially mighty and sure poetic vision that had been reinforced by the most intensive reading and chanting (he was no closet poet, when we were high he raised his voice to the reach of his mind and the blind world around me became ignited with light and blessed mental music!). Milt nevertheless was so perfectionist and self-critical that he refused to risk himself upon the page until he could bring forth a cathedral work. He had let trickle out a few poems in the ultraclassy literary mags since the age of 19, but these—subtle, tricky, indirect stabs at his great target which to my mind were not fully committed and were deliberately soaked in the "inwit" and chinese-box effects he knew so brilliantly from his intellectual immersion in seventeenth-century English verse—weren't the major part of his output.[2] Only his own head was the private spectator at his greatest work, witnessing and ultimately rejecting the unfinished feats of poetry that his creative monster threw up for inspection. Instead, to make bread, to keep writing until he congealed sufficiently unto himself to attempt his extraordinary poetic bid, he wrote "excellent" prose for *Commentary* and one or two other academic highbrow outfits—prose on the Village, Brighton Beach, money-changing in the Paris ghetto (he had met the all-time Yiddish caricature there in a hook-nosed beret during six or seven months spent abroad), etc. This prose was and is fine of its kind, superior in its choice of language and gravity but not quite the kind of stunning and grand expression I had expected of him. In the area of prose—which in a kind of rough simple way I always separated from poetry—I had strong self-confidence and a definite point of view, since I had been writing and publishing sentences from my second year in high school on. When Klonsky invaded my terrain so to speak, splashed around in the same common

2. *Inwit* is an archaism meaning conscience or wisdom.

trough of communication in which I felt myself an easy and knowing pro, I tried to see the literary greatness that I knew to be in the man glow through but found myself carping because he was doing his work in the same medium that had always been swimming-water to me. I suspended judgment, always waiting for the time when he would switch to his native poetic vision or what I conceived as such. But it came only haltingly, in droplets, and it was then that I slowly understood that the enormous expectations we lovers had of him plus his own terrible high standards—"Klonsky was a polished poet at 17," Anatole Broyard once told me with something close to awe, which I well understood because Broyard meant precociously adult, aware, responsible, heavyweight as well as polished—had made him fearful that he might never bring off what he seemed fated by his unique combination of brains and soul to do.

The American Novel Made Me

"The American Novel Made Me" is a passionate addition to the rich literature that celebrates and wonders at the young Jews of the 1930s, whose extraordinary bookishness was indistinguishable from their budding patriotism. Like Alfred Kazin's A Walker in the City *(1958), Charles Reznikoff's* By the Waters of Manhattan *(1986), Alexander Bloom's* Prodigal Sons *(1986), and James Atlas's biography of Delmore Schwartz (1977), Krim's essay powerfully captures how "an isolated, supersensitive N.Y. Jewish boy," found in John Dos Passos, James T. Farrell, William Faulkner, Richard Wright, and many other novelists "the America out there and more than anything I wanted to identify with that big gaudy continent and its variety of human beings who came to me so clearly through the pages of these so-called fictions." But this essay is also a full-throated argument for New Journalism as the inheritor of the space once occupied by the novel. Krim argues that the ambitious writer's "only choice is to insert himself into these events through his writing, to become an actor upon them instead of a helpless observer." That is a good description of what New Journalism became from the mid-1960s to the late 1970s, a period that has been called the "last, great good time of American journalism" (Weingarten 2005, 8). Krim pioneered such writing, and in this piece he is one of the first to define and defend it.*

I was literally made, shaped, whetted and given a world with a purpose by the American realistic novel of the mid to late 1930s. From the age of 14 to 17 I gorged myself on the works of Thomas Wolfe (beginning with *Of Time and the River,* catching up with *Angel* and then keeping pace till Big Tom's stunning end), Hemingway, Faulkner, James T. Farrell, Steinbeck, John O'Hara, James Cain, Richard Wright, Dos Passos, Erskine

Caldwell, Jerome Weidman, William Saroyan, and knew in my pumping heart that I wanted to be such a novelist. To me, an isolated, supersensitive N.Y. Jewish boy given the privacy to dream in the locked bathroom of middle-class life these novels taught me about the America OUT THERE and more than anything I wanted to identify with that big gaudy continent and its variety of human beings who came to me so clearly through the pages of these so-called fictions. I dreamed southern accents, Okies, bourbon-and-branchwater, Gloria Wandrous, jukejoints, Studs Lonigan, big trucks and speeding highways, Bigger Thomas, U.S.A., U.S.A.! Nothing to me in those crucial-irredeemable years was as glamorous as the unofficial seamy side of American life, the smack, brutality and cynical truth of it, all of which I learned from the dynamic novels that appeared in Manhattan between 1936 and 1939.

They were my highschool, my religion, my major fantasy life; instead of escaping into adventure or detective fiction—there were no groovy comic books then, such as Pete Hamill writes about 10 years later when Batman flew into his head over in Brooklyn, or if there were I was already a kid snob tucked into my literary American dreamscape—I escaped into the vision of reality that these fresh and tough pioneering writers were bringing to print from all corners of the country. In an odd way, even though most of these books ended bitterly or without faith, they were patriotic in a style that deeply impressed my being without my being able to break down why: they had integrity to the actual things that people did or said, to the very accents of frustration or despair voiced by their characters, they were all "truthful" in recreating American life. This was a naked freeshow about my real national environment that I damn well did not receive at home—a home full of euphemisms and concealments, typical, with the death of one parent and the breakdown-suicide of the other hanging over the charade of good manners—or in the newspapers, radio or at the movies. Except for the fairy tales read to me as a bigeyed child and an occasional boy's classic like *Robinson Crusoe* or *Treasure Island* or the Tom Swift books this was the first body of writing that had ever really possessed me and apparently I would never (and will never) get over it.

How can I communicate the savage greenness of the American novel of 30 years ago as it was felt by a keenly emotional teenage boy?—or girl,

I guess, although it was primarily a man's novel but certainly not totally. I and the other members of my generation who were given eyes and ears and genuine U.S. lifestyle by it knew nothing about its father, Theodore Dreiser, and his beautifully pensive younger brother, Sherwood Anderson, until we became intellectually smartassed and history-minded 10 and 15 years later. We lived in the perpetual present created by those men named in the first paragraph and were inspired to become prose writers because of them. It wasn't really a question of "talent"; if you responded to the leaping portrait of American life that these craft-loving realists (superrealists in actuality) were showing with professionally curved words you created the talent out of yourself; at first in imitation of what you creamed over in their style, point of view and impact, then later in painful effort to do equal justice to your own personal test tube of experience.

The deservedly legendary American novelists of this raw-knuckled period before the war (they were our celebrities, on high!) encouraged an untested, unformed young guy to dig into his own worst personal experience and make something exciting out of it in the form of a story. The whole movement was in the finest and least self-conscious sense the story of myriad personal lives in this country, it encouraged everyone caught in its momentum to look hard at the unique grain of his or her life and its interweave with other lives. None of us who in the late 30s were swept up into the romantic-heroic fantasied career of novelists were in any sense fated for this role, in my opinion; we were baited beautifully by the gusher of skilled novels—Maritta Wolff, John Fante, Dorothy Baker, Bessie Breuer, Daniel Fuchs, Pietro di Donato, Josephine Herbst, (the early) Robert Paul Smith, Tess Schlesinger, Frederic Prokosch, Gladys Schmidt, Irving Fineman, Gale Wilhelm, Albert Halper, Nathanael West, Oakley Hall—that seemed to be goosing each other to shine more truly than the next. To a young, hungering mind once hooked by the constantly fresh stream of national lives that made their debut in these novels—characters from all parts of the country, waitresses, fishermen, intellectuals, lesbians, truck drivers, salesmen, alcoholics, nymphomaniacs, jazzmen, generals, athletes, everything—it was impossible to call it quits; once the "real" American scene entered your imagination through the eyes of these standup individual recorders and native consciences who seemed to loom up, suddenly, hotly, with a rush before the 30s decade ended in World War II, there was nowhere else for the youthful truth-maniac to go but to the new novels hurrying each other out of the New York publishing womb. New fiction was the hot form, contested, argued, encouraged from *Story* to the *New Masses* to *Esquire* to the (then) *Saturday Review of Literature* to *The New Yorker;* the city buzzed with the magazine-unveiling of any new talent, it was news that traveled with enthusiasm (Irwin Shaw in *The New Yorker,* Di Donato in *Esquire,* James Laughlin telling it like it was down at his family's Pittsburgh steel works in *Story* before he became publisher of *New Directions*).

It is very true that as the 30s drew to a vicious close with the Spanish Civil War and Hitler's preparations for the new blood-and-iron stomping of Europe, the politicalization of the U.S. novel became more acute and the bleak international scene seemed to throw its heavy shadow over our comparatively virginal literary pinethrust. But all of this is seen from the cool view of later years whereas if you were just coming alive as a human being in the late 30s it all seemed like one nonstop fictional ball. As a highschool boy, although I bought my *New Masses* every week because the Communists were truly involved with fresh fiction (O Meridel LeSeur, where are you now?) no matter how slanted their typewriters, I found the political-propagandistic implications of the new novels much less important than the powerful concrete punch they delivered. Each of the exciting 30s novelists, it seemed to me inside my comet-shooting young head, were pioneers; they were tackling unrecorded experience in each hidden alley and cove of the country that I wanted to be a part of, bringing it to ground for the first time, binding it up and sending it East for exhibition before the rest of the citizenry. Certainly their moral flame was ignited and burning steadily or they would not have gone to the huge labor of making almost the entire country and its people accessible to fiction; but apart from the explicitly political base of men like Farrell and Wright (and the poignant Odets in drama, although his politics was a left cartoonstrip compared to the flashing originality of his voice) this flame was used to warm their faith in the value of writing truly rather than held aloft as a defiant gesture.

Their moral integrity—Weidman to his New York garment center, Saroyan to a Fresno poolhall, Faulkner to his luxuriant decaying cottonwood swamps (of the soul)—was concerned with how to verbally break the back of unarticulated and unacknowledged truth, that which has been seen, smelled and suffered but never before written. They were to my imagination outriders, advance scouts, and what they brought back from the contemporary American frontier was as rare and precious to all of us who were waiting as the information now hugged to earth by an astronaut.

I saw it in even more private terms; as a boy of 10 or 11 I had wanted to be an explorer, my fantasy-life taking off in the magic snowtracks made by Robert Peary and F. A. Cook who fought over discovering the North Pole and Admiral Byrd and Roald Amundsen who independently reached the southern one. It was no accident, I believe, that the American novelists of the 30s took over the explorer's role in my mind after the merely geographical aspects of exploration had faded into the bottom drawer of childhood. Who else but these self-elected—self-taught—self-starting—gutsy men and women with the sniff of glory in their proud nostrils were the real explorers of this country's unadvertised life? The novelists who electrified me and hundreds, perhaps thousands, of young kids like myself between 1936 and the outbreak of the war were idealists in the most adventurous sense no matter how stained their material seemed to be on the surface. If you said to somebody, as I soon began to after breaking into print in the DeWitt Clinton highschool lit. magazine, that as an adult "I wanted to write" it could only mean one thing: the novel. A bigness impossible to recapture in 1968 attached to those three power-words, "wanting to write." One had the image of climbing the jaggedest of the Rockies alone, flying solo like Lindbergh, pitting one's ultimate stuff against all the odds of middle-class life and coming out of the toughest kind of spiritual ordeal with that book-that-was-more-than-a-book, that was the payoff on just about everything, held in your hand. It was heavenly combat the way I pictured it, self-confrontation of the most hallowed kind, and if my vision of it was ultra-ultra then the legendary American Novel itself at this time was the most romantic achievement in U.S. life for the dreamer who lived inside everybody with a taste for language, style and—justice!

To have wanted to be a writer in this country in the late 30s had about it a gorgeous mystique that was inseparable from the so-called American

Dream on which every last one of our good writers was first suckled before being kicked out in the cold to make it come true. If that phase, A.D., American Dream, meant going all the way, that the individual in this myth-hungry society had the option to try and fly above the sky-scrapers, then writing toward "the great American novel" was not only an act of literature but a positive affirmation of the dreamdust that coated all of us born under the flag. All the driving personal ambition, energy, initiative, the prizing of individual conscience and courage, that operated or was supposed to operate in every other branch of national life entered strongly into wanting to be a novelist—but with a twist. The act of writing a novel made use of all these widely broadcast qualities, yes, but the reward one sought in it was not palpable gold; bestsellers as such were sneered at unless they occurred by accident; the goal was one of absolute truth to the material, to make a landmark on the unmapped moral and esthetic landscape of America that would somehow redeem the original intentions of the country and the selves made by it and represent the purest kind of success story for the person who brought it off.

This meant that being a typical good American novelist in the 30s, even wanting to be one, was *not* finally dependent on having an extraordinary gift for telling a story in print. Certainly there were narrative and stylistic "geniuses" like Faulkner, Hemingway, perhaps even the early O'Hara, James Cain, Djuna Barnes, each buff and lover of the period will name his or her own, and their overpowering skill with the craft produced virtuoso performances that set standards and became models to aim at. But the American novel only became a great art in its outward finish and skill, in the 30s, because of the internal spiritual motivation that made wanting to write it perhaps the sweetest gamble in national life. You might almost say that the romantic promise of the country as a unique society of total justice for all, pegged on the limitless possibilities of each individual—all the raging hope that the American Dream meant to the imagination of its most ardent dreamers—was all part of the religion of wanting to be a novelist when I got the call while in highschool. If the idea of the mystical American novel had not been bound up with all of these big national feelings and aspirations that writhed around in the direct center of one's being, if that novel had not been more than "literature," I doubt if I and so many prose writers my age would have chosen the written word as our badge.

It was the ambition (when the time came at 15 or 16 to tell yourself what you "wanted to be") chosen in the pride of the secret imagination by rebel fantasists, now in their 40s, who believed they could rebuild reality closer to the American soul's desire by writing in the light of a final faith that would transform their portraits of frustration or injustice into the opposite. By this I mean that because they wanted to believe in the promise of the country, were inseparable from its myth, were tied up emotionally and psychologically and every other way with "America" almost as if it were a person—with their own fulfillment as human beings actually dependent upon the fulfillment of the nation at the poetic height at which they conceived it—they felt they could let go in the novel to the full extent of their negative imagination. Everything bad, awful, unjust, painful, stupid, outrageous in their own lives or theirs in relation to the lives around them could be discharged at full intensity in fictional form with the underlying implication that it was just and right to give such ferocious bite to negative expression because it was all an attempt to redeem an invisible, psychic Bill of Rights. Towering idealism, paradoxically shown by the extent of the dark "realism" in the characteristic novel of the time, was the climate in which the fictional life of the 30s grew to bursting; the more the novelist envisioned The Way Things Should Be the more he and his readers felt he had the duty to show the ugly side of the land, the failure of the ideal, the color of the pus, the company goons beating down the strikers.

We kids who wanted to write the American novel knew without analysis, responded totally with our sharpened feelers, to the unspoken values that lay behind any particular book in question; if Weidman's *What's in It for Me?* or O'Hara's *Hope of Heaven* showed heels and weaklings with special corrosiveness of scene, dialogue, action, nailing them to the wall with the brilliance that comes from a mixture of contempt and pity, we shared enthusiastically in the experience because we knew that in writers of O'Hara's and Weidman's stripe the moral judgment was implicit rather than explicit as in a Steinbeck or Wolfe or Wright. It didn't matter to us, implicit or explicit, because we were instinctively clued in to the intention of all the late 30s novelists just by wanting to make the same nittygritty comment on our own experience; we knew by feel that even if a specific book baffled our haughty teenage heads it thrust at us a segment of the country's experience, it was criticizing America under the table in order to purge and lift it, it was forever encroaching on the most taboo, subtle and previously undefined aspects of our mutual life to show a truer picture of the way we lived.

Those of us, then, who couldn't forget what we had already been through—who remembered each hurt, black skin, Yiddish nose, Irish drunk, wop ignorance, too short, too tall, too poor, afraid of girls, afraid of boys, queer, crippled, sissies, young-bud neurotics/psychotics, the most vulnerable and stung of the new generation who could fight back with words—it was we who thought that being novelists would hero-ically reclaim us by recreating the bitter truth about our personal lives and our environment. Obviously it took sensitivity of the most piercing kind to provide the openings in the personality where painful experi-ence could lodge and stick, so that one day it would all be poured forth in answer against frustration (personal and social both); you must never forget that we who wanted to be novelists not only thought it was the most free and ultimately ethical means of American expression, we were also squeezed by the very existential nuts into *needing* fiction in order to confess, absolve and justify our own experience. The majority of us who "wanted to write" were already middle-class losers who couldn't make it inside the accepted framework; the thinskinned minority who were set apart in our own psyches to observing when we wanted to act and to thinking when we wanted to participate—the kids who were constitu-tionally unable to do the saddle-shoed American Thing during the smok-ing acid-bath of adolescence.

Do I therefore mean, to hit it squarely, that writing fiction for me and my breed was a pimply kind of revenge on life, an outcast tribe of young non-Wheaties failures getting their own back, all the shrimpy, titless, thicklensed, crazyheaded dropouts and sore losers of American youth resolving in the utter misery of the dateless Saturday nights to shoot down their better-favored peers in the pages of a novel? Yes, I flatly mean that in part; the mimetic ability, the gift to recreate lifelike scenes and

dialogue, to be good at acute description, even to have one's moral percep-
tions heightened, is spiced and rehearsed by unhappiness. Wasn't the novel
to those of us caught in the emotional hell of American teendom a wish-
fulfillment device for would-be lovers banished from the sensual playland
that taunted us via radio, billboard, movie marquee and our own famished unconscious? From (in my case) the big, smooth, "in" gentile world
of blue eyes and blond hair and supple tennis-racket bodies that I felt I
could never be part of and that then seemed like the top of the heap?

Yes, the American novel for those of us who were precocious outsiders—and there were a thousand reasons why each one of us failed to
measure up to the gleaming Robert Taylors and Ginger Rogerses who
star-touched our Loew's Saturday afternoons and made us silently weep
into the bathroom mirror on Sunday—was a magic, lifelike double in
which we thought we could work off our private griefs, transform them
into messages of hope and light, and remake our lives themselves by the
very act of writing. This artform, then, for us, was many things: the fre-
est and most total kind of expression for reality-loving idealists; the place
where "truth" could be told as it could not in real life or in any place but
one's mind (psychoanalysis was still a decade off for most of us); and a
form so close to living matter itself that the illusion of personally con-
trolling experience instead of being its fallguy or victim could not have
been stronger. Sure, the novel was a legitimate "artform" even for those of
us who wanted to use it for the redemption or glorification of self; but it
was a yielding female art that was responsive to the most private subjective needs and it provided the only complete outlet for the being that was
choked and distorted in our waking relationship to society. To us it was
the golden cup of a modern fable—one which we could fill to overflow-
ing with all the repressed hunger in ourselves and also one which could
announce our fame, toast us to the sky because of our verbal triumph over
the weights that near crushed us, make come true in imagination what
could not be realized in the bruising action of daily life.

Of course it *was* action on a literary level, action with words, but in
the final sense it was substitute or dream-action carefully clothed with the
wrinkles of a photographic realism. The facade of the great realistic style of
the 30s was documentary, bang-bang-bang, everything as hard and metallic

as the shiny unyielding materials turned out in our most modern factories; swift as a biplane, lit up like a radio tube, driving as a racing car on the Salt Lake Flats ("James Cain's style is like the metal of an automatic. You can't lay his story down."—*Saturday Review of Literature*). But this was only the outward enameling that we swung with and mentally caressed because it was all so new, fresh, a prose like the artifacts of the country itself—stream-lined. Our stripped-down, whipped-down appreciation of power loved that clean line bulleting across the page. Yet behind the lean, aware, dirty knowingness we were stylistically tuned in to was that assumption, as if by divine right, of impossible freedom—the novelist working out his total hidden life before our eyes—which made novel-writing in America such a tremendous adventure no matter how pinchingly personal the original motives might be that drove you to your desk.

I am certain that those of you reading this who came of age in the same late-30s period recognize the excitement about the novel that I am trying to recapture because it made me what I am essentially. Can you imagine a human being actually molded by something as abstract as a literary form? Yet it was quite real, not only in my case but in that of the vulnerable cream of an entire generation who graduated from high-school when the U.S. novel had grown so big that it literally stretched us with its broadshouldered possibilities. Our values, coloring and slant as people were dominated by the overwhelming idea of being novelists, the beautiful obsession that kept us secretly, spiritually high like early Christians. It puffed us up with humility, humbled us with pride, made us into every character we imagined and put us in every story we could cook up; but within, not outwardly as an actor might express it (and there were strong correspondences although we novelists-in-embryo toughly put down actors as childish narcissists) and we coolly loved ourselves for the infinite range of life that easily gave itself to us and you could be god-damned sure to no one else. When I flunked out of college in 1940 a year after finishing highschool, for example, this was not even remotely seen as a failure by me and mine but rather as a new and soon-to-be-significant phenomenon which I would be able to write about from firsthand experience. The first time I got laid, drunk, smoked "tea," shipped out (and jumped ship before we left Sandy Hook), saw death, spent the night in a hospital-clean Pittsburgh jail, masturbated over the fantasy of going to bed with my sister, put on women's panties and silk stockings for kicks, got into my first adult streetfight and almost had the mortal shit kicked out of me—all of these "firsts" and a hundred others were special, fated, grand experiences for me and those like me because I was a novelist-to-be and I was on a special trip!

What a dream it was, what a marvelous hurtproof vest we all wove in the name of the novel (which was another name for religion or faith in the nonchurchly modern sense).

2

I did not, finally, write novels as anyone familiar with my output knows; but I was made as person and mind and writer in their image, just as a newer generation (and even my own exact contemporary, Tony Curtis, ne Bernard Schwartz) has been created by the movies. The reasons why I never added my own byline to that passionate list are many, some personal as well as cultural; I may not have had the "talent"—although I published my small share of vivid short stories—or what is more likely the needs of the post–World War II period *shifted* in my eyes and those of my friends and we put much more importance on trying to understand the new world zooming up around us than expressing what we already knew. We became, in manner, crisply intellectual instead of openly lyrical but much of that same apocalyptic sense of possibility that we once felt in the U.S. novel now went into its examination (the name of the game was literary criticism) until the work of fiction became for us a means to examine life itself. Wasn't that what it was all about anyway?—at least so ran our sincere and often troubled rationalization at the time. But even though the form began to slowly change in the late 40s and the early 50s for a radar-sensitive minority of us, nonfiction instead of fiction, the goal remained essentially the same: the articulation of American reality by individuals who really, personally cared because their own beings were so helplessly involved in this newly shifting, remarkably unstable, constantly self-analyzing and self-doubting society that had shot up after the war.

I sweated the national anxiety out in myself, what direction was I going to go in? the idea of the novel still hanging over me as a kind of star but getting further and further distant as my ignorance in other areas—politics, poetry, sociology, history, painting, etc.—was exposed and I tried powerfully to educate myself now that as a non-novelist I was being challenged socially and even in print. The dream of being a novelist, the dream that being a novelist had been in this country, had kept me warm for 20 years; now I was torn from this sustaining fantasy by my failure to act and was forced to fend for my self-esteem in a hardboiled intellectual community (the literary-political magazines where I published) that had no sympathy for my little inspirational couplet on What The American Novel Means To Me. They either thought it was a put-on, because I had written none myself, or a sentimental indulgence. Therefore whether it was because I temporarily allied myself with the so-called New Criticism in its more cerebral search for reality—and there were a number who had wanted to be fictionists (even wrote their one or two novels) who took this further crook in the country's prose road along with me—or because basically I did not think "novelistically" which in all honesty I am forced to doubt or else all my former covetous years were pitiably unreal—or as I believe because "truth" no longer seemed to *me* to reside in my beloved American novel as it had in my young manhood—I began in the mid 50s to regard the novel as a used-up medium.

For a person like myself, confessedly given great hope and direction by this medium, justified in all my agonizing human goofs by its very existence because I thought I could one day redeem them through it, the beauty of knowing the novel was there like a loving woman for me to go to when beaten to my knees, it wasn't an easy emotional matter for me to say in my mind, "It doesn't sing for my time the way it once did." But I said it—at least for myself. What had happened, not only to me but I'm certain to others who came from my literary environment, was a fundamental change in our perception of where the significant action lay: the fictional realism on which we had been shaped seemed to lead almost logically to that further realism which existed in the world of fact; we had been so close to the real thing with the *style* of superrealism that it was now impossible to restrain ourselves from wanting to go over the edge into autobiography, the confessional essay, reportage, because in these forms we could escape from the growing feeling that fiction was artificial compared to using the same novelistic sweep on the actual experience we lived through every day.

In other words the very realistic 30s novel that had originally turned us on made us want to take that giant step further into the smellable, libelous, unfaked dimension of sheer tornpocket reality—my actual goodbye-world flipout in 1955—James Agee actually pounding on his small car in Santa Monica a year before he died and telling a friend of mine who had casually quoted a line from Agee's first and only book of poems, "I wasted it! I should have written only poetry!" sobbing while he banged on the hood with his fists—Elia Kazan looming tightfaced over Paddy Chayefsky and me at the Russian Tea Room saying moodily that he had to see the isolated Clifford Odets, Golden Boy with cancer, who had crept back to New York to sniff the ozone of dead triumphs before perishing on the coast—my remembering while Kazan spoke with disembodied flatness how I had met Odets at 17 at the U. of North Carolina and how he had taken me for a drive in his fast Cadillac (?) and switched me on so that I rapped pre–*On the Road* about speed and how the strange iodine odor came from his antiseptic-smelling body and wiry brillo hair—all these once-reportorial facts now became the *truer* story for those of us whose appetite for what it had been, built up to a point no longer satisfied by fiction.

In addition to this feeling of irrelevance that I increasingly had about the novel as a meaningful statement for the late 50s and 60s, the audience for it in America was no longer as loyal and excited as it had been (as I had been!) when we were first mentally-emotionally bowled over by its momentum. TV, movies, electronic communications of every sort were cutting into the time that people who were totally alive to their era could spend on prose fiction; if it was *story* you wanted in the old *Saturday Evening Post* sense, you could get that dramatized for you on the Late Late Show while you did a multimedia thing with your companion in bed, and it was only the specialists, critic-teachers, the people in the book trade, who seemed to me to hold out strenuously against admitting that the novel's dash was being taken away from it by the new media. These electronic whispers of tomorrow could in a momentary flash do what Flaubert and Conrad spent their lifetimes trying to achieve with words: "Above all to make you see."

Of course, you can say that the post-Faulkner U.S. novel was no longer sought out for story-values per se but rather for radical insight into existence; that the form provided a framework for an attack from a completely different "existential" or "absurd" quarter than the realistic 30s novel; granted—and also more than granted that extraordinarily talented writers were opening up this form and "making it as limitless as the ocean which can only define itself" (Marguerite Young), writers such as John Barth, Young herself, Ralph Ellison, William Burroughs, Joseph Heller, Norman Mailer, Hubert Selby, Donald Barthelme, etc., the list is big because there were and are that many highly imaginative writers who have been doing remarkable things with fiction during these last 15 years. (Ironically, as the novel has shed its effectiveness in our society, there has never been since the 20s such a yell of native talent, wild originality, deadly challenge.) But the basic fact I noticed as the deluge of new fictional expression increased and readership became a frantic duty rather than the great thrill it once had been—and the practical impossibility of keeping up with the diversity of new books (new lives!) became obvious—was that the impact of the novel on our beings, on my being, was no longer as crucial as it had been. From my own changing point of view tremendous stateside writers could still appear in what was loosely called a novel—and what form has become looser?—but *I* felt that the entire role of the American novelist as I had originally heroized it had to be transformed into something entirely different if it was to be as masterful to the imagination of the 60s as it had been to me in the 30s.

In this sense: writing fiction for me and my breed was not an entirely realistic, naturalistic, rational human enterprise in spite of the authentic-seeming imitation of reality on which we were indoctrinated; underneath the accurate surface it was all bathed in dream or myth; we who wanted to mythologize ourselves and America (and they were inseparable) were trying personally to lift the national life into the realm of justice, we were attempting to use the total freedom of our imaginations to rearrange the shitspecked facts of our American experience into their ultimate spiritual payoff. We wanted to "build Jerusalem" (Blake) out of America's "fresh, green breast" (Scott Fitzgerald) and the novel was our transcendent, our more-than-could-ever-be vehicle for fulfillment of both ourselves and the national seed that had begotten us. In other words, *our* novel was a form of imaginative action. If you, the novelist, couldn't make it to the height of your vision in so-called straight or nonliterary life because of one handicap or another, then you did it through your books even better; but the goal was the same as the man of action's, your books were deeds that came out of your mixture of vision and moral commitment (Hemingway, Farrell, Wolfe) and they stood as the seal of where you were humanly at as clearly as if you had sewn your psychoanalysis into the binding. There could be no faking about taking a stand and you were measured every step of the way by readers who took your fictions as acts that influenced the world of the U.S. spirit until they were outdistanced by new and more penetrating fictional commitments. It was a soul-contest of the keenest kind, with the country as beneficiary.

But the effectiveness of such "imaginative action" today seems to have been reduced to mere toenail-picking by the tornado voices of the mass-media. Whether you and I like it or not we have all—novelists as well as readers—become pawns in the newscast of each day's events. "Our" novel can no longer affect these events in even an indirect sense: almost every ounce of my energy (for example) is used in coping with my own life, things happen too fast for me to be affected by the stance of some protagonist in a fiction, I am spun around by each latest threat to my survival, and what was once the charismatic lure of the American novel now becomes for me and countless others an extravagance instead of a necessity. But isn't that what makes artforms change—when life leaves them in the lurch? When concern moves away from them, not by design but by a gut-barometer whereby we seek out what is most vital to us and jettison the rest? Because of my existential impatience with fiction as it related directly to my life—and I concede that this could be a flaw of temperament although it is backed up by my professional work as an editor of new writing—I was and am forced to believe that in varying degrees my experience is true for readers all over the country; and I felt and feel that prose must find a form that can meet this reality and win readers back to the crucial excitement that I experienced when the novel was more than a novel and evoked a mystic response that molded being itself as well as an author's reputation.

But what happens then—I have had to ask myself—to our significant writers who are still either in love or "imprisoned" in a traditional form that is losing its cultural importance in spite of their brilliant personal fights? What happens—I must ask myself again—to that awesome authority of the imagination that encouraged, demanded, people who called themselves novelists to create human beings (like nature itself) and dictate their lives and fate (like gods or supreme justices of the universe)? What happens, further, to that great ton of submerged American experience locked inside themselves, more raw, subtle, potential human riches than the combined knowledge of sociologist-psychiatrist precisely because it was garnered by their blood as well as brain? What happens, in short, to that special mission, what to me for many years was almost a holy mission, of making an imaginary American world that would be more real than the actuality itself?

And where, as a final question, does the legendary U.S. novelist go when except for a handful of individuals he is no longer a culture-hero in a radically new environment, when his medium is passing into the void of time, and when he is still stuck with a savage inner need to speak, confess, design, shape, record—the whole once-glorious shmear?

3

There is one drastic way out and even up, as I personally see it now, and that is for the American novelist to abandon his imitation or caricature of a reality that in sheer voluminosity has dwarfed his importance and to become a communicator directly to society without hiding behind the mask of fiction. (I must make it clear that what follows represents my own need and desire imagined out of the confusion of our time and my unwillingness to accept a literature that is primarily a reflection of our era's helplessness; committed novelists, and some very sharp ones too, will doubtless block me out of consciousness and continue to make an ever wilder art of their materials to match the nuttiness that fevers our days; I will always be a sucker for their spirit and bow to the new images they will offer us, but my compelling feeling that now as never before is the time for writing to become direct action and cause things to happen makes even potentially great novels grow small compared to what I can envision if the novelist puts his power into speaking straight to his audience.)

The American novelistic imagination as I received it with open heart and mind 25 and 30 years ago was really the most fully human expression of this society at that time; and it is the new humanizing of American writing by the boldness of direct communication, the revolutionizing of the writer's relationship to his reader, that seems to me tremendously more needed right now than the pale echo of fiction. Instead of "novelists" I believe we now actually have only literary individuals themselves, men and women struggling with their own destinies as people in relation to other people and with the problems that threaten to swamp us all—emotional, sexual, political, racial, artistic, philosophical, financial—and that these should be stated to the reader as candidly as possible so that he, too, can be brought into the new mutual non-novel of American life and make possible a truly democratic prose of total communication which can lead to new action in society itself.

I believe the ex-novelist, the new communicator that we can already see in the early and various stages of his making (Mailer again, Tom Wolfe, Norman Podhoretz, Dan Wakefield, Willie Morris, Frank Conroy, Jan Cremer, Erje Ayden, Fielding Dawson, Irving Rosenthal, Ned Rorem, Taylor Mead, Frederick Exley, myself) should speak intimately to his readers about these fantastic days we are living through but declare his credentials by revealing the concrete details and particular sweat of his own inner life; otherwise he (or she) will not have earned the right to speak openly about everything or be trusted. He should try and tell the blunt truth as in a letter and this includes the risk of discussing other individuals as well—no one should be immune from the effort to clean house, undo bullshit, lay the entire business of being an American right now on the public table without shame. So that the new communicator's statement—about himself, his friends, his women (or men if he's gay), people in public life, the cities, the war, his group therapy, wanting secretly to be a star, wanting to sleep with Mamie Van Doren (or Susan Sontag), still hoping to love and be loved, putting his being directly before the reader as if the page were a telephone and asking for an answer—will be evidence of the reality we are *all* implicated in, without exception, and be in itself a legitimation of this reality as a first step to changing it.

How can we suffer from too much truth? Who isn't heartened to see it when an author respects us enough to tell us where he really lives and by the very nature of his writing asks us to reciprocate? But there is a more significant reason for total leveling than moral straightforwardness in a time famous for its credibility gaps, and that is the power that can return to literature as a daring public act which has to be respected by even those pragmatists who habitually reduce words to playthings. If I write about my own being in relationship to other, real, named, social-security-numbered beings and present it to you, the reader, it is inevitable that you too will be pulled into the scene (at least a few hundred of you will know either me or one of my real-life cast of characters) and must take up an involved position about what you're being told and experiencing. You are interacting with me and my interactions with others so closely—assuming I have the ability as well as the stomach for truth—that you have become part of the experience whether you seek it or not. You Are There, now included in the network of my life as I am included in yours, and what you have seen and heard and identified with in my communication will not be put aside like a "story" because it is an extension of the same reality that unites us both; I will have established a sense of community with you about the destiny of both our lives in this uncertain time which becomes as real as if we were communicating in the flesh—and as existentially suspenseful. Reading then becomes a crucial event because something is *really happening* in existence and not in "literature" alone; due to what I have written our very lives will touch, the reader is just as much a participant as the writer, your isolation or indifference has been penetrated by reading just as mine has by writing and the alienation of our mutual situation has been broken through by my need to make you experience what I have and share my consciousness.

In other words, I want American prose to again become a potent force in the life of the individual in this country and not just his novelty-seeking mind; I want it to be necessary and important once again—even more important, since I see its purpose as having changed—as I knew it when it shaped me; and I want this selfishly because I have devoted my dreams to this business of words, and my own self-respect as mere human refuses to accept that what I once took vows for can be written off as a second-rate art, which "madeup" and irrelevant writing often seems like now in the aftermath of the electronic-visual explosion. But apart from my own investment in literature—and I can't rationalize and say that the source of my ideas doesn't spring from my own unappeasable imagination as a would-be American novelist who was once promised the world and shall never forget that fact—who can deny that once a gifted writer tells it to his equals exactly "like it is" we are moving into a new dimension where writing is used to speak directly to being? And where the talents of reporter and pamphleteer are now usurping those of novelist to awaken individuals to the fact that we all share a common bag as probably never before?

It seems plain to me that the man we used to call the American creative writer is now beginning to express living history through himself so urgently that he is becoming its most genuine embodiment. The imagination that once led him to build a stairway to the stars has been forced into coping with his own imperiled life on the same quaking ground that holds us all. Out of necessity he is being pushed toward a new art of personal survival and as a result he must move ever further into the centers of action to fight for his fate; if he left the crucial decisions of our time to The Others while he concentrated on his "work," as in the old days, he would be living a lie because he is now too personally a part of each day's events to pretend they don't shake him and dominate his existence. His only choice is to insert himself into these events through his writing, to become an actor upon them instead of a helpless observer, to try and influence the making of history itself with his art so that he can save himself as a man. His driving need for direct participation in our national life *now* makes the new communicator want to change America in a pact with his readers, and to begin by changing his own life in the commitment of laying it on the line.

For myself time has shown that the vision I saw or read into the American novel which immediately made me a character in it, the "hero" who wants to be a novelist, could only be fulfilled if the novel was real and was acted out. Perhaps—in the light of this late recognition of my own need to personify what to many others existed solely in the imagination—I was scheduled all along not to write novels, as I always thought, but to try and put their essence into action. If this is so, I embrace it willingly as the more exciting and now necessary of the alternatives; for just as I once believed that art was the highest condition that a person could attain to, I now believe that if this is true it is the duty of those who conceive such an ideal to use it on society itself and take their literary lives in their hands, if need be, in the dangerous gamble to make The Word deed. That's where the new prose action is 30 years after I got hooked—for real, chums, for deadly real.

The 215,000 Word Habit

Should I Give My Life to The Times?

This article about the New York Times *and the power it has over its readers was published in* The Nation *in 1988 and reprinted in* Best American Essays *1989. It is an excellent example of how Krim—like the best comedians—turns exasperation and complaint into laughs. The article lambastes the* Times *for its outrageous girth, which humbles the poor reader who equates its consumption with intellectual respectability. The great model for the Beat generation—Krim included—was Walt Whitman, who praised the beasts of the field because "not one is respectable" (1944, 67). Krim never met an intellectually respectable position he liked and never gave one a break. Nothing beat the* Times *for respectability, so Krim tears into it. Readers secretly wish to put the paper down "for a minute and look out the window. But you just can't do that, it's like masturbation used to be for the current senior-citizen generation—God is watching."*

Laughs aside, Krim here continues his worthy attack on the ideal of endless self-improvement through education that he started in "What's This Cat's Story?" (chapter 1). Krim's work has offered me many opportunities to think about Saul Bellow, and here is another one. Bellow identified Herzog *as a "negative* Bildungsroman." *Moses Herzog does not educate himself, said Bellow. He de-educates himself. As Bellow put it, over the course of the novel Herzog "comically divests himself of an appallingly bad education" (Cohen 2008, 11–12). Krim also understood how important such a de-education project could be.*

Excuse me while I put my *New York Times* aside and try to write this piece. It's now 8:35 in the evening, absolutely no baloney, although we used to use a shorter word, and I'm still working on Section B, page 4—"For Ferraro, Lost Friendships But Stronger Family," continued from page Bl. I've already had my supper (broiled tilefish, little potatoes, bean salad, a glass of Boucheron blanc de blanc), not my breakfast, and I still have twenty pages of Section B to go plus Sections C and D. Let me not wring out the page count here—the real situation is monstrous enough—actually, the upcoming eighteen pages of Section B are nonreading materials, only classifieds. But what with hard news, features and reviews, tonight I still have forty-three pages to mow down before tomorrow begins in three hours and fifteen minutes and the same torment awaits me!

What's happened? What's going on? Was *The Times* always like this except we didn't notice—of course not, even I know that, but when did it start becoming pointedly pathological as a daily read? When did it really start getting out of hand for all but the professional human mice who spend their days in the stacks nibbling away at print? There's no exact telling when it passed over the line, but obviously it first began during the tenure of A.M. (Abe) Rosenthal as executive editor, 1977–1986. Rosenthal himself has said that he picked up new journalistic finger foods from that preppy innovator Clay Felker, when Clay was at the helm of *New York* magazine during the 1970s—before Mad Dog Rupert ate little Clay up and spat him out for jaw-strengthening exercises.

But what did Rosenthal pick up that has now made *The Times* into such a Frankenstein of unrestrained virtues, or did it turn into a noble glandular case for other reasons also? What we know is this: Rosenthal took from Felker all the magazine-type concepts he could newspaper-ize—things that Mr. Prep had originated as consumer service features, like The Passionate Shopper, The Underground Gourmet, Best Bets, How the Power Game Is Played, etc.—and fleshed out (why? why?) what was already a portly paper. The answer to the mystifying question posed just now flashes in: yuppie readability, entertainment. If you're in print, why should the mags have it all in the Age of Plush and newspapers continue to trod the same old grim rut of who, what, when, where—how square!

At the same time old shrewdie Abe was adding ice-cream colors to his paper's sober garb, that garb itself was also draping an increasingly voracious global waistline, until the weekday *Times* now averages around 215,000 words of hard copy, and Sunday's close to a million.

Two hundred and fifteen thousand words is what you're trying to grapple with every day; so am I, buddy, and it makes me want to cry at the torment that publisher Punch Sulzberger is inflicting on us. Could it be that Punch is one of those legendary "Jews without mercy," as some hard-liners of that beleaguered faith have been called? Is it necessary that a human newspaper be this size? But while you ponder that, keep in mind what an obsession, what a massive hanging goiter, the very thought of this great paper has become in the minds of its cringing readers. Just as I have my own forty-three unread pages of today's *Times* in escrow until I can gut out a first draft of this article—don't worry, I'll redeem those pages if it kills me before I permit my eyes to close tonight—so there must be untold thousands throughout this city (country?) who are fiercely trying to finish up before the new day arrives with its new 215,000-word responsibilities. Few regular readers have the chutzpah to snub the paper entirely for a day, never doubting they will be punished in some mysterious way, yet few can get through it without psychic confusions about what to skip, whether to read on (onward!) at the expense of earning a living, vacuuming the rug, writing a letter to the phone company, etc. I kid you not, it's become a weird confrontation for many people, this *New York Times,* all of its sheer mass comprising nothing less than an alternate reality—but too fearfully much for people who don't want to devote their lives to it, as James Joyce asked his readers to do with his books.

Not only does *The Times* stagger its own readers with the enormous weight of humanity dumped on them every morning; things have reached the point where it has become America's number-one commissar of the real. If it doesn't appear in *The Times,* such is the unconscious reflex of the faithful, it isn't worthy of existence. To the extent that now it even reports on itself as a necessary source in the making of news. For example, the day after I started flinging my own frail frame against this graven idol—the day that occurred three hours and fifteen minutes after the raw beginnings of this piece, a while back—the chesty confidence that holds power in place was exercised in full view without a hint of shame. Reporter Herbert Mitgang, doing a story on a new one-volume encyclopedia called *Chronicle of the 20th Century,* interviewed its editor in chief for no particular reason except that he had once been a managing editor of *The Times.* His name is Clifton Daniel and he is, incidentally, married to Harry Truman's daughter, so why not chuck him and his new brainchild a PR bone?

Fine, but then in the very same issue reporter Mitgang was himself interviewed by yet another *Times* reporter, Edwin McDowell, for writing a *New Yorker* magazine article (see how the old-boy network widens!) about American novelists who have been harassed by the Federal Bureau of Investigation. Reporter McDowell tells us the article was inspired by a book that Mitgang has put together called *Dangerous Dossiers: Exposing the Secret War Against America's Greatest Authors.* Did that end it? Not on your life. William H. Honan, until recently cultural editor of the newspaper, was then quoted by reporter McDowell as saying, ominously, *"The New York Times* was not aware of the article or book until today."

Ah, *The New York Times!* It quotes itself, it interviews itself, it sometimes seems to get confused with the world itself, which is reflected in the knit brows of the earnest—especially that flock of briefcase-carrying young women one sees on lower Manhattan buses, wrestling with the four windmill sections of you know what, too overpowered by duty to put the whole thing down for a minute and look out the window. But you just can't do that, it's like masturbation used to be for the current senior-citizen generation—God is watching.

I wouldn't dare say that *The Times* isn't the most incredible 30-cent buy in New York (a Snickers bar would have to come down 20 cents even to get in the running), but do dare say that it is at a perilous subjective cost. One can easily imagine actual madness and suicide resulting from an impossible attempt to read all of this newspaper every day, and I wouldn't be surprised if some CUNY social psychologist isn't already working on a grant proposal. If reality in our time has gotten out of hand—the new science of disorder, Chaos, can serve as a clue, correct?—then the newspaper has followed suit; but like the old naturalistic novel it has resorted to accretion of detail to keep up, rather than initiating a counterinsurgency against the flood.

There is a crisis at *The New York Times*, nor should my saying this make you guffaw when you look at the profit statement. If a reader feels that only by brilliant eye-editing (quick hop/skip here, forget this one, now should I plunge?) can he reach the last page without putting a sixty-foot trench in the middle of his day, something is gravely out of whack. Would it take a nuclear wipe-out to make *The Times* start all over again, lithe and quick? Is it crazily advisable to get even bigger and more impossible, an intimidatingly honored but unread monument, like William Caddis's *J R* (National Book Award, 1976), totally cowing the reader with its vision of absolute coverage? Or is it obvious, as I concede it is, that this indefatigable machine of money, talent and heedless pride will continue on its way even when its desperate readers are cudgeling their brains, looking for a formula to cope? Even as a new day hints at its arrival in the predawn Eastern skies with Sections C and D of yesterday still barely skimmed? Is there to be no end to it, seriously, even unto eternity and beyond?

5

Remembering Harold Rosenberg

Krim at first seems an unlikely choice for a tribute in Commentary *to Harold Rosenberg, the influential art critic known for his appraisal of the Abstract Expressionists. But the 1978 article is a distillation of Krim's twenty years of misgivings about and appreciation for the Jewish intellectuals that once ruled New York. The recrimination of Krim's "What's* This Cat's *Story?" (chapter 1) is not on display here, though in earlier years Rosenberg's success and status would have been enough to generate a verbal blitz about how these achievements set off powerful currents of envy that unman lesser writers. Instead, this reminiscence is an almost loving portrait of Rosenberg and the Jewish intellectual world he was part of, "the New York radical/highbrow milieu with all its fanatical scholarship and ironic, jesting humor."*

He moved very slowly in the last couple of years, this towering figure who could have passed for Captain Ahab, rising and dipping with his cane in hand as he inched his way up Tenth Street toward Third Avenue to get a cab. That's when I mostly saw him when he was in town; he and his wife May had a place in East Hampton for at least half the year, and for another two months he also taught in the Committee on Social Thought at the University of Chicago, along with Saul Bellow and some other celebrated types.

I usually caught up with him on the street, or invited him over to my little place diagonally across from his big World War II bargain apartment, where he couldn't resist pointing disgustedly out of his window to the sloppy, *New Yorker*-cartoon back yard of his neighbor. But it was easier to be with him on neutral turf—the sidewalk or my place—than

in his own musty fortress, where you felt hemmed in by the claustropho-
bia of his artifacts and history, thirty-odd years in one place, and where
he had the advantage over you for his own fun and games. Besides, the
phone was always ringing and that made me jumpy and even jealous.
Harold Rosenberg was a very popular man who had carved out his own
loyal circle of friends and flatterers after a lot of lean years bucking all the
Establishments.

"Now that I'm famous," he once said, "they all want a piece." He wasn't
the most modest of heroes, he even gave in to some embarrassing moments
of public self-caressing, but it was all easily forgiven (as one would a hungry
kid). W.H. Auden, born a year after Harold, had once been called the most
intelligent poet writing in English; one could say the same about Rosenberg as a critic. I never thought of him primarily as an art critic, although
that was where he made his celebrity, and with justice.

But he brought to it that long, ascetic involvement with literature and
ideas that characterized all of the *Partisan Review* intellectuals, a kind of
World War II *Magic Mountain* group who scrutinized the Western world
from 7,000 feet up in the Alps of the New York mind. Rosenberg was never
one of the power-hungry politicians of the *PR* group, like that frustrated
culture commissar, Philip Rahv. As a matter of fact, he was one of the most
skeptical, lancing, anti-political iconoclasts I've ever run into, for all his
expert Marxmanship. But you could no more disassociate Harold from
the *Partisan Review* enclave than you could two of his keenest competitors,
Clement Greenberg and Dwight Macdonald.

No particular love was lost between Macdonald and Rosenberg,
Yale vs. Brooklyn College, if you will, but the amusing thing was that for
almost a quarter of a century they lived in the same four-story whites-
tone across from me, Rosenberg on the second floor, Macdonald on the
fourth, often barely grunting hello. And then both these brilliant unaf-
filiated radicals followed each other onto the *New Yorker*—once for both
of them the incarnation of vapid luxury values—where each became a
star in successive decades. O. Henry would have had field day with a plot
that began like this.

As for Harold and Clement Greenberg, I never heard either one mention the other, but I knew through the Village grapevine that they were

engaged in a bitter intellectual battle over the Abstract Expressionists—as to which one would represent the movement to the baffled public, or even to the AbEx's (as we called them) themselves, who could certainly use a lucid explicator. But neither Rosenberg nor Greenberg was about to step aside and win a nun's award for self-effacement. Clem was warm and homey, red-faced, going prematurely bald, the very image of a kindly vulnerable uncle to jittery young writers and painters on the scene. But he was known to use his fists, not just his mouth, when he felt he had been wronged.

■   ■   ■

Harold looked and shone like the Lion of Judah. He was about 6'4", a really heroic-looking prince among the bookish intellectuals, added to which he had a congenital game leg that had to be propped up like a bayonet when he was sitting. It gave him a Byronic wound, which increased his romantic air—the ladies were not immune—and probably made a number of his thick-lensed intellectual peers as defensive as hell.

But Rosenberg was not taken in by much of this. He had a workaday absurdist view of himself and the world, once telling me with matter-of-factness that when he was looking at some art in Paris during the 60s a French war veteran spotted him limping on the street and thought he was a fellow victim of the carnage. He made Harold get into the wheelbarrow he was pulling and pushed the celebrated oversized critic to a gallery four blocks away.

I'm not sure Harold had the dogged patience of Clement Greenberg in the long-range contest for contemporary American art—life as a sort of matinee idol of the intellectual underground had made him impetuous, mustaches bristling—but he was by far the more intense, ideologically dramatic writer. When he coined the famous phrase, "Action Painting," for the emerging New York style, Greenberg answered with a bit of cool sarcasm that Harold was trying to sell the new movement as "not actually art, or at least not art as the stuffy past has known it." Clem prided himself on knowing more about the traditional history of oil painting, which he probably did, and tried to put Rosenberg down as a slick mystifier who wanted to sound "very profound, and most art critics have a special weakness for the profound." Between the two of them, these formidable polemicists more or less sliced up the original AbEx crew into the Rosenberg and Greenberg camps—a phenomenon that later gave Tom Wolfe mischievous fuel for *The Painted Word*—with Harold becoming the unshakeable lifelong champion of Willem (Bill) De Kooning and Clem going to bat for Jackson Pollock, at least for a while.

One story that filtered back to the Village from East Hampton in the late 40s must have given Greenberg a chuckle. It seems that Harold had ticked off the super-sensitive Jackson Pollock by saying in an *Art News* article that there were a few people in the new movement "who can't draw." Pollock, a neighbor out on the Island, immediately thought that he had been singled out. He brooded over these three little words all day, after reading the piece in the morning, either with or without consolation from the bottle. (Reports differed; he was then going to an analyst and some said he was ferociously sober.) At any rate, around twilight he stormed into the Rosenberg's modest compound and shouted for Harold to come out of the house, where Jackson would then take him apart like a fillet. After an electric silence May Rosenberg stepped onto the porch and is supposed to have said: "Jackson, stop picking on poor Harold, he has a bad leg!"

The idea of this huge colossus, Rosenberg, being stopped from defending himself with his hands because of a stiff leg was slightly ridiculous to those of us who knew how he towered above the opposition. We also knew that Harold could even be a bully on occasion, so quick and overwhelming were his ideas allied to that intimidating, royal size. But Pollock was an inspired wild man when the mood was on him, and he had wrecked the Cedar Tavern more than once; May Rosenberg probably had the right idea, although I would have been curious to see Harold in action. Using your typing or painting hands for another lowdown purpose was not a strange sight on the New York lit/art scene of the 40s and 50s.

But Wyoming-type head smacking (Pollock hailed from Cody) was about as far from the dazzling machinery of Harold's urban intellect as you could get. He often struck me as the embodiment of the pure, passionate mind itself, like those great French modernist poets—Baudelaire, Rimbaud, Mallarmé, Valéry—whom he revered. Even in his last published article in the *New Yorker*, when the first martini (his quick test of health in the last years) must no longer have tasted good, he speaks with chaste feeling about "the light, calm, order, and sensuality of Baudelaire's classical paradise." He was loyal to his pure aesthetic brotherhood to the end.

Most people who knew of Rosenberg as one of the incontestably big critics of the day had no idea that he wanted above all to be a great poet. He even published the usual slender volume, *Trance Above the Streets,* but his poetry never really bit into the age as did his prose. Yet the poet was always there, in the neat titles of his collections and articles—*The Tradition of the New,* "The Herd of Independent Minds"—and in his "prestigious way of compressing and interweaving his metaphors," as the *Saturday Review* once put it. It was a poet's sensibility, toughened by all the years spent in the calculating world of prose, which led to that extraordinary style he eventually mastered, where every word is pared to the bone and the bones themselves have been soaked in the last forty years of New York intellectual life.

Yet I got impatient with Harold's style before he died, and wonder whether he hadn't reached his limit a few years before and wasn't just repeating himself at the end. I knew him to be a simultaneously funny, brilliant, immensely provocative, emotional man, and yet the prose face of his *New Yorker* pieces always hid the emotion, was as smooth as oil, set as a mask. You could always anticipate the measured calmness of a Rosenberg piece, even the trenchant dynamite of the thinking tucked knowingly under the surface. It may be that the time we are now living in wants the "dynamite" out front, but whatever the reason, the impact of his unique style had worn off for me and came to seem more and more an unflappable virtuoso performance.

Since I always thought of Harold as an almost wickedly Houdini-like thinker, one who could only have come out of the New York radical/highbrow milieu with all its fanatical scholarship and ironic, jesting humor, I don't know how valuable his work was strictly as art criticism. Time will tell its usual tale; as will the other art pundits and rivals, who may have been stifled when Harold was riding high, wide, and handsome. But I would think that for the major painters of his generation and the one directly behind it, just as for younger writers like myself, he was a goad and a leader by virtue of owning one of the most scintillating intelligences of the period.

Still, whether he did justice to the newer American art movements that followed AbEx, and whether he really *saw* what the younger artists were doing—I have my doubts. In fact, I think it all to the good that his influential *New Yorker* column will now be opened up to a new generation, even though he made it a platform for some of the most original ideas ever published in that magazine about contemporary art and its effect on contemporary life, meaning us. He never wrote at a level beneath his thinking.

Rosenberg's going sweeps a period with it. Most of the survivors of the *Partisan Review* heyday are now tired or quiet, and of the original Abstract Expressionists only De Kooning, at seventy-four, is still painting his dreams. Harold came out of a context of Depression radical politics and mandarin poetry and Greenwich Village painters' cabals that will never come again in the same zebra-striped package. And as one of the "kids"—at fifty-six!—who inherited the beauty of stunning, prodigious minds like his, I feel that a vital fiber has now been torn from my being forever. It is a loss that is impossible to communicate: those we could never imagine dying are passing into mist, and we who are left feel naked and unworthy, no matter what good things might come our way.

PART TWO

Whites and Blacks

6

On Being an Anglo

In the 1990s, multiculturalism became a boon to scholars investigating Jewish identity and, specifically, how Jews came to be perceived as white and whether that is an identity Jews should wear.

In the following four essays Krim shrewdly sizes up the ironies of his own white/Jewish identity, the pitfalls of white/Jewish admiration for black life, and the language of black rage that saturated American life in the late 1960s and 1970s. This 1978 piece, "On Being an Anglo," is a neat introduction to the section because in it Krim knowingly embodies his two identities, white and Jew—making it clear that the former was not his idea.

Taos, N.M.—There are only four recognized breeds of people out here: Anglo, Spanish, Indian and hippie. At 55 I'm naturally an Anglo, which would have furrowed the brow of my innocent, trusting mother, whose maiden name was Ida Goldberg. But it amuses me to be stuffed into the identity of the ruling American archetype that helped make my life miserable as a kid.

Being an Anglo, I begin to see, is not a joyride. Local Mexican-Americans (Spanish) resent your stuffy, seemingly secure sense of yourself so much that they go out of their way to embarrass you. Like the curly-haired, smiling, slightly loaded guy who parked his pickup truck in front of my friend's art gallery the other day and urinated on what was left of the season's sunflowers.

He gave me a wink and a shrug as I came walking across the gravel carrying my Anglo-type attaché case. I shook my head in a solemn, condemning way and confirmed every feeling that this mischief-maker was brought up with, namely that I was a prude and a hypocrite who probably picked his nose when no one was looking.

As an Anglo, I protest that. The only reason I don't go making my toilet all over the place is that I have these awful standards to live with, not because I'm a snob. If this freewheeling Chicano was as surrounded by as many books on genealogy and responsible gardening as we Anglos, he too would have thought twice about using the sunflowers as a commode.

It's not an Anglo's fault that he's been conditioned to clean between his toes at night and repress strange noises at the table. A number of us have recently made secret trips to the new town psychiatrist, Dr. Dennis Wood, just to learn how to express ourselves more openly without feeling unnerved. But it's not easy to slay the habits of generations.

Like every Anglo, I resent the Indians and Spanish playing up to me with their imitation of Anglo courtesy and then laughing behind my back. In my other incarnation, as a New York Jew, I was once or twice laughed at to my face, and that stung me into belligerence. But I now see that Anglos have a much subtler form of meanness to contend with.

When I asked for a pack of "hard-top Marlboros" at the local 7-2-11 grocery last week, a man with a thick Spanish accent waiting in line behind me mimicked my words to himself without looking up, his lips sarcastically caressing the weird Anglo cadences. I silently bit the bullet—my bottom lip.

People rarely insult an Anglo head-on, of course. But we're made to know in a hundred little ways out here that the good American earth won't be ours much longer. As a new Anglo, I know deep down that we don't want that power anymore; it's a burden to us and deeply offends our sense of simple justice. We're tired of being singled out as privileged when we often feel as pale and ordinary as a dish of pudding that's been forgotten in the fridge.

Truly, in my new Anglo bones I know very well that I don't have the desert starkness of the Indian, the raw vitality of the Spanish, the nose-thumbing perversity of the hippie—even the drive of the energetic Jew! I just want to do everyday things correctly and quietly, without taking advantage of anyone or calling attention to myself.

But a lot of the country doesn't see it that way. I'm what they want to bring down. Yet I can't finally blame them. We Anglos have become somewhat colorless and predictable, I'm sorry to say, unfair advantages have probably nestled in our dried-out hands too long.

I can even feel it by the way I smile at the hippies in the plaza as they throw the first snowballs of the fall at the pole-high American flag, hoping to score a direct and brutal hit. I should speak out, if I weren't so timid, but the time-honored Anglo response is to make your judgment privately, then be on your polite guard when the hippies push into my friend's gallery to keep warm.

■　　■　　■

In two months I won't be an Anglo anymore. I'll be back in New York on the same Village streets where two relatives of the Roosevelt family get out in work clothes and sturdy gloves, mop and bucket, every Saturday morning, and for three hours tirelessly clean the entire block of dog dung, cigarette butts, etc., then open the hydrants and wash it down.

I'll be standing on my stoop along with a casual black neighbor, watching the show and smoking a Marlboro. We'll smile to each other as this couple performs the work we'd never dream of doing, then surreptitiously flip our butts in the glistening gutter. What the hell, these little butts are so tiny they'll never be seen. And even if they are, those Anglos won't dare say a word.

7

Anti-Jazz

Unless the Implications Are Faced

In his 1961 review of Krim's Views of a Nearsighted Cannoneer, *James Baldwin wrote that Krim is, "God bless him, almost the only writer of my generation who has managed to release himself from the necessity of being either romantic or defensive about Negroes" (6). Baldwin was impressed by "Anti-Jazz" and its companion piece, "Ask for a White Cadillac" (chapter 8). Eric Sundquist overlooks this evaluation in* Strangers in the Land: Blacks, Jews, Post-Holocaust America, *where he assumes that Baldwin would have dismissed Krim as a "real sweet ofay cat," the way Baldwin did Norman Mailer and his essay "The White Negro" (2005, 69). Such an oversight is typical. Krim's achievement is almost completely ignored by the massive literature on blacks and Jews. A notable exception is Seth Forman's* Blacks in the Jewish Mind *(1998, 108).*

"Anti-Jazz" appeared in 1957, the same year as Mailer's "The White Negro." Both essays investigated how blacks influenced whites through jazz, but Mailer took the romantic view that the influence was profound, that white hipsters "had absorbed the existentialist synapses of the Negro" (1959, 341). Krim drew different conclusions. He saw a superficial imitation of manners and language among whites that "give up their own personalities, or distort them beyond recognition." This debate is timely again. The popularity of rap music has led many to note that whites are copying a black style that grows out of conditions they do not share or understand.

Krim's chief concern here is "with the crucial human problem of what one's identity is." He takes it for granted that identity is not endlessly malleable. We cannot choose to be anything we like. History and culture exist, they shape us, and we must acknowledge these influences to live an authentic existence. Jewish life can be a strong incubator of this idea. Philip Roth denounced the false "tolerance" that seeks to erase the differences between people, differences that are sources of power (1985, 201). Saul Bellow mocked the view that people can overcome "the limits of heredity, nature, and tradition" (1995, 173). Krim signals that he is writing from a Jewish perspective by citing the Jewish jazz musician Mezz Mezzrow as an example of someone who recklessly tried to overcome those limits. Mezzrow "did everything but paint his face black in his effort to behave and be like a Negro." Krim poses a simple and challenging question: Do such people "truly realize what they are doing?"

Jazz is the music of U.S. colored people. It came out of squalor, ignorance, the most ignoble and pathetic kind of conditions, which ultimately produced its beauty and excitement. But do white jazz-lovers who experience the warmth or brilliance of the music, who adopt the "philosophy" of jazz, truly realize what they are doing—do they want to embrace the values of life that helped produce this music?

From college kids to intellectuals one sees and hears people playing with the terminology of jazz, hot or cool, using the colorful language, snapping their heads back and forth as they listen to the music, having a grand time experiencing the sensations that the great rhythmic beat of the music sends out. But have they—we—earned the right to speak its language or adopt its casual ways of expression without facing the basic issue behind it? That issue, in my opinion, has to do with the crucial human problem of what one's identity is.

Jazz, the greatest cultural contribution of the Negro thus far to this country, cuts through all classes, job distinctions, political differences, American racial backgrounds. It is now known all over the world and was the original creation of what until just recently was the lowest class of citizens in this country. Into it was poured all the frustrated love, humor, the hardness and softness of a group of people who were forced to live and love apart; it was musical talk from outcast person to outcast person. But it transcended its beginnings and began to catch the ear, perhaps even mold the ear, of potential young musicians from all over America, regardless of race. These young musicians, now in their 50's—from Condon, Bud

Freeman to Benny Goodman or Krupa—began to pick up not only the fascinating American-Negro rhythm and notes (since the colored man taught the jazz instruments to sing, as was said of Mozart and the instruments of the symphony) but the spoken language as well. An afterhours spot was a "late pad;" the drum was "the skins;" a girl was "a chick;" marijuana was "charge" or "tea;" the examples are endless, but they were all improvisations and verbal inventions of the Negro, and the white men who played the music used them in their language and in their *thinking*. It is impossible to believe jazz would have blossomed so strongly without this soil beneath it; it was an attitude, a philosophy, indeed a way of life. And through it came the Negro triumphantly striding into American life, barred from no home, making of his athleticism, his pleasure-loving, his violence, yes his "shiftlessness," his geniality, a potent force.

Jazz said: Love my music, love my philosophy, which lies behind it. So we had white men and women imitating the Negro philosophy of life because they loved the music from which it inevitably and naturally came.

But few people probed this giving up of one's own identity or tradition to adopt that of an underdog people; nor will there be an attempt here at a psychiatric explanation of why any certain individual did so, because I believe it was the *style* of the music that was so impressive that it dominated other so-called psychoanalytic considerations. But regardless of the reason we had the phenomenon, put so plainly in Bernard Wolfe's book on Mezz Mezzrow, *Really the Blues*, of a Jewish man who did everything but paint his face black in his effort to behave and be like a Negro. It seems to me that this permanent problem is at the bottom of every white man who plays jazz and those non-Negroes, both men and women, who love it and listen to it.

Does the reader think that jazz, that great beat, those beautiful melodies, the way a blues singer belts a song, the way a sax man raises up on that platform like an athlete and lets the combinations fly and flow from his horn are anything but Negro in their central heart? They are the Negro in America thus far, the humor, wit, easy stride, subtle rhythm, great power; but also, *which is harder to accept,* the awful ignorance, poverty, violence, lack of constancy, me-firstism, and all the other facts that open-minded people who know Negro life well—the inner lower-middle-class communities of Harlem, or Newark, or Durham, North Carolina—see all too often. And that too is part of jazz.

When one reads *The Village Voice*'s graceful and worldly jazz columnist Mr. Reisner write about "the titans" of jazz, and all sorts of romantic business about the greatness and sophistication of jazz instrumentalists and the hipness of its philosophy, one can't help remembering nights in the Harlem apartments of unlettered Negro acquaintances where the music—the beautiful jazz music—came from unpaid $400 Philco combination radio-phonographs with the husband and wife at each other's throats over the money (before she got hit) and the four children screaming at the sight. Or the jealous husband, another time, who thought his drunken wife made a friend of his in the bathroom (where the john was stopped up and had been for two months because the landlord of this rotten end-of-hell trap wouldn't fix it) when he went out for a pint of whiskey. And again the slugging of the wife, the grappling on the kitchen floor, the screaming of the kids, and the final hop out of the first-floor window by a 5-year-old little toughie to get a cop on 125th Street and bring him back. And the cringing of the white man, me, during all this.

All this went and goes into jazz, too, especially the lyrics and beat that seem so rich and hearty to white appreciators; essentially it is this kind of wild, violent, bitterly unjust life that produced what we know as jazz. What would you white jazz-lovers say if you saw your own people, thousands of them, enslaved to the hocus-pocus of various Father Divines—still operating by the carload in Harlem and Philadelphia—buying furniture and especially the needed music-boxes, phonograph or radio, on time, time, time, the girls buying earrings and the men booze or sharp ties when the kids need medical help or the ex-wife is forced to "go into the life," become a prostitute, "because my old man don't give a shit what happens to me."

Here is a life, to the uninitiated reader, that at home, in its intimate relationships, its man-woman relationships, is as sordid, as painful, as grotesque in its accumulation of miseries as anything in Maxim Gorki's autobiography. But it was out of this that the art of jazz music came, it was the pit of ugliness and frustration being made beautiful and attractive *as hell* through the release of music.

But think now, if you will, of the many white people one knows who use Negro expressions, talk the language of jazz, imitate the drawly Southern Negro's voice (like my friend Jazzbo Collins on the radio, or for that matter even that modest master of good musical taste, Crosby) and you will see the contradiction that exists. These people, the white jazz-lovers, hear only the extract of the kind of life that produced this music; its sensuality, rhythm, humor, passion, even closeness and intimacy. It is especially attractive to young people who are disillusioned with the values of white society. But no matter how beat they are themselves, the majority have literally no idea of the conditions of life that lie behind this music. They hear and appreciate its externality in the sounds; but that part of "the life" which they see, no matter how many Negro friends they number in Greenwich Village or in the entertainment or literary worlds, is misleading. It can never tell them of the background of jazz, which would actually revolt some of its greatest propagandists.

But to return to the central problem, which I make no attempt to solve, what of the white musicians or jazz lovers who give up their own person-alities, or distort them beyond recognition, just out of the influence of the music? Do they truly realize what they are doing? Most young Negroes who come from the environment that produces the language and man-ners adopted by the people I am speaking of want to escape from it, better themselves in the white world; and yet the white cat or chick wants to immerse him or herself in the very thing that every sane, sensitive Negro knows only too well, to the point where the beauty of the music is no com-pensation for the bitterness of the life, or at least a large part of it.

Are the white jazz-lovers, especially the vocal ones in print, being truly responsible, are they ultimately entitled to love this music so enthu-siastically without mentioning either with anger or, better, soul-searching, the life from which it comes, which still goes on with a vengeance in every all-Negro community in our country? One is forced to think of people like Mr. Reisner, who recommend books and models of the "jazz philosophy," which if you happen to know their authors or any of the "titans" of jazz makes you realize that there is a sadness in this whole business of hip-ness, and broadly in all of jazz, that is just as real as the attractiveness of the music.

I would like to conclude with a few observations for which I see no solution, but seem to me at the root of all that has been said here. How "Negro" should white musicians and jazz-lovers allow themselves to become? Can they maintain a balance of self-identity even while loving the music? And more important, does it follow that to be influenced by the music you have to adopt Negro values, some of which are not as great as they're cracked up to be by romantic white liberals because they came out of poverty, superstition, ignorance? Further, does just loving the music mean that immediately you become part Negro, as it were, turn your back on your own inheritance? Can we who love the music allow ourselves to embrace "the way of life" that lies behind it when an outraged realistic head can see it clearly for what it is?

And finally, when you use or glorify the jazz language and manners, are you trying to trade in your identity like the dramatic example of Mezzrow, or are you giving it a bigger and perhaps better dimension? One would like to believe the latter; but almost every true, religious jazz-lover I have ever met who is white has stretched and perhaps even perverted a part of himself to be something he can never totally be, nor would ever want (nor would his colored friends want him) to be if he looked at it coolly.

It seems to me that all white people who are magnetized by jazz should face and discuss these unglamorous life-problems that its "legalization" has left in its wake. They are more real than further deification of jazz artists or their literary disciples; they have to do with the ultimate problem of what a person's identity is. Is it even possible to play the music with feeling without "feeling colored" yourself? And if out of love for the music a white person tries to think and feel colored, isn't it a distortion, doesn't it provoke distrust and some contempt on the part of Negroes—even wonder?

Most ordinary Negroes, whose emotions are naturally put into jazz, know only too well that the ecstasy of their music came out of a rough and often abysmal life; many would gladly have sacrificed the music to a white skin and a less brutal standard of living. The next time we act *hip* and *dig* the joys of jazz expression, musical or verbal, we could do worse than pause and ask ourself if we are prepared to accept the price and implications of this seemingly groovy way of life. It comes from something further down and wayer out than I think you dream of . . . man.

8

Ask for a White Cadillac

Krim wrote "Ask for a White Cadillac" as a companion piece to the "Anti-Jazz" article that rankled Greenwich Village with its unorthodox views on the pathologies of black life that, in part, informed jazz. Far from the apology that some of his critics wanted, Krim in this essay furthers his exploration of white fascination with and attraction to black life by setting aside any pretense of objectivity. Here the "I" is front and center. This is Krim's own story of his love affair with Harlem and how the passion burned itself out. For the student of black-Jewish relations, it is rich with insights and suggestions. Krim writes almost glibly that his "notions about the natural greatness of Negroes" stemmed from his "being the unreligious modern American Jew who feels only the self-pitying sting of his identity without the faith." Despite the offhandedness, Krim was saying something new: that there was a vacuum at the center of postwar Jewish life that was filled by identification with blacks. Years later, historians wrote about this vacuum. Herbert Hill noted that the Jewish Labor Committee, founded in 1934 to help victims of the Nazis, was without purpose after the war. "In an effort to justify its continued existence, the JLC tried to become a civil rights organization within the labor movement" (Hill 1998, 265). Another writer saw that during the 1950s, the left as a whole—with Jews prominently represented—"seized upon [Martin Luther] King and the Civil Rights Movement to regain some of its vitality and popular support" (Friedman 1998, 122). Krim here suggests, in 1959, that a similar lack of vitality existed within individual Jews attracted to black life.

He was also early to understand that his "fixed" nose was like the hair-straightening products used by blacks to copy white models of beauty. And when he says that among blacks "good looks are earned by the way in which you bring art (dress, a cool mustache, the right earrings) to shine up an indifferent nature.

100

The Negro has been and is an artist out of necessity," he offers a way to understand the prominence of Jews in the cosmetics business. Helena Rubinstein, Charles Revson, and Estée Lauder may also have felt they had to earn good looks through artistry in a Christian society that did not value their natural attributes.

After I wrote my article on the white jazz hipster and novelty-digging people of every stripe who imitate the Negro's style I came in for biting criticism in Greenwich Village, where I live. Friends of mine, and newly made enemies as well, accused me of being anti-Negro; the influx of tense, self-conscious, easily offended Negroes who have recently hit the Village has made any frank statement about colored life extremely delicate and often full of double-jointed guilt feelings; in fact I myself began to have grave doubts as to the truth of what I had written when I saw the reaction.

I now believe (a year and a half later) that my comments were essentially valid—in spite of my own, and every man's, limited angle of vision—and therefore of value, since any ounce of truth that can be dug out of the world and placed on the scale of justice wins you a moneyless prize, but one that gives point to your days. After the anger, sentimentality and truly hurt communications that I received after my original piece, I felt compelled to investigate the whole bruised subject in more depth and background, to search for my own true attitude in relationship to the Negro. More than most white or non-Negro men I have haunted colored society, loved it (and been stomach-kicked by aspects of it), sucked it into my marrow. I aim here to tell as much of the truth about myself in connection with Negroes as I am capable of, with the knowledge that while it will no doubt expose my weaknesses of mind and temperament it will be another small step in destroying the anxiety that makes us try to balance on eggshells and bite our tongues and souls for saying the wrong thing. Complete equality for Negroes (and more subtly, for whites in relation to them) will only come when writers and speakers level down the whole dirty highway of their experience—level all the way.

Having been born in New York City in 1922—Washington Heights, to be exact—the image of the Negro first came to me through jazz and a colored maid (how proud young Negroes must burn at that—I would!)

who took care of me as an infant. As to the maid's influence, it is unconscious but surely present; I remember nothing except for the dim feeling of warmth, big soft breasts, perhaps honeyed laughter with the head
thrown back in that rich queenly way of buxom Negresses which has
been typecast to death but is too vital to succumb. But I do recall vividly
the beat of jazz rippling through our household from morning until night.
My mother played Victor Herbertish light classics on the piano and my
father sung them in a proud-peacock way, but my older brother and sister,
during the 1920s, got right on board with the new jazz music and the big
beat pounded away from both the bedroom (where my brother blew his
tenor sax) and the living room (where my sister edged my mother off the
piano seat and made the keys hop). What fascinated me as much as the
music itself, even as a boy, was the verbal style that accompanied jazz;
the easy, informal play on words that instinctively crept into the voice of
people who spoke about or sang jazz. This was a Negro invention quite as
much as the music itself, a wonderful, melodic, laughing camp with the
hard white words that took the lead out of them and made them swing.

But it was translated into white terms, or middle-class lingo, by the
easy-throated, golden-rhythmed Bing Crosby, whose voice dipped and
flirted and slurred with great beauty to my 12-year-old ear when he introduced a tune over the radio or played with some lyrics while singing. It
always seemed to me that Crosby had a powerful effect on the lovely
small-talk of this country, its inflections and casualness, and that this
came from The Groaner's being the almost unwitting ("I was a wheel
that rolled uphill"—Crosby) ambassador from the black-belt to the white.
He dug instinctively and with great fluid taste—in spite of his collegiate
front—what lay behind jazz: the good-natured mockery of stiff white
manners by Negroes and the sweetening of dry attitudes into rich, flex-
ible, juicy ones.

The Negro to me, then, in my kid-ignorance, was jazz and fun; this
was due to the accidents of my personal history—the fact that I came from
a northern, comfortable, Jewish middle-class family and was shielded
from any competitive or side-by-side contact with Negroes. Colored men
and women were exotica to me during my childhood, magical, attractive aliens to the normal rhythm of the world. I take no pride in saying

this. But because of my background and that of thousands like me, we couldn't know Negroes as the rounded human beings they are but saw them through a particular porthole of wonder and odd fascination. Unfortunately, Negroes were thought of as being the servant class by people of my economic bracket; but because my family was Jewish and in some ways (in others not) compassionate because of the endless history of trial of the Js, Negroes were never mistreated in my home. To be fair, however, I have heard numerous Jews from lower economic groups—not to mention people from every other race in America—heap verbal scorn on the *schvatsa*,[1] even at this late date. It goes without saying that such people are bucking for a future red harvest of bloody noses, both for themselves and more thoughtful people.

When I was about 15 the Negro came into my life with a wallop directly connected with the sex drive. It should be no secret that until the war the colored girl was the great underground sex symbol for the U.S. white man, the recipient of his trembling mixture of guilt, leer and male-sadistic desire. Feeling inferior due to what I thought was my physical unattractiveness (where have you heard that before?), I had never been able to make it with the pretty, aggressive Jewish girls of my own environment; not only was I an awkward, fear-haunted, savagely shy kid, my ego had been blasted full of holes by my being orphaned at the age of 10 and my having lived in a state of psychological panic all through my adolescence. I took refuge in heartless masturbation (yes, in technicolor!) and the Negro chick in all her stereotyped, Cotton-Club majesty became my hot partner for imagined sex bouts of every exciting kind.

There should be nothing shocking in your reading this. Thousands of white American men have done the same, I'm positive, and the reason why they selected Negresses hinges on the double taboo of both sex (long explained and still life's quivering ice-cream) and physical intimacy with a colored person. Together, the behind-the-shed appeal to a *timid* and therefore *prurient* white kid like myself was dynamite. Thus it was that the Negro girl became my jazz queen, someone who loved (in my

---

1. *Schvatsa* (or *schvartze*) is Yiddish for black, often used derogatorily.

imagination) to ball, could never get enough, was supreme physically, rhythmically, ecstatically—"Oh, baby, give it to me!" I know only too well that this is a standard cliché and that my blunt picture of it might be offensive; I also know that for historically and psychologically understandable reasons there was, and still is, some truth in this stereotype.

My love of jazz and raging enslavement to sex came together and focused burningly on the colored girl, but it wasn't until I moved down to the Village—already violently pro-Negro-radical-crudely White-manesque—in my early 20's that I first slept with a Negro chick. This baptism was a nothing experience: the girl was Villagey, neurotic, affected, unswinging, among the first of the colored pioneers to make it downtown. In those, my early Village days, she was just one gal among several whom one made and then lost in the merry-go-round of kicks that whirled me and my buddies. Days and nights were lost to us in an almost fanatical pursuit of pleasure during the war-ruptured mid 1940s, with booze, tea (pot), literature, psychiatry and sex leading us headlong into the foam of ever-new experience. But this wild hedonism played itself out in time both for me and my friends. We had to cope with our private selves. Weaknesses in each separated us from the pack, and our lives became more private, secretive, smaller, pettier. Things we had hidden from one another and from ourselves began to obsess us, and I in particular found that I had no genuine confidence toward women and could only make them (or so I thought) by not wearing my glasses and not being myself. I could no longer go on the charm and boyish good looks—as synthetic as not wearing my specs, since I'd had my nose "fixed" when I was 17—that buoyed me up when I first climbed aboard the Village kicks-train. I was becoming lonelier, more introspective, and hung up to the ceiling in my relationships with women. But my hunger for sex (warmth! light! life! the complete holy works!) was as cancerous as ever, and I craved, needed, burned for the gratification. It was then that I first began to go up to Harlem and really see dark society in its own hive.

2

I naturally went to prostitutes in Harlem, but I eased my way into this way of life—for it became that—by enjoying and digging the sights and human scenes of Harlem for their own sake. Here was the paradise of sensuality (to my thirsting eyes) that I had dreamed of for years, but had never gotten to know except for fleeting, half-scared trips through this no-man's land. Now, nerveless because of the heat of my desire (and even when this hot temperature in me waned I never once felt the anxieties on Harlem streets that my white friends tell me is a normal fear) I began to sidle up to my quarry from several sides—listening to jump music from the fine box at the Hotel St. Theresa bar, seeing the show in the small room at the Baby Grand on 125th St., going to the Friday night stage shows at the Apollo, getting the rhythm and feel of the place by stalking the streets and being perpetually slain within by the natural style of the men, women and whizzingly precocious kids. Harlem to me, as I got to know it, was a mature wonderland (until I saw the worms behind the scenery). Not only was the sex there for the asking—provided your wallet was full, Jack— but the entire place was a jolt to anybody with a literary or even a human imagination. The streets hummed and jumped with life right out in the open, such a contrast to the hidden, bottled-up phobias that I knew so well. You can't hide your life if you're a poor or scuffling Negro and live frankly among your own people. Jesus, it broke out everywhere, the crip- ples and amputees I saw begging or laughing or triple-talking someone out of bread (loot) on street-corners; the high heel-crackling (with metal plates so they can be *heard*, man!) sleepless hustling chicks on some mon- ey-goal errand in the middle of the afternoon, wearing shades against the enemy daylight and looking hard and scornful of tragedy because they knew it too well; the go-all-night male cats gathering around some mod- ernistic bar in the late afternoon, freshly pressed and pomaded and ready to shoot the loop on life for the next 20 hours, crap-shooting, card-playing, horse-playing, numbers-running, involved in 15 mysterious and button- close deals with women—either girls working for them in "the life" (hus- tling), as I got to say, or sponsoring them in some gambling bit or this or that. The whole teeming place was alive to me in every foot of every block, for there was everywhere a literal acting-out of the needs and desires that all of us are condemned to cope with until we quit the scene, but here in Harlem there could be no false pride about doing your dirty-work behind a screen. Even when I cooled my sexual heat there many times—in a cellar near a coal-bin, lying on a pallet, or in a room with four other men and women pumping away on three cots barely separated from each other—I felt little or none of the shame I would have had in downtown Manhattan doing the same thing. On the contrary, I began to think that this was more real, natural and human, given the situation of Harlem as I knew it and as people had to live it out to *make* a life for themselves.

I began to feel very much at home uptown—and felt thunderbolt excitement, too. As a writer as well as a frustrated, needy man, I could never get over how Russian the amount of dramatic life I saw was. Here were the same radical contrasts of money and poverty, of tremendous displays of temper and murderous emotion, of hustlers and johns making their arrangements next to funeral parlors where last night's balling stud had perhaps just been laid out. (I obviously mean Russia before the Revolution of 1917.) Humor, the most quick and subtle shafts of wit, shot like sabre-points of Mozartian sparkle across street corners and bars where hostile or drink-angry people were mouthing the favorite Harlem curse for all frustration, "Motherfucker motherfuckin motherfucker!" And through all this street-embattled life ran the perpetual beauty of clothes, threads, duds!—bold, high-style dresses and appointments on the girls (flashing jewelry, dyed platinum-blonde hair over a tan face, elbow-length white evening gloves handcuffed with a fake black-onyx bracelet) while the guys were as button-rolled and razor-sharp as hip clotheshorses stepping right out of a showroom. Certainly I saw poor, frayed, styleless people and outfits: but the percentage of sartorial harmony and inventiveness was keener, perhaps out of the need to *impress,* than I had ever seen in any other single New York City community.

In fact I learned about clothes in Harlem—more than I ever had in college or fancy midtown Manhattan, when I worked on the *New Yorker* surrounded by smooth Yale-Princeton-Groton boys. Clothes merely seemed an external decoration to me then, and the pork-pied smoothies often seemed like phantoms with little or no personality. But in Harlem clothes literally make the man and woman: every hair of imagination, flair, nerve, taste, can be woven into your garb, and the tilt of a hat on a hustling, attractive spade cat will be pretty nearly an unerring clue to the style you'll run up against when you speak to him. The girls love a big approach in dress, stagey, rich, striking, and when you consider the color they have to work with you understand the way they'll pour on reds and yellows that smite the eye and make the average white girl seem mousey and drab by comparison. My own style of dress when I first hit Harlem was the casual approach which I wear in the Village and also uptown in the 40's—shined loafers, button-down shirt with a decent, perhaps regimental-stripe tie, a suit jacket and odd slacks (mostly the GI khaki type that can creep by as smart if the crease is truly alive). When I made my opening passes at the whore bars in Harlem—which you get to know by keeping your ears open, following a smile, seeing the number of chicks lined up at the mahogany—I felt embarrassed by my outfit in contrast to the tailor-made cordovan-shoed jazz that the bar-jockeys were showing. My embarrassment was correct to feel, for one or two of the frank hustlers I ran into soon after I made my play—within the first week—wondered "why the hell don't you dress, man?" (I later found out that in Harlem there are three gradations of male dress: clean, pressed, and "dap"—for dapper. Everything can be squeezed into these three categories, and by Harlem standards I was barely clean for any kind of swinging night-life.) After I had been properly put down about my clothes, which were slightly insulting to the dress-tight colored hustling chick and the sharp male studs, out of misunderstanding, I had to think about drapes in a new way.

I was taught that in Harlem if a man wants to make out with women he has to behave like a man, not a boy or a half-vague intellectual: he has to dress like he knows the score, is not afraid to be bold and flairful in the eyes of women, and wears a slick, capable look about him. Probably Negroes who have scored with money uptown wear the insignia of it on their back as a sign of pride or superiority; certainly some of it is narcissistic strutting and over-obvious, but in a rough community like Harlem there is nothing wrong in proving who and what you are by your appearance. You can't be a self-effacing Shelley or a Chopin—even the homosexuals in Harlem, which is bursting with them, are brash, daring, cop-baiting individualists—when you're competing with other lean and hungry cats for the sweet cream of life. After I was given a fishy eye because of my dress a number of times, my refuge in casual Village-type clothes underwent a change, and I dressed as rifle-hard and classy as I could when I later did my uptown balling.

What had happened inside me was this: I realized that downtown, in white society, especially the knowing, introspective, intellectual-literary kind, we put much value on "good looks" in the sense of paying excruciating attention to wart-tiny details of face and figure, and going into a tailspin when someone has facial one-upmanship over us. But up here in Harlem, where everyone is sunburned for life and can have little of that false self-love in what a blind fate has dealt them, good looks are *earned* by the way in which you bring art (dress, a cool mustache, the right earrings) to shine up an indifferent nature. The Negro has been and is an artist out of necessity, not necessarily a fine artist but a human one; and if you want to score in Negro society you have to compete within the rules that an *original* kind of tough life has laid down. I wanted to score. The romantic-fantasizing me had lain flabbily undeveloped on its Villagey couch of yearning for too long, and I knew that if I wanted the chicks and the heart-deep kicks I had to get with it in a hurry.

I learned not only to dress but to bargain with hustlers, keep my appetite in my pants and not show it, and develop all of the masculine wiles that I had once attributed to philistines with grudging acknowledgment of their effectiveness, but scorn as far as I was concerned. I became careful about money after I had been suckered out of perhaps 50 dollars, either by girls who promised two tricks and gave only one (or none) or "guides" who maintained they knew great flesh-parlors, and then disappeared over the squeezed-together Harlem roofs after letting me wait on a fourth-floor landing while they made the "arrangements." I was being shaped by the environment in which I was trying to make it, and while I never yielded up my total personality I cut out many of the affected, indecisive mannerisms that almost seem to be the norm in bookish white society.

Pleasure was my business in Harlem and I had to approach it like a businessman; I had to control my wandering kicks and appreciation to a technique for getting what I wanted. Along the way I picked up, almost without knowing it, a hundred small bits of advice and know-how: never turn your back on a bar when standing there, it makes you conspicuous and is in bad taste; come on slowly and coolly with a hustling girl after looking them *all* over (Negro bar-buddies hammered this home), since you're a man and have the good money in your pocket or you wouldn't be there; ask for no favors, butt into no fights or arguments ("You might get hurt bad, Dick!"), show courtesy and good humor when put down by some h-high or drunken chick climbing a peak of meanness within herself; always buy a bouncer or bartender a drink when you can afford it; remember that music, sports and money are driving, magnetic topics in Harlem and will always get you an interesting conversation if you're hung up or ill at ease.

I had come uptown with a predisposition. Not only did I love the girls and the music—which reflected each other in warmth, drive, flashing humor, lusty beat—but my eye and heart had always been a pushover for the stylish, spirited Negro ace as well. It was therefore no strain on my grimly introspective makeup (a complaint I heard from several other isolated white writers who were drawn to Harlem but felt hurtingly awkward when they tried it) to make my way into colored society, to dig the tasty food, kibitz easily in the luncheonettes, listen to the finest and hippest jukeboxes for hours and be a happy addict with my quarters. I felt I was being educated and given a human feast at the same time; nor did I prey on it. I gave both spirit and gold and the greatest appreciation for what I got, and can say now, without self-consciousness, that the human exchange was equal. Most of the Caucasian men who come to Harlem to get laid are looking for easy eats, and carry their stiff marriage of caution and superiority so squarely that they are verbally speared in a dozen ways without knowing it. All they hear is laughter and they wonder why. The other greys who come, including myself, are the imaginative, sensitive, troubled, daring kicks-seekers who the hipper local Negroes take to without any break in stride, recognizing masculine brothers in the eternal war with fate, chicks and George Washington's dollar. There was no segregation once I got in. The masculine brother idea, like the female sister one, is a reality in Harlem, not just words; broke and drunk I found no trouble or shame in borrowing money for carfare back to the Village, which I repaid the following week, or even getting my ashes hauled on credit (which is difficult and embarrassing to set up with the average, where's-my-next-movie-money-coming-from hustler unless she digs you in the boy-girl moonlight sense).

But I also saw by about my third month in Harlem the low, cruel, igno-rant, selfish, small-minded side of uptown life. I was first cheated out of money by lies and juicy come-ons which never matured. O.K., one expects to be played for a sucker in the tenderloin unless one keeps one's wits, and I learned what every pilgrim through the thighs and breasts of Fleshville and Champagne Corners has had drilled into his bank account since man first sought pleasure. I accepted it. But my finer senses, if after all this I can legitimately use the phrase, were humbled time and again by the sight of men beating women, hustlers drunkenly cursing and clawing each other, friends of mine (Negro men and women both) boasting of how they had cheated Con Ed out of money by fixing the meter or how they had boosted goods from Macy's and Bloomingdale's, or how some date I was out with was afraid to go home to her old man (the pimp she lived with) because he'd take three-quarters of what I gave her and beat the living jazz out of her if she held out. (This particular girl once hid in my apartment for three days out of fear, narcotizing herself among other ways with watch-ing Darren McGavin as Mike Hammer on TV and impatiently waiting for Darren to "get to that dirty fighting, man, cause it's *too* much!")

I saw the most fantastic lying—not the exception but the rule with the gang I traveled with—to get money for H (heroin), jewelry, clothes, whisky, pot, the latest Big Mabelle record, money out of a sucker, stranger, relative, brother, mother; it made no difference. Yet side-by-side with this I saw the human good that lay just an inch away from its flip into unargu-able nastiness. For example, the great naturalness and wit of most of the people I got to know—their fluid ease, generosity, life-shrewdness, laugh-ing philosophical fatalism—when taken a notch to the left became reck-lessness, hostility without restraint, the pettiest haggling over coin, the most sullen selfishness. The qualities I dug in Harlem nighttime Negroes often became, in other words, the viciousness I repudiated in all human beings who were bent on degradation of another, the violence of those who whined, fibbed, stole, backed out of jams, played others for fallguys, the gold in their teeth and back pocket. Apart from my jazz and sex self-interest—my plain thirst—I came to Harlem with an open mind that was ready and willing to find beauty in much that the squares, or engineers as we called them, backed away from. I found that I, too, backed like a trooper. I should have realized that I couldn't get my kicks, my needs fulfilled, without a corresponding loss on the other side of the human balance sheet. *Was it, then, people like myself who helped degrade the Negro by coming to his community in order to cut myself a piece of the Pleasure pie? Was it my needs of ear and flesh that helped make some of the colored whore themselves, and understandably cheat and con on the side, because they knew why I was there and laughed up their mutual sleeve at my so-called decent ethical standards?*

These were rough thoughts and I had to try and face them. I came to the conclusion that we fed each other, the Harlem nighttime Negro and myself, but that the revulsion and often amazement I felt at the lying and cheating couldn't be my responsibility because, what the hell, I wasn't God. It went on when I and no white spy was present, in this Lenox Avenue hotbox, not because of any Gene Talmadge bullshit about colored inferiority but because the people were dollar-hungry, haphazardly educated, often ignorant (hardly stupid—I've got the scabs of many a mental thrust!), street-Arab tough, and ruthlessly indifferent or *foreign* to middle-class morality. They lived by night, in the old movie title, and they hustled their bucks and jollies any way they could; they had lied, spat, fisted, grabbed their way up from five in a room, rats, bugs, the unflushable toilet and the leaking ceiling, the misery-drowning bottle and the magic needle, mama doing the two-backed bit to make the rent and new-compact money ("I'm the third generation of prostitutes," a businesslike Negro mother told me with flat dignity) and their attitude towards getting what they wanted was the hardest, most selfish, screw-the-ethics approach I had ever been up against.

3

I was hypnotized by it for a while—the way the sheltered sissy-rich kid in movies always is by brushes with the underworld—but after a year of hitting Harlem three or four times a week, day and night, the fascination wore itself down and hardened into skepticism and suspicion. My heart no longer winced at the sights of misery and humiliation that I saw on the streets; I looked for the further truth, behind the too-glib appeal to my humanity, where before I accepted hard-luck stories on their running-sore face value. (As James Baldwin and Richard Wright have both pointed out, the Negro's suffering has been so full that it's often hard for him to refrain from using it, actor-style, to make it pay off. And who's to blame him from the distance of this printed page—while, similarly, who wants to be suckered and played the jerk close up?) I got to know, by my uptown education, something of what it's like to be an average Negro in any of the big-city ghettoes, how you harden your heart, your jaw, your stomach, take what you can get away with, spit at fate, laugh at wounds, conceivably dance at funerals to keep your own spirits alive. I appreciated the life-induced toughness of the hustlers I knew, by the dozen, even while their callousness and ignorance never failed to scrape against my upbringing like sandpaper. They had begun life, before American society had been wrenched open to make way for the man of color, as the very social garbage of U.S. existence; and if they didn't nastily laugh or scornfully sway with the right-is-white whip the very humanity in them would have said nix, nix, this can't be, and they would have used razor or gas to find pride's haven. And I, also a poor up-against-it mortal (but in a different way) had once too been ripe for the big sleep when my hope of happiness had fled, and here I was trading on the dirty pleasure streets with these my sisters and brethren in hardship!

Even after I had lost my girlish, milky notions about the natural greatness of Negroes—a defiant liberalism and sense of identification stemming in part from my being the unreligious modern American Jew who feels only the self-pitying sting of his identity without the faith—I was still haunted by Harlem. True, irony and slitted eye had replaced to some extent my former urge to dig all the sights and sounds. I was more realistic, cynical, harder and even nastier on occasion with the hustling girls than I would ever have dreamed I could be when I first entered paradise. I would no longer allow myself to be taken for quarters or drinks by one-armed and one-eyed beggars and bar-jockeys (who were actually less handicapped with the facts of life than yours truly). The promise of a wild blow-job by some outwardly gorgeous mulatto chick was now tempered by experience, by the coldness that could freeze the bed once the money had been paid, the quickness, indifference, cop-out; I could no longer sweepingly arc my dreams of sex and desire on to a Harlem that I had gotten to know from the spare-ribs up. I was more like Sam Spade now than Stephen Dedalus, or his crude U.S. equivalent. But even so, I still got a special boot out of walking the streets of Harlem, of mingling in its life to the depth I did (which went beyond the whore and bar-type acquaintanceships to two fairly solid friendships with working-class Negroes) that I never received downtown in white society.

This next is an uncomfortable point to write about: but it's true that when I strode the Harlem avenues I not only had an absence of the physical fear my buddies tell me they feel above 110th St., I had a sense of *security* and well-being precisely because of my color. For the first time in my adult life I felt completely confident and masterful in my relationship to both sexes because society judged me the superior, just as in a different, Irish-bar—type scene it made me stand out unto myself because of the Yiddish bit. In other words, I was the human worm turning; even more true and paradoxical is the fact that I was a better, more capable, objective and gentlemanly person among Negroes (for the one big reason that my security could never be threatened) than I was among whites. So oddly enough my Harlem experience made me feel both how and why many uptown Negroes act as they do and also made me feel like a southern white, understanding for the first time the tremendous psychological *impregnability* to the cracker (every white man has a built-in colonel-kit!) in having an "inferior" class beneath him. It was an astonishing revelation to realize that you could be a better person—more attentive, calmer, happier, and that last word is the truth—for the *wrong reasons,* that is by realizing that the people in Harlem wanted you to like them, and that if they permitted themselves any expression of hatred it was clear that it was an aspect of themselves they were crying out against rather than you.

I am not proud to write this: but it's true, or was in my case, and since I like you am wantonly and unmitigatedly human, I took advantage of this psychological reality to give myself the basic happiness I wanted. It brought out my best as a person among other people, and yet it's likely that my very security helped reinforce the *insecurity* of many of the Negroes I knew towards whites! (Thus does one human being use another for reasons that are deeper than morality—because of our inconsolable life-needs as individuals.) I was the predatory male in Harlem, which means the true male, refined, amiable, sure-footed and sure-minded because I knew that fulfillment of my needs (not downtown blockage and anxiety) was right around the corner whenever I wanted it. In the Village I always felt, like most of us, that I was in equal competition so intense that it brought out my worst and made me want to withdraw rather than come out in all my potential manhood and therefore complete humanity. I can only justify this Harlem-using by my need as a human being, and if I didn't know how desperate the necessities of life can be—to the point where the impossibly jammed-up contemporary person must hunt in every offbeat street and alley that the mind can conceive to assuage them—I would feel more guilt than my picture of total justice says is right.

4

It is unrealistic to think the same attitude holds in Harlem that exists downtown in the Village, or in midtown, or any of the new mixed housing projects, where Negroes are increasingly your neighbors, friends, lovers, wife, husband, landlord—Christ, your goddamn analyst! Harlem is Harlem, the brutal, frantic, special scene of the big-city Negro in America until this time, and the white–black contrast still maintains its unique, soon-to-be-blended (as Negroes increasingly crash out) charge for the pioneering ofay who crosses the line with nerve-ends humming. You are entering Negro America, man, and you carry with you—despite your personal courage or lack of it—an unspoken message stamped on your skin, Jim! You are there for a reason, as are the second-rate white dentists, real-estate finaglers, jewelers, optometrists, pawn-brokers, and so are the colored, because until recently they were hemmed in as neatly as an enemy. Why dodge the sociological exoticism in your being there? But why, also, dodge the needs that led you there? If you love music, beat, chicks, color, barbecue, wild inventive humor with the stab of truth in it—why shouldn't you be there when your own life has denied you these things? But, hungup human that you are, you can never mate the pleasure of Harlem with the pain; your mind doesn't want to see that the kicks you love breed in a white-ringed pest-hole (I exclude the secret few upper middle-class hideaways) whose stink offends your very soul, like an unaired bathroom. I could never immunize myself (nor should I have!) to the garbage in the streets, the obsessive ads and shops for hair-straightening and beauty treatments (not so unlike my own nose-bobbing, is it, in the attempt to gleam like a clean-cut White Protestant beauty?), the pawnshops five to a block, the rat-infested tenements, the thousands of dollars spent on TVs and radio-phonographs at the sacrifice of medical aid and sanitation, the feverish traffic in drugs, the hordes of sullen-faced, corner-haunting hustlers, the waste of money on adolescent trinkets, the wild red rage on the broken-beer-bottle 5 A.M. streets and the ceaseless stealing (how many times have I had my change stolen from bar and lunch-counter while I was feeding the juke and trusting my nighttime friends!). And yet, my conscience sneers to me now as I write this, what did you expect, what could you have rightly expected—a heaven of sensuality without the pissmire of sociology?

I sincerely doubt that even God could marry the discrepancies: namely, the boots and joys of Harlem life for soul- as well as penis-starved human beings like myself, who could get the needed equivalent *nowhere* else in this greatest city on the globe, along with its ugliness, .45-calibre toughness, and kick-him-when-he's-just-getting-up attitude (not when he's down—that's too easy). The life-scarred pavement that reaches from 110th and Lenox to 155th breeds the one intergrown with the other. And yet if you look at Harlem without any attempt at morality at all, from a strictly physical and blindly sensuous point of view, it is the richest kind of life one can ever see in American action as far as the fundamental staples of love, hate, joy, sorrow, street-poetry, dance and death go. The body and texture of its solid reality is a 100 times stronger, sharper to the nostrils, eye, ear, heart, than what we downtown greys are used to. And within a decade (some say two) it will probably end as Negroes become increasingly integrated and sinewed into the society around them. I will truly hate to see Harlem go—where will I seek then in my time of need, O merciless life?—and yet I would obviously help light the match that blows it out of existence.

At a buzzing bar I used to go to on Lenox between 110th and 115th Streets, where the bait paraded boldly, drunkenly, or screw-you-jack around the circular wood, wanting your wallet but trying to size you up as a plainclothes cop or not, the makers of Hennessey Whisky had put up a sign which I'm sure was designed for the neighborhood trade all over Harlem. It said: "Ask For A White Cadillac." This bizarre drink was just good old Hennessey along with milk, mixed together in a highball glass. But the name, the music and color and swing of the image, was a laughing ball to these pleasure-bored sports and duchesses, who were belting White Cadillacs (and perhaps the cat next to me was an off-duty chauffeur) at 3 A.M. while the rocking box dealt out sounds like hip bullets, and the entire bar shrank into a black-and-tan fantasy of booze, wailing laughter, the crack of palm on face, tears, the bargain of bucks for ass, and the lusty, caressing accents of "You can take your motherfuckin drink and stick it in your motherfuckin ear, darling!"

So long, dark dream mistress of my adolescence and educator of my so-called manhood!

Black English, or
the Motherfucker Culture

With the eruption of black anger and Black Power in the late 1960s, a torrent of aggressively foul language was turned like a fire hose upon white America. The black poets of the time joined that language to art. In Amiri Baraka's 1969 poem "Babylon Revisited," white culture is compared to a deadly animal, a bitch, and Baraka wishes that all such "receive my words / in all their orifices" (1976, 468). The obscenities directed against America were fed by an underground stream of obscenity in black life that came to the surface during the 1960s. The poet Don L. Lee cleverly employed this obscenity to criticize the pretensions of black revolutionaries in "The Revolutionary Screw," also published in 1969. A woman propositioned by a self-styled revolutionary replies, "go fuck yr / self nigger" (1975, 1296). For the poet, it was the woman's response that was revolutionary.

In the following unpublished essay from 1969, Krim addresses the unrefined raw material of black obscenities heard on the streets of New York and the effect it had on whites and blacks. The essay frankly records the brutal words that carried black anger, and while Krim freely admits it has legitimate sources he also predicts that such language will have a corrosive effect on black life itself. Above all, Krim is adamant in his refusal to ignore what he knows about the human condition that affects everyone, regardless of what banner they march under. "However beautiful black may be it still disguises a lot of unbeautiful pockets of individual confusion, neurosis, obsession, inability to come to terms with oneself."

You must learn the American language if you want to understand the
American people.

—Thomas Chandler Haliburton,
Judge Haliburton's Yankee Stories

Probably the most paralyzing assault of the black masses on
white America is not in the actual physical violence of burning cities, riots, the new melodrama of the streets that makes taking a
walk an existential experience, but in the battering use of what ordinary
middleclass people call dirty language.

The proliferation of muthafuckas, shit, piss, prick, white bitch suck my
cock, white faggot eat my pussy, the insistent drone of this speech that can
freeze comparatively sheltered white hearts and turn the stomach around
in a hardened Jewish civil rights lawyer is a new development in the use
of the American language as a deadly weapon of attack. I write this from
Spain, where except for minimum needs I am ignorant of the language, but
this very lack allows me to replay the speech I left behind just a few months
ago and in my ear I hear echoing the words of a six-foot-six black supercat
who was terrorizing a White Tower joint in my neighborhood (Third Ave.
& 14th St., NYC) a few days before I left. "Muthafucka," he told the small-
boned, pasty-faced, rimless-eyeglassed counterman, "if you ever do that
to me again"—carelessly take away his coffee before he was finished, then
refuse a second cup free—"I'll make you eat all the shit out of my black
ass." The counterman was silent as a ghost, taking it, and the cat, about
25 or 26, then stormed out of the restaurant. The rest of us, including two
middle-aged Negro women, said nothing, the words probing each of our
stomach-linings in a different way but all equally profound.

There has really been nothing like this kind of expression in public
within my memory and probably within the history of the States; certainly
it is not recorded before the 60s, when it began to make itself known out
in the streets of all our major cities and in subways, buses, trains, stores,
movie theaters, wherever people from every so-called walk-of-life gather.
As a boy growing up in New York and Newark, N.J. in the late 1920s and
30s, the first one of the classically tough capitals of the world, I can recall
occasional "Fuck you's!" hurled into a public space by Dead End kids and

on Saturday nights the drunken mumble of oaths like "You bag of shit" and "You yellow cocksucker" spilling out of the windows of Amsterdam Avenue bars as the Irish and German manual workers got into their weekly alcohol bag. But these were unusual occasions. All public cursing (that word itself seems dated) was then limited to special provocation, and there was always some little well-dressed guy sitting on the sidelines who would valiantly get up at some point and offer to fight unless the verbal shit-slingers quieted down and paid some due regard to the "women and children" within earshot. This always seemed to sober the cursers, many of whom were Roman Catholic.

But now it is often the black chick herself and precocious black children who paralyze white cops and dockworker types with a blast of gutter talk that totally unhinges them, mocking President, country, Christ, the Virgin, mother, wife, family, "dignity," "self-respect," every single holy brick they've mortared together to build their lives. As a matter of fact, I'm fairly certain that some working-class white men who once exulted in their raw masculinity by the use of four-letter words have now cut them out entirely as a reaction to the almost professional vulgarity of many blacks; they can't hope to win because they now have more to lose in their own ideal of themselves than the people fighting for RECOGNITION ("look at ME when you talk to me, muthafucka!") by the use of inflammatory language—the way they themselves once fought against the educated upper-middleclass Wasp who acted superior but was embarrassed and helpless against speech that threatened the fabric of his life, from bodily fear to less tangible anxieties.

Is this, then, what we're living through these days, the fight for recognition at any price on the part of blacks using the roughest English that can be dredged up or invented to knock the white man off his toy pedestal, make him back up, admit his poor humanity, smear some of the excrement on him that they feel has been unjustly fed to them? I feel, as someone who has been on the blunt end of this new rhetoric, that this must be true in part; the overwhelming need, the compulsive need of the aggressive kamikaze black man, woman or kid to tell it like IT is, not to alter a syllable of his experience in communicating to whites, even to paint it BLACKER than it is, can't be separated from that general lightning-bolt upsurge of spirit known as black is beautiful, black pride, black self-aware-ness, etc. In the Negro's social indignity lies dignity, is the underlying mood, and the only way this can be made evident is to wail on the basis of your own gut language and the life that it growls out, not try any longer to hide on the basis of some two-faced alien standard imposed from without and foreign to what you know. When the contours of life change, so will the words, whitey, and until then you can expect a stream of the rankest truths that you've hidden from consciousness and that we will remind you of night and day without letup.

If there is thought behind the inexhaustible hammer of black obscen-ity—and often it seems unconscious, by now a reflex, automatic, the con-tempt shown to whites equaled by the contempt shown to everything—the ease with which I or anyone on the other side can identify with it by put-ting ourselves in black shoes would be part of the argument for its sub-jective validity, and it is not an easy one to refute. Certainly the white American has laid the seeds for this revenge of language that reddens his ears by having stuffed them up, in the past, along with his mind, to what was happening right in his own backyard, basement, kitchen, men's room, to all the smelliest and least attractive parts of his land. As we know only too well by now, he never shared that land as he constitutionally vowed to do and now each unshared moment—count dem, white debbils!—is cursing him literally as well as in less audible ways, laughingly pepper-ing "Bullshit!" in his face, blaspheming out loud his impossible to defend structure of what is decent behavior and what isn't. On what grounds can white rules of public decency, verbal etiquette, be enthusiastically sup-ported with first the enslavement and then the humiliation of a people—social, economic, psychological—at the base of the pyramid that has led to the present moment? The moral reasons that lie behind the fierce use of what used to be called immoral language can be found without any devious logic, they can be argued as the recourse of a subterranean nation within the U.S. to ridicule and destroy what has caused it incalculable pain and suffering, to inflict shock and embarrassment on those they know are vulnerable to it, to achieve fear and respect for their capacities by tormenting their former tormentors with a torrent of shame-producing words that draws the blood from most white faces.

I think it is fair to say that in America today the driven black man has become the true lord of free speech, out of necessity, to win power and consideration for himself by any means necessary; but the quality of this speech, its usual strident one-sidedness, indifference to the mildest amenities, recklessness and pounding obsession with the bathroom and the bed, the toilet and the sex act, shitting and fucking with incest the prize turd stuck in the hairpie, all the guilt themes of the English-speaking nations doubled and tripled in their almost ritualistic usage, has sent out radiations that have had electric effects on different whites. The earnest practicing white Protestant and Catholic man and woman, as well as the college-graduate Jewish liberal who is atheist but socially sensitive, have all reacted with psychological pain of the highest order to judge by my own family, their guilt toward what they have wittingly or unwittingly done to Negroes in America and their subjective desire to make amends struggling with an aesthetic loathing of "filth" that makes them helplessly schizophrenic toward this aspect of loving your brother.

Far over on the other side, in fact within the ranks of the alienated sons and daughters of these very Protestants, Catholics and Jews, black utilization of all the once-taboo language with such boldness and aggression toward the accepted code of public talk has had the reverse effect. White revolutionary groups beginning with the Beats, of which I was a member, running for 10 years all the way up to the Peace & Freedom Party, also a temporary home for this uprooted writer—with hippies, Yippies, SDS,[1] Up Against the Wall Motherfuckers (a direct imitation of black language and black rage), various rock groups and underground newspapers in the forefront now—have been tremendously turned on by black verbal style and its continuing savaging of "the Man": white American government, white capitalism, soulless white IBM computerized attitudes. Everything implied by Eldridge Cleaver when he said "ofays don't know how to shake their asses" has been adopted by young white radicals who talk black, think black, fuck black or try to. Norman Mailer's "White Negro" has metamorphized into *Village Voice* reports from Berkeley of

---

1. SDS stands for Students for a Democratic Society, a 1960s radical group.

white "niggers," happily self-defined, and some of the wisest young white revolutionaries I met in PFP—including the dedicated Stephanie Oursler—were sorry from the bottom up that they hadn't been born black and come by their "muthafuckas" at birth instead of secondhand.

And between these two poles, the established hedge-trimmed white community who are truly jarred and frightened and repelled by the public use of language they forbid at home, and the young white niggers who groove with it as the most potent weapon around in the dislocation and destruction of authority and the creation of a free city of the streets, there is that great stone mass of American whites not taxed by religious scruples or revolutionary ones either who consider blacks an inferior people and whose prejudices are I-told-you-so confirmed when they hear the stream of underlife pouring from black mouths, black beards, unforgivable black condescension to the way they live.

But these culture blocs are almost predictable in their reactions, a social scientist could chart them for a year with 99 percent accuracy, although the division of feeling they display can give one a suggestion of how deep is the wound within the country to this new black style. More revealing to me, however, is the position held by that independent minority of white intellectuals and literary martyrs who through the years have defended free speech as a sacred principle and are now resisting at the offense to their own sensibilities that the shit-fuck-muthafucka routine brings in its wake, even though they can justify it intellectually. Many of these whites as well as a lesser number of black literary intellectuals like Ralph Ellison and Albert L. Murray—writers, teachers of literature, newspapermen, editors, poets 40 and over, men and women who live by words—are turning conservative by the minute in the face of the black word barrage: not politically so much as linguistically, humanistically, personally, feeling a surfeit of the very naturalistic language they once went to court to defend. These include men and women, some of them acquaintances of mine, who fought literary censorship of every kind—from Joyce's *Ulysses* through Sherwood Anderson, Dreiser, James T. Farrell, final American acceptance of D.H. Lawrence and Henry Miller right up to the prosecution of Ginsberg's *Howl* in San Francisco and Hubert Selby's *Last Exit to Brooklyn* in London—and who now exist in a state of limbo or confusion as to the genuine value of total freedom of expression when its result seems only to have been (to them) a debasement of the general language, in fact a debasement of life as it is comprehended through language, rather than a blow struck for the good old human spirit.

It is important for me to go into their dilemma because as courageous literary spokesmen they have always felt the protection of the word was in their hands, that by their absolute refusal to allow any abridgement of its complete expression they were guarding the mightiest tool of man's inquiry into his condition from the blind wrath of the prejudiced, timid, hypocritical deniers of truth who block the self-awareness of each succeeding generation. Now they themselves are put in the position, not only by the more belligerent of the verbal freedom-riders, but by their own sense of bitter irony, of being the reactionaries; even further, the "daring" modern literature that they so conscientiously defended now seems to them a little like a sick joke when confronted with the raving street culture, especially when you consider the solemnity with which they fought for a "fuck" from court to court and how they risked their reputations and livelihoods to stand up for a "cunt." It seems ridiculous to some of them now, wasted, all the years having gone down the drain to advocate what a 10-year-old kid from Harlem can give them lessons in! In fact if this is what modern literature was all about, one of the new white niggers might say, black men and women uptown and their ofay young brothers and sisters downtown are writing *Howl* and *Tropic of Cancer* every morning, noon and night and nobody's making a fuss about it anymore; the freedom has been WON, baby. Tell it like it is, muhfuh.

But I have no illusions that what I take responsibility for calling black public speech came into being by itself without the white boy's gamy participation in a much less intellectual way than those devoted people discussed above. Americans have always cussed, as people used to say, and the GIs of WWII brought back Henry Miller and the institutionalization of the all-purpose "fuck" on a bigger scale that it had ever been known before. And among white American word-brokers since the war that huge list including James Jones, Mailer, Ginsberg, Burroughs, Selby, Lenny Bruce, Michael McClure, Ed Sanders, Charles Bukowski, Hells Angels, Beats, Grove Press—the list is endless—have certainly dug into the forbidden fruits of the tongue and produced veritable banquets of crotch and asshole that owe nothing to black influence and rejoice in their own guilt and its attempted exorcism through language without help from anyone else. For it seems to me clear, if not the total story, that indigenous, virginal American shame toward the ancient facts of life, puritan inheritance on the part of all of us no matter what our stock, and a kind of wild individual experimentalism that we're driven to—the attempt to undo our shackles, conditioning, beyond anything ever known because in our society we just can't live with the burden of pain that our all-embracing primitive consciences create—leads to the fanatical attempt to turn guilt inside out, to spit out everything that haunts us, in the hope that total evacuation will cleanse the soul and bring momentary peace.

The burst of black street talk upon the ears of everyone, then, as I see it, is a bitter exaggeration of language and preoccupations—sexual, psychological, materialistic—that couldn't be more deeply in the American grain; if it is obsessed with the bed and the toilet, then so is the undersoul of the country; if it is offensive, then so is the secret mind of America; this language was not created by blacks but by the heterogeneous mass of all of us, churning with our own inverted idealism, our disgust and violence towards ourselves and each other, that compound of fear and shame and inability to live with ourselves which makes us create the ongoing language of our jostling discontent. There are no boundaries to what we can do, say or be because there are none that each of us will accept, such is our uniqueness and our suffering. What is new about the savagery and nastiness of the muthafucka style is the deliberate but understandable employment of every word calculated to embarrass and paralyze the victim—but knowledge of where to push the button comes from black involvement in the same embarrassment, he or she is more possibly calloused in the tender areas of guilt but equally a partner; if some street-cat verbally brings me down to the color of my shit when I'm walking with my 60-year-old sister he is demeaning himself equally but it is worth it to him right now to see me reduced. Can I blame him, knowing what I know? "It would be better to be dead than to exist like this," Ishmael Reed once wrote about black life in the *East Village Other;* if you can accept the depth of that statement as being true, not simply rhetoric, the unprecedented invasion of your own sense of propriety that you've run into from black strangers on the streets can be philosophically swallowed even if it makes you burn. As LeRoi Jones, Archie Shepp, Cleaver, Reed, any number of barbed black voices would dryly say, the people you've made into men's room attendants in one form or another by the thousands smell the shit, eat shit and talk shit every day, baby, because you've put them there, and they'll continue to do so until we stop you with words that make you wish you hadn't been born so hypocritically clean.

I accept this is true, but at the same time as a user and lover of our common language I protest as much as anyone the self-indulgence of its wallowing, the attack on my standards and privacy, the unwanted bath in street-corner biology, the unasked-for intimacy that the user's imagery creates, the nerve, the *chutzpah*, presumption, contempt with which my ear is used as a free toilet bowl by some cunt-struck black cat who wants to impose his sadomasochistic fantasies on the world, thinking that by yoking them to a clenched fist he has the right to smear my head with ignorance, obsession, the meat-view of life, hammering down every nuance and creative possibility into a monotone of one-syllable appetite and force. And yet I know, as I think we all secretly do—call it penance or fear or even curiosity, which is stronger than one normally thinks—that I must submit to this and learn from it until my own humanity is forced to include common black humanity on a perfect level with myself, until I participate in the shit up to my ears, until the black street-actor participates in those parts of life that are not connected with the men's room up to his ears. Isolation has produced the language that offends us and participation will reduce it. If you feel brutalized by it, think how members of the Negro community brutalize and bore each other with it. But to me it is too late, historically speaking, for moralizing; the common usage of every dirty word in the book has broadened our ear, made us tougher in relation to the ugly facts of life than we have ever been, and has added new range to our speech—our experience—which we protest against but which lodges in our national ear.

If the muthafucka culture rains down upon us griming our experience, it is to be expected that it will one day grime black experience as well and the language will ease up, pass on, metamorphize into something new; until then it has to be accepted in the pit of our speech and experience with the knowledge that it is the explosion of all our guilt and rage, not just the black man's, but the culture which binds us all. We must face our guilt towards the bed and bathroom more directly than any other English-speaking country because it obsesses us more and is now out in the open, never to be again hidden; we must understand what our compulsions are made of or we will never be rid of them; if the white man has defiled the black in this society the black man must nevertheless come to understand that he is perpetuating his own blindness, his own compulsive immaturity every bit the equal of the white bastard he scorns, by the endless catechism of biological enslavement that he reveals with each breath. These are our national metaphors of guilt, shame, sadism, comic strip notions of sex; these are our fantasies. They cripple the user as much as the recipient, they dull the ear, numb the mind, imprison all of us in adolescent hang-ups that are now being fought out for the most adult stakes, the future of this society. I think some intellectual whites— let alone the vast non-intellectual majority—are ashamed to have their cherished little pornographic secrets revealed by the strident blacks and this can only be healthy; but the obsessive nature of the attack, its one-dimensional level, its attempt to redefine all experience within the limited range of A to B (ass to balls) is, to me, a confession of failure to tell it like it really is and more of an expression of a state of mind. If there is terror or fear in the white camp, why not go all the way in applying your own sex revulsions to white behavior? Why not legitimatize your own insecurities by expressing them in the now quite fashionable and acceptable hostility to the white? Why not, in other words, get rid of your shit by making it seem like the other man's? All of this, too, don't kid yourself, goes into black speech when it is aimed at white ears and it has to be accepted and admitted by the more thoughtful of the militants, by black intellectuals and especially the conscious language-hurlers—black speakers and writers. It isn't all one-sided. However beautiful black may be it still disguises a lot of unbeautiful pockets of individual confusion, neurosis, obsession, inability to come to terms with oneself, and while white America is no doubt responsible for having kept "the nigger down," using that fact as an excuse to wallow in your own nightmare vision of reality traps the black who spews it out as well as the ofay who backs up in the face of it. The immediate thrill of seeing the white man blanch, and it must be a great satisfaction for the formerly invisible black man to see it happen, is not enough to sustain a self-strangling network of words that indict the user, finally, as much as they wound and awaken his former enemy.

But all of this is theory, cerebration; the FACT is that no matter what I or anyone else writes black men and women, and their white imitators, are going to continue using the roughest English in public that has ever been used before until they themselves weary of it. And that weariness, boredom, shrug and grin at former excesses, will only come when the champions of muthafucka culture realize that language and what it identifies, the reality to which it points, is bigger and more various that what they have reduced it to—just as the older defenders of literary realism, the ones who are now cowering before the storm they helped unleash, have come to realize that their equating of naturalism with reality was a very human mistake based on the appeal of the obvious. They had to fight for this freedom of expression, and I would guess that if each had it to do over again they would do the same, for the issue was clearly cut from the 1920s to the beginning of the 60s: the truth must out. Well, now it IS out, everywhere, and instead of making for a paradise of openness and decency it is closer to a hell of the under-mind, to add another notch to history's file of ironies. "Dirt"—which I don't believe in, but which has its points in this context—for its own sake, that which is demeaning, damaging, ugly, spiteful, painful, low, rank, physical to the point of a new metaphysics, is now being hosed out of the system and the fact that it has no letup at present testifies to the infinite human disgraces that we are inside. But until it stops of its own accord, until the energy of verbal violence and defamation is gotten out and its users are exhausted enough to look around them, to see the new mythology they have created, I say let it roll! The American language, like the American spirit itself, has always been capacious enough to absorb each new cultural uprising and make itself a bigger instrument for expression as a result. Unwittingly, black Americans in their wild wrath are doing the country a favor by enriching it even where it doesn't want to be enriched—at the groin-level. We can never again, black, white, young, adult, go back to pre-Black language, pre-Black manners just as we can never go forward on their basis alone; a corner in America has been turned that the majority would never have ventured past on its own, that some will resent until their dying day, that already is the object of the equivalent of pulpit denunciations, but which can no more be erased or blocked from the ear and thus the heart and mind than the social situation which gave rise to it. If the American soul has been stretched, so has its language. And while language originally comes from what we are, it finally shapes us in its image. The extremism of the new cursing, even the reverse holy quality it seems to have—blasphemy in the true sense, not with God as the victim but with all the "civilized" cover-ups that shield the raw physicality of life and the raw obsessions that make their overthrow so dramatic to one's guts—is a sign of what is going on in the American psyche. A great war is being waged. The words are the evidence.

PART THREE

Success
and Failure

10

Making It!

"Making It!" kicks off Krim's career-long public struggle with his desire for suc-
cess, his doubts about its worth, and his inability to achieve it. His five essays on
success and failure—written between 1959 and 1974—amount to one of the post-
war era's most important and honest records of this crucial American theme. And
Krim often ponders how being a Jew figures into what he saw as his failure.

In "Making It!" the classic Krim voice—demanding, hyperbolic, and com-
ic—is in top form as his wise-guy alter ego belittles the high-minded artist.
"Man, I know what I'm doing! I'm swinging instead of standing still, I'm racing
with a racing age, I'm handling 17 things at once and I'm scoring with them
all!" This 1959 essay marvelously captures the language of the hard-boiled and
anticipates Saul Bellow's depiction of the brutal Reality Instructors who torment
the hero of his 1964 novel Herzog. *It is Krim's appetite for this tough-guy lingo,*
combined with his higher cultural yearnings, that stamps his work as belonging
to a classic moment of Jewish-American writing. Irving Howe identified a hall-
mark of that writing as a mixture of "street energy with high-culture rhetoric"
(1977, 15). It is all here.

When has an inside phrase like "making it" or so-and-so's
"got it made" shot with such reality through the museum
of official English? In this terse verbal shorthand lies a philosophy of life
that puts a gun in the back of Chase Manhattan rhetoric and opens up,
like a money-bag, the true values that make the Sammys and Susies of
modern city life run today. *You've got it made.* How the words sing a swift
jazz poem of success, hi-fi, the best chicks (or guys), your name in lights,
pot to burn, jets to L.A. and London, bread in the bank, baby, and a fortress

built around your ego like a magic suit of armor! You've got it made. Royalties pouring in, terraces stretching out, hip movie starlets strutting in butt-parade, nothing but Jack Daniels with your water, your name in Skolsky's column, Tennessee for lunch, dinner with—somebody who swings, sweetheart! And tomorrow the world (as a starter).

Middle-class ideals of success once curled the lip of the intellectual; today he grins not, neither does he snide. Columbia professor, poet, painter, ex-Trotskyite, *Partisan Review* editor, G.E. engineer, Schenley salesman— they all live in the same world for a change and that world says, go! The Marxist, neo-Christian, romantic, humanitarian values of 20 years ago are great for the mind's library and its nighttime prayer mat; but will they fill the cancerous hunger in the soul for getting what *you* want today? Softies become tough, toughies get harder, men dig that they'd rather be women, women say to hell with lilacs and become men, the road gets rougher (as Frankie lays his smart-money message on us) and you've got to move, hustle, go for the ultimate broke or you'll be left with a handful of nothing, Jack and Jill! What happened to the world out *there*, the one you always thought you loved and honestly-couldn't-get-enough-of-without-wanting-a-sou-in-return for your pure and holy feelings? *Baby, that world went up in the cornball illusions of yesterday! Forget it just like it never knew you were alive. This bit about being a fine writer, a dedicated actor, a movie-maker with Modern Museum notions of heaven, a musician because you truly love it, a painter because you die when you smell the color? Don't make me laugh—it's not good for the stitches, dad. This world (nuts, this rutting universe!) is a Mt. Everest, kiddo, and you've got to start climbing now or the dumbwaiter of this age will slam you down into the black basement. Use whatever you've got and use what you* ain't *got, too!*

Throughout the jumping metropolis of New York one sees vertical fanaticism, the Thor-type upward thrust of the entire being, replacing pale, horizontal, mock-Christian love of fellow-creature; the man or woman who is High Inside, hummingly self-aware, the gunner and gunnerette in the turret of the aircraft that is Self, is watching out for number one with a hundred new-born eyes. He or she has been slicked down by the competition to a lean, lone-eagle, universe-supporting role. Hey Atlas, did you ever think that common man and woman would be imprisoned under the burden of your heroic weight and find it the ultimate drag rather than the godlike stance, without value, nobility or purpose? The ancient symphonies of Man have lost their meaning. It is hopelessness that drives the modern whirlwind striver to put such emphasis on personal achievement.

In every brain-cell of intellectual and artistic life the heat is on in America today no differently than it is in business. Values? Purpose? Selectivity? Principles? *For the birds, Charley! I want to make it and nothing's going to stand in my way because everything is crap, except making it! I want my ego to ride high, my heart to bank the loot of life, my apartment to swing, my MG to snarl down the highway, my pennant to wave above the scattered turds of broken dreams for a better world! Why don't you level and say you want the same, you hypocrite? Be honest for Chrissakes!*

With the blessings of psychiatry, enlightened (so-called) selfishness has become the motto of hip city life; the once-Philistine is admired for his thick skin and wallet, the poor slob who translates Artaud but can't make his rent, a girl, or hold his own at a party is used as a dart-board for the wit of others—not by the "enemy," either, but by his very Village brothers who have forsaken a square idealism for a bite-marked realism. The only enemy today is failure, failure, failure, and the only true friend is—success? How? In what line? Whoring yourself a little? Buttering up, sucking up, self-salesmanship, the sweet oh-let-me-kiss-your-ass-please smile? *Don't be naïve, friend. You think this hallucinated world is the moonlight sonata or something? You think anyone cares about your principles or (don't make me puke!) integrity or that they make the slightest ripple in the tempest of contemporary confusion? Go sit at home, then, you model saint and keep pure like the monks with your hands on your own genitalia! Because if you want to make it out in the world, baby, you have to swing, move, love what you hate and love yourself for doing it, too!*

The one unforgivable sin in city life today is not to *make it.* Even though the cush of success may seem hollow to the victor as his true self sifts the spoils, alone and apart from the madding cats who envy him, he knows that his vulnerable heart could not bear the pain of being a loser. Wasn't success drummed at him every day in every way in relation to women, status, loot—Christ, the image of himself in his own eyes? Didn't he see those he admired in his tender years flicked off like so many flies because they'd never made a public victory of their talents? My God, man, what else could he do except be a success (or kill himself)—the world being what it is?

For *making it* today has become the only tangible value in an environment quaking with insecurity and life's mockery of once-holy goals, which the bored witch of modern history has popped over the rim of the world for sport, like an idle boy with paper pellets. *How can you buy grand abstractions of human brotherhood for that daily fix needed by your ego when Dostoevsky and Freud have taught us we hate our parents, brothers, sisters, and wives, as well as friends? Oh, no, you can't snow us, you peddlers of fake hope! We know you for what you are: Vaseline-tongued frustrates who wanted to make it and lost. Man, how the wound shows behind your pathetic rationalizations!*

The padded values and euphemisms of a more leisurely time have been ruthlessly stripped away under the hospital light of today's world; honesty, integrity, truthfulness, seem sentimental hangovers from a pastoral age, boy-scout ideals trying to cope with an armored tank of actuality that is crumpling the music-box values of the past like matchsticks. It is not Truth that is pertinent today, in the quaint dream of some old philosopher; it is the specific truths of survival, getting, taking, besting, as the old order collapses like a grounded parachute around the stoney vision of the embittered modern adult. *What is left but me?* mutters the voice of reality, *and how else can I save myself except by exhausting every pore in the race with time?* We see in America today a personal ambition unparalleled in fierce egocentricity, getting ahead, achieving the prize, making a score—for the redemption of the self. Are the ends good? Does it matter to the world? Will it pass muster at the gates of judgment? *Such questions are ridiculous: they presume a God above man rather than the god of life who thumps within my chest for more, faster, bigger, conquests for me, me, ME!*

As the individual stands his lonely vigil in the polar night of the desolation of all once agreed-upon values—as they have receded like the tide, rolling back into the past—where else, he cries, can he turn but to his own future? Who else will help him? What can he or she do but mount the top of personal fulfillment in a world that has crumbled beneath the foot? Upon the neon-lit plains of the modern city comes the tortured cry of a million selves for a place in the sun of personal godhood. As one by one the lights of the old-fashioned planets Peace, Love, Happiness, have flickered and gone out, plunging all into the spook jazzglow of a new surrealist dawn, the only believable light comes from the soul-jet of need that burns in the private heart. *Let the lousy world crash like a demented P-38! What can I do about it? I'm merely a pawn of this age like you. Man, my only escape-hatch is making it at the highest pitch I can dream of!*

An individualism just short of murder has replaced the phantom of socialism as the idols of the recent past shrink into mere trophies on the mocking walls of history. In an existence so dreamlike, uncertain, swift, the only nailed-down values that remain are those that can be seen in the bankbook of life. *Can honors be taken away from me? Fame? Money? The beauty I can possess (by name or dollar) in both flesh and leather? No! Don't croon to me of art or soul in a world that has flipped loose from its moorings, seen the futility of truth, the platitude of spiritual hope, the self-deception in innocence, the lack of discrimination in goodness, the pettiness of tears! You only live once, Jack, and if you don't swing with the fractured rhythms of this time—if you hide behind the curtains of a former, simpler, child's world of right and wrong—you condemn yourself to the just sneers of those who dig the real world as it is! Baby, there is no significance today but* you *and the sooner you wake up to the full horror of this fact, the better!*

By time-honored esthetic and moral standards the knowing modern man, and woman, is a barely polite gangster; his machine-gun is his mind, ideas his bullets, power and possession his goals. The reduction of the real to the usable has been whittled into a necessity by the impossible number of potential choices within himself: he knows, after juggling more thoughts than he can reach conclusions about, that he must snap down the lid on fruitless speculation and use the precious energy for making warheads on the spears of practicality. Victims of their own subjective desperation, pygmies under the heavens of thought that dot the roof of their minds with a million perverse stars, converge upon the external prizes of life like hordes released from prison: eager to bury the intolerable freedom of the mind's insanity in the beautiful sanity of—making it! *Yes, yes, I will convert the self that bugs me into an objective victory in the steel and weighable world! I will take the scalding steam of my spirit and hiss it outward like an acetylene torch upon the hard shale of life, and cut diamonds for myself! You say this therapy of mine adds brutality to the gutter of modernity, that I care only for my private need at the expense of the world? That my fuel is desperation and that I'm marvelously indifferent about adding my shot of cruel self-interest to an already amoral environment? I don't deny it. Survival at its highest conception means making it! To live you must conquer if you're normal enough to hate being stuck with your futile being and smart enough to know you must trade it for success!*

For what else is there? Dying at parties, as I used to, when I saw some headliner bring the fawn out of even the best people, who swooned around this living symbol of magic? Eating my heart out because I didn't have the admiration, the quiff, the loot, the attention I and all human beings demand out of life? Suppose I do know how cheap and unlike my original ideal it all is? You want it too, you envious bastard, you know you do! Spit it out that the ego is the world today for all of us and that without its gratification living is a hell, roasting on the skewer of frustration as you watch others grab the nooky! Jack, life is too far gone—too man-eat-man—for your wistful moralizing and pansy references to the cathedrals of the past. It's only the present that counts in a world that has no foreseeable future and I'm human enough to want to swing my way to the grave—sweetheart, you can have immortality!

In an age that has seen the abandonment, because they are too costly, of cherished political and personal hopes, hypodermic realism inside and businesslike efficiency outside becomes the new style. The address-book replaces the soul, doing is the relief of being, talking of thinking, getting of feeling. *I've got to numb myself in action, exhaust this inner fiend, or else all the hopelessness of this so-called life of mine will come bursting through its trapdoor and overwhelm me! I've got to swing, plan, plot, connive, go and get and get some more, because what else is there, Buster?* The frenzied tempo of achievement is matched only by the endless desert within; the futility-powered desperado drives himself ever forward, trying to find in action some publicly applauded significance that is freezingly absent in solitude. Does it matter that he finds his buddies who have made it as rocket-desperate and unsatisfied as himself?

Hell, no. Doesn't the world admire us and isn't it obvious that it's better to be miserable as a storm-trooper than as a Jew? Wasn't my picture in Look, *wasn't I on Mike Wallace's show and didn't I turn down an invitation from Long John?*

Doesn't my answering-service hum with invitations, haven't I made it with that crazy-looking blonde who sings at the Persian Room as well as that distinguished lady novelist who lives near Dash Hammett's old apartment on West 10th? Don't I jive with Condon as well as Wystan Auden, Jim Jones (when he's in town) as well as Maureen Stapleton, Bill Zeckendorf, Bill Rose, Bill Styron, Bill Faulkner, Bill Basie, Bill Williams, Bill de Kooning, Bill Holden—just on the Bill front? Don't I get tips on the market, complimentary copies of Big Table *as well as* Holiday, *didn't I put down Dali at that party for being square and get a big grin from Adlai Stevenson for doing so?*

Man, I know what I'm doing! I'm swinging instead of standing still, I'm racing with a racing age, I'm handling 17 things at once and I'm scoring with them all! Life's too wild today, sonny, to worry about the fate of the race or private morality or nunlike delicacies of should-I or should-I-not; anyone with brains or even imagination is a self-aware marauder with the wisdom to know that if he hustles hard enough he can have a moat full of gravy and a penthouse-castle high over life's East River! I'm bartering my neuroses for AT&T (not crying over them to Beethoven's Ninth like you, you fake holy man!) and bemoaning my futile existence with Mumm's Extra Dry and the finest hemp from Laredo and my new Jackson Pollock and my new off-Broadway boff and my new book and my new play and my new pad and this TV show they're gonna build around me and— Jesus, I've got it made!

. . . while down below the lusting average man and woman sweats in jealousy at the sight of these Dexedrine angels, the very inspiration of what he and she can become if only they too can put that last shred of shame behind them and swing, extrovert yourself, get with it, make that buck, make that chick, make that poem, make this crazy modern scene *pay off.* O my heart, so I too can sink my teeth in the sirloin and wear the pearls of hell!

11

Norman Mailer,
Get Out of My Head!

In this 1969 article about Norman Mailer for New York *magazine, a hub of New Journalism then run by famed editor Clay Felker, Krim again wrestles with his demons as he simultaneously pants after and rejects success. "Norman Mailer, Get Out of My Head!" is a shrewd evaluation of celebrity culture and how it makes the anonymous feel less real. Krim fights back by targeting the celebrity whose fame made him feel less real: Norman Mailer. The essay bristles with the aggrieved ego of the would-be famous, a category that has become even more prevalent today. But its energy and tension are probably owing to the daring gamble with success and failure that went into its making. Krim's friend and editor Peggy Brooks, who helped republish his* Views of a Nearsighted Cannoneer *in 1968, urged him not to publish the piece. She felt it was career suicide to go after Mailer, especially since Mailer had written a generous foreword to Krim's* Cannoneer. *And the piece did largely end Krim's contact with Mailer, damaging Krim's prospects. It was not the last time Krim would write an article that burned his bridges. But from today's perspective what stands out is Krim's clear-eyed understanding that celebrity, fame, and glamour is a poisoned apple no American can resist eating.*

I sit with Mailer's *The Armies of the Night* to the left of my typewriter and *Miami and the Siege of Chicago* standing straight up beyond the roller so that it can look me right in the eye but I know that the books will be incidental to what I must say. These are Mailer's latest writings and as an engaged literary man I must deal with them, especially with

138

the inspired journalistic-novelistic *Armies* which acts out themes that have
been obsessing me for the last several years about the literary artist being
in the center of actual history and shaping it with his voice, but the books
have also become an extension of Mailer's presence in New York life and
it is this that is smothering me, raking me, bringing to the surface raw
competitive feelings which have nothing to do with literature as an end
in itself.

For example: I had a good chance of getting planked one night about
three weeks ago, I was looking forward to it because the girl was dark-
eyed, salty and keen, quick to judge and flaring in opinion but this seemed
merely to open up wider the potential excitement of rocketing with her,
when she started to rave about Mailer's *Barbary Shore. Barbary Shore!* The
novel is 17 years old and I have never done it justice; it struck me as a failure when I read three-fifths of it in 1951, a potentially fascinating probe
into the shadowland of ex-communism but novelistically a fallen weight,
and now this hip young literary snatch was carrying on about it in a way
that would have offended Mailer himself. I lost my trick of the evening
because of the stone I turned to after this Mailer-infected preacherette
thrust him at me like the sacrament and now I must reread *Barbary Shore*
myself to discover, beyond my ego, the worth of the book. Without wanting to I will become a Mailer scholar because I can't move in Manhattan
life today without having him imposed on me, and my own honor as a
"man" demands that I break my behind to be just (or at least to try) even
when my gorge is packed and rising.

I have almost always been cool and appreciative of Mailer, for a decade
now, and have felt detached and unruffled when brother bigtown editors
and writers have told me of his being everything from a superficial and
flashy writer, an overrated fighter, a potential suicide to a loudmouth, a
prick, a maniac (literally), every conceivable rasping putdown with which
we block off those who threaten us. We are all imperiled egos on the make
in New York, the bigger the emotions we hold the more we suffer by being
cramped and squeezed out of our ideal shape by someone else's filling the
available space at the top, and I have listened to such comments medita-
tively; in my own smaller public orbit I have also been called crazy, arrogant beyond belief, a tiny talent who whacks off publicly, etc., it seems

that any writer or individual who is hard to classify today must breast the worst tongs of the psychiatric vocabulary by which others try to wrench you into place in a world without a scheme.

So I have never been seriously shaken by any of the comments I've heard about Mailer, except to take momentary pleasure at some of the knocks because of inevitable feelings of envy brought on by his domination of the foreground; yet these malicious tidbits of satisfaction at another's putting his foot in the turd have never lasted long because of my respect for Mailer's powers of recuperation, like those of the now-dead poet Delmore Schwartz, and when we were closer and there was real trouble such as the stabbing of his second wife Adele I stood by in court with his then young protege Lester Blakiston ready to do what I could, which was nothing.(I recall the midnight that the news of the stabbing hit the air-waves, he was about to run for Mayor of New York, I was to be "publicity campaign manager"—according to a grinning flower thrown me by Norman at a party—and then, suddenly, we were all at a cocktail scene at the Village Vanguard the next afternoon for a new Vance Bourjaily novel and at that very hour Mailer was being hustled from the courthouse to Bellevue for observation; I had been through the same pride-stripping machine in 1955 and as I sipped the martini in the dimly lit Vanguard where Mailer would have been cavorting and heard and saw 40-odd people totally absorbed in the New Moment, Mailer's name on no one's lips within my hearing, I realized how quick the reversals of "power" are and how quietly satisfied some would-be lit stars in the drinking mob were because Mr. Brassballs Mailer was getting what was coming to him.)

But now I can no longer be cool, appreciative, observant, philosophical, certain of my own identity in the face of Norman—no, for the life of me I can't help feeling uptight myself. When my sister recently came to town from St. Louis she plied me with questions about Mailer ("Is he really as intense as he appears on TV?") and her brother-in-law, a New York lawyer, told the livingroom at large what a competent businesswoman Mailer's mother was and as a clincher, "HE's obviously a brilliant man." Here is what's left of my family, decent media-washed people who with possibly one exception don't read Mailer, who stand for everything he presumably does not—with the crucial Jewish middleclass exception of "success"—telling me how brilliant he is! I am now at the age (46) where I resent this until my nerves sing; yes, I want them to understand my brilliance as well, to allow my literary pride to breathe, to try and understand the remarkable effort I put into my own work and what it signifies. Of course I don't really expect them to "understand" (sympathize with?) these things, but don't they have eyes and ears and can't they see or project their imaginations into what it must be like for me, or even A me, to, sit still under this kind of pressagentry? Because it is not Mailer the author they're creaming about nor was it the writer sans a whole shimmer of extraliterary goodies that turned on the young clit I wanted to make it with.

No. It is Mailer the Individual who has now sizzled over Manhattan in a way that I imagine he always wanted (hell! that 95% of us would have wanted) and if he survives the current suffocating prevalence of his personality will probably no longer want, and it is just this Mailer—the multiplied image of a man with every person outside of what they think is the charmed field of force adding his or her own frustrated hope for excitement to N.M.'s own need—that is suddenly, bewilderingly, finally, driving me to the wall. I DON'T WANT to walk around the city constantly being Mailerized by my friends (and even dim acquaintances) who use me as a bridge—D. D.: "I hear Norman is acting impossible again, have you seen him?"; S. M.: "I saw two of his wives [Adele and Beverly] at a party when we were playing that small theater in Provincetown but I didn't see him, if you had been there you could have introduced me"; B. R.: "Could you give me the Great Man's phone number, daddy, my kid cousin from the West Coast is here with big eyes to meet him and a Ph.D. thesis on his work?"— because it brings into the open the throwback emotions of defensiveness that reduce me when I've got to stand fully tall and that hammer me into selfprotection, frustration, anger, when I need every ounce of the freedom that is my savings bond as a human being.

Human being! It is this essence, my identity in the world as a person, that is hurled into a tight knot by all the talk that swirls around me concerning Mailer-this and Mailer-that and which now triggers every protesting hope of my own birthright. If this is an indication of my own insecurity as a man, of my own marginal position on the New York status scale, of every wound and hangup of my own which Mailer now brings to a head because of his aggressive ubiquitousness in the literary-sexual-intellectual-avantgarde Manhattan environment where I must live my life, so be it. I will cancel nothing out of my possible motives in resenting Norman's imprisoning effect on me because I want to know too, I'll whitewash no conceivable unpleasant impulse—envy, jealousy, wishing I had the same gift and the same attention, the applause, charisma (it was Mailer himself who first told me the meaning of that chic word so representative of our period in a bantering exchange we had in 1961), frontpage reviews, "in" national reputation, I'm scraping the brain sac to try and come clean here—and yet I truly feel it is none of these things in themselves and not even the total that punishes my spirit and makes it necessary for me to declare myself. Believe me, I can put up with over-whelming fame or notoriety in my business and not let it eat away at my days and work; and of course YOU HAVE TO PUT UP WITH IT if you don't own it yourself, so that as a writer ages he has to come to terms with the actuality of the landscape he exists on or he will be driven mad with envy and frustration; it is not Norman's "fame" that bugs me but the quality and type of it, because it is not based on works alone (Ellison, Nabokov, Lowell) but rather on an imperialistic personality that gobbles up territory that I want for myself.

This is no accident: when Mailer said 10 years ago that he wanted "to hit the longest ball in American letters" the appetite of his personal ambition was defiantly announced to everyone (honorably, it seems to me, instead of the secret insanities that keep others going), and yet it is the grandiosity and collegiateness of this conception of writing-as-personal-superiority that is at the root of his effect on other wordmen, myself included. This last sentence stinks slightly of moralism, as if I were above the compulsions of "grandiosity" and "collegiateness" and since it is particularly suspect or could seem hypocritical in a case like mine—when I have used the "I" as assertively and with as much apparently cheeky chutzpah (according to the young director Leo Garen, at this writing one of Norman's sidekicks) as anyone using words in New York today—it is worth exploring further. When I say that Mailer's use of writing for Personal Competitiveness, Personal Power and the Proclamation of Personal

Superiority is a pain in the ass to other literary strivers on the scene I am not exonerating myself from probably having such needs.

No one is writing today with any impact who doesn't load his lines with every inch of his private needs, either directly or some other way, and how can you have had an American life with its emphasis on sports, money, politics and the other sex without having had competition and the itch for power reamed right into you from the start? But I am saying that Mailer's naked and often proud emphasis on competition, being the best, beating you in the arm-wrestle or any of the half-dozen games he used to initiate, comes no doubt out of a heightened boy-fever within himself but it is also the reaction of a man so VULNERABLE to the sweeping power-drives of this society, vulnerable to the point of determining to get on top of them at almost any price, that you can only understand What Makes Norman Run by your own perception of the enormous contradictions in this wealthy, earnest, corrupt, endearing, irrational, glamour-oriented bad dream of a society.

Mailer the guy, the individual whose insatiable needs, successes, grandstand plays and endless performances have penetrated my life whether I will it or not by the unsolicited remarks of my friends, other writers ("Doc" Humes: "Did you know your prose is closer to Mailer's than anyone else around?"), fellow newspapermen (Pete Hamill, Al Aronow-itz, Charlotte Curtis, Jack Newfield), women I would like to sleep with, my fragmented family, etc., this Mailer can only be understood by the novel-ist whose precise and tormented intuitions have exposed so much that is paradoxical in this country. Understanding that, that the fantasy-rich novelist is necessary to understanding the behavior of the man, under-stand also how the man now uses each sidepocket of his novelistic imagi-nation to extend the presence of himself in a world he no longer trusts to literature alone. The resources of the highly creative writer in Mailer are now almost exclusively at the service of the man, his writing (and films, plays, statements) at this moment takes second place to the gyrating real-life novel he has been living out through his use of all the available media, and it is this EXTENSION of Mailer's being in the very airwaves that invades MY being to the point where I must consciously fend him off, hide my resentment at his everywhereness, adopt a strategy in relation to the inevitable drop of his name, devote time and energy to coping with his invisible presence which is unlike my picture of myself and yet is real, God knows, burningly, frustratingly real.

And yet it has got to be made plain that this has nothing to do with Mailer's prose, which I enjoy, admire, reread for gut pleasure (especially the firstperson gold that runs from *Advertisements for Myself* to *Armies of the Night*) and would find literally painful to be without, although the Germanic bloat of the last section of *Armies* seems to me to vitiate the buoyant originality and superb deftness of the first three-quarters. No, Mailer the writer is most often a positive credit to the life of this time and his excitement, surprises, wit and brilliant ease of expression aerate my brain like the keenest menthol. Not only am I indebted to Mailer for his writing, the gift of one man's life to another, but I personally received nothing from him but open generosity and the most silken perception when I was painfully putting together my first collection, *Views of a Nearsighted Cannoneer*, to which Mailer contributed a passionate small foreword. Therefore in a poignant way it is not Mailer as he actually is that for my own selfrespect and breathing-room in the world I must rebut, because what he is as a writer and active nerve of our time can only heighten the quality of prose and perception around him and make consciousness a more exhilarating experience for me and my contemporaries, it is rather the uses to which his drive is being put because of the aggravated needs that are blasting him: those unwanted American super-hungers and skyscraper anxieties which as an author he can articulate with surgical touch and control but as a cat on the scene has to act out for immediate and bigger and bolder and deafening rewards.

Stay with me in case you think I'm primarily interested in puritanizing Mailer here: I have no illusions that we'll go back to a period of "pure literature" in the decade ahead but every hope that the writer-in-action will become an increasingly significant figure in the hub of U.S. life, not merely as a "celebrity" but as an active influence in the interpretation and even creation of events themselves, using his imaginative involvement and independent voice as the highest articulate measure of everything that happens in this country. If ever there was a time and a need for the literary imagination to prove its greatness in a madhouse period like ours that time is now, and Mailer's swiveling engagement with every day-to-day eruption seems to me right and necessary for dealing with the landslide of phenomena that confronts consciousness. Putting aside his flamboyance, he takes it all on like the gamest of stalwarts, is faked out by none of the tracer-bullets of a multiple reality that fires in upon him from all angles, and copes like a standup dock boss until he is drenched in psychic sweat and exhaustion—only to renew his taunts and jeers at the impossible load an hour later. His stamina in the face of the contradictions and incongruities that contort us and our society is unique, a startling example for us not to throw up our hands in recoil or drop out but rather to direct our moral grenades at the conditions that have made us what we are—and because of this he has excitingly glamorized the role of literary activism for the 60s.

But Mailer is, when you look at it closely, a transitional figure in "the Movement," not a true steady flame of the moral activism that has come to ripeness in this time, although (when you look back) he was a singularly shtarke[1] maverick who stepped out of a premature, certified, middle-class success at the start of his career to pursue his wild ghost absolutely wherever it took him. Yet everywhere he traveled literarily or polemically after *The Naked and the Dead* he trailed the specifically American banner of a man who has been a public winner ("Mailer hated to put in time with losers" he tells us chestily in *Armies*) and with it that even more telling dividend, the person with an image, a glow, the radiation of adult magic; which is more effective in the daily life we live here than the depth of one's work—a hundred times more effective. Images usually come to people because of spectacular or well-advertised achievement, but in the insecure heart of this country they stand for more than the event or even the lifestyle (Marilyn Monroe, Toots Shor) that bestowed the image; they become additions to Being itself, as though one's very substance were giantized through an electronic magnifying glass to the entire land and every other human being susceptible to this image then walked around with your face and soul in his head. The man or woman with an image

---

1. *Shtarke* is Yiddish for manly, strong, and tough.

becomes a psychological phantom who hovers over the secret life of others; he is their invisible companion, the embodiment of their need and the target of their competitiveness, the standard by which they act and judge themselves. So that, for example, when Nat Hentoff tells Mailer in *The Village Voice* (as he recently did) "Yes, you are the best and most honest writer in America," it is probably as gratifying to Hentoff to feel free enough to finally say this as it is reassuring to Mailer to hear it.

Such an act means—if I can interpret from my own catfooting experience in this minefield—that Hentoff now feels so secure as a public presence himself (deservedly) that he can honor Mailer's image without any loss to his own; and by complimenting Mailer to the far point of his literary taste he shares in Mailer's most recent success, becomes part of it by perceiving it with generosity, and defuses his own hostility to a possible competitor by absorbing him—absorbing the image into his own security of status instead of fighting it, an often sincerely unconscious strategy that makes life simpler as you penetrate further into the boobytrapped thicket of celebrity, fame, ego-moves and above all trying to live at minimal peace with oneself in a time increasingly haunted by the images of others.

And I say this as a man who has obviously been haunted by the image of another.

2

I was not immune to the power of Mailer's name when I first met him in 1959; but as I've suggested, names have different power to each of us depending on whether or not they sum up an area of fantasy that has been coveted in our separate heads. To my own imagination, or projection of myself into the limitless continent of possibility, Mailer was fascinating to meet in the flesh because he had engaged the American world as sulfurously and totally as I had always conceived of myself as doing but never had with anything like his breadth and vision. Even closer to home, he had done it as a New York Jewish novelist who had crashed out of the parochial Brooklyn-Washington Heights-tea-and-wisdom orbit which was our mutual ethnic hashmark into the splendid chaos of everyone's U.S.A., and based on my own inability to honestly transcend myself in writing—that is, whatever I wrote in those days had to emphatically come from my personal experience or I disowned it—I admired him doubly for being free enough from the overwhelming experience of self to lose it in the faith of his own creations.

He, in turn, was surprised and impressed by my stubborn commitment to my own subjectivity when we discussed it briefly once after my *Cannoneer* book came out in 1961. But it was I who measured Mailer much more closely than he did me because he had PULLED IT OFF, I was hypnotized by the fleshly presence in front of me of what I thought of as my own dream-vision of myself, and I related tenderly and uncompetitively to it. I was glad that Mailer existed, as I think down deep we are of every human evidence of heroism, because it gives hope and credence to our own projection of ourselves; as Mailer already knew, he had become the focal point of other people's frustrated sense of themselves and he peered out from behind the external neon face of his presence to make shrewd inner judgments that his fans were unaware of. My point is that Mailer soon learned after the public success of *The Naked and the Dead* that he was the tempting apple of certain people's inner eye; even austere literary types who could legitimately criticize the book for its reliance on the spadework done by previous American novelists (Melville, Dos Passos, Farrell) were impressed by his achievement at 25; and then more than impressed by the extraliterary vibrations that bounced off Mailer, a seemingly juicy combination of celebrity, money, good looks, swift, boldness; and within this network of projection, magic, goodwilled (and not so goodwilled) envy, identification and symbolic leadership, being the recipient of every hidden genital emotion that his eager congratulators poured onto him, Mailer was in a position to see some of the slime of contemporary inner life denied to those who were not in his unique situation. The same could be said of Ginsberg, Dylan, Tim Leary, Joan Baez (although "slime" doesn't exist for that sweet dove) or any of our present-scene Dream People but I doubt from their public statements that they have observed the reactions to themselves with the careful third eye of Mailer and probably Baldwin and Capote as well; the business of the novelist and now the novelized New Journalist is people pure and unsimple, and the opportunities for insight into the most private reactions of others can be profound when you yourself are both the writer and the throne, the articulator-definer and also the charge itself that animates the room and produces the psychic undress which feeds your mind and then your pen.

I'm certain Mailer saw into me with this builtin fame fluoroscope parts of my mental anatomy that I could never see for myself, because when I introspected I did so on a solipsistic turf relating only to itself, not itself in relation to a broader, bigger field of operations where the very size of your mental frame and its shape is more apparent to others than to you. Norman was often amused but thoughtful (always thoughtful unless he was stoned or turned on by the spurt of the moment to climb it like a steeplejack and roughhandle anyone in his way) at my sober insistence on being my self, using only the "I," as a literary credo; but by inference and silence he suggested a wider area of possibility than the one I allowed into the intense but comparatively narrow strip of experience I was guarding like an Israeli machinegunner. Yet neither of us really gave that much to the other—I don't want to mislead—he because there were always voracious ears offered to his lively-mouth when he chose to rap and because he had long before decided on his inner scoreboard how much to reserve and when and where to give, a scheme which often went up in smoke because of the combustion of the chance moment but a general strategy nonetheless; I because I had to preserve my integrity or consistency in the face of his aggressive charm while at the same time relaxing my literary spine all the way so that it could be responsive to the faintest touch of new sensation that Mailer was capable of delivering. But unfortunately my friendship with him was never balanced because although I was as singleminded about my own cause as Norman was about his when I was alone, or with my own collection of friends, it immediately changed when we met in a group or anywhere in public where there were more than just the two of us; when that happened he assumed (and I didn't contest it) the central role that was his right based on actual holdings in the world—performance, rank, notoriety, money, applause-volume, all the goodies—while the major part of my possessions were invisible and tangible ONLY to that comparative minority who knew my work and intentions. As for the rest, the majority, especially that flashy fringe cinched together from Madison Square Garden, Broadway, off-Broadway, TV, the outer rim of

Mailer's fluctuating expansiveness—we shared another hard core of raunchy Provincetown–East Village friends which I'll get to shortly—I was considered just another vaguely known ego-hustler who had attached himself to the Mailer fount in order to find a substitute identity and mystique absent in his own bleak life.

I therefore had to walk a tightrope between my own selfrespect and my fascination with Norman and recognize that as cutting as I might be as to why others wanted his friendship, I also was a pushover for tight association with that particularly mindblowing seal of American success which has been confirmed by the media and all the other mirrors that multiply the godhood of the Chosen One in our society. This hardly means that we don't genuinely like the star of our choice when we get to know him (her); in fact we're so prone to begin with that we can easily LOVE the chosen one at the modest lowering of an eyelid (what dignity!), the beginning of a smile in our direction (what humanity!), a kind word— any crumb that we can gobble up, because to love the Star is to love what has been rated the best of our time, to feel that lucky you are participating in the most precious moments available to your generation. But, of course, how much of this love is selfcongratulation, convincing yourself of your own reality and worth by finding it in close contact with another harassed human, but one whose "reality" and "worth" can't be doubted WITHOUT DOUBTING ALL because it is attested to by every playback machine in our culture? I feel I can now say from the pit of my sensitive gut that the drives which circulate around the concept of the "celebrity," both being one and its effect on the inner lives of others, are more crucially revealing of what men and women in our time are really made of than any other phenomenon of the 60s: because if it were not for the conspiracy of his court (you, me) who admire the attention and power that the celebrity wields he would not possess it; the celebrity is finally made by others into the unique figure he is in our world because he represents the hidden desire of each person who wants to protect and serve the celebrity as the eventual possibility of their own lives.

My own relationship to this "possibility" when I was seeing Mailer was ambivalent: although I was fascinated by fame as an American of this time and place, where the very idea to a people living on the edge of confusion and unreality sometimes seems like the only security that the primitive ego in all of us can understand—"fame" then becomes such an extension of personal recognition and approval that the private miseries of the artist, or American-in-extremis, seem to his imagination justifiable or bearable only by his measurable impact on masses of people—I only wanted it on my own terms (I thought) and as a result of the individuality of my own vision. If it were to come to me as the result of pounding my own beat to the point where I broke through to a new china of imaginative truth, fine, I would glory in it like every American whose heart and head have been shaped since childhood by stars, stars, beautiful stars, to quote L. Bruce in another connection; but I had nothing but contempt in those days for anyone in literature who would deliberately seek it (contempt has now been replaced by a crooked smile of understanding) when the stakes seemed so different from showbusiness or any other outlet of hardboiled selfadvancement. In relation to Mailer, which was eerily special because of the closeness of our age, background, the Jewish thing, jazzedup urban experience, etc., and with people like Saroyan, James Jones, Willem (Bill) De Kooning, Joan Blondell and Anthony Quinn both before and coequal with Mailer, I was as interested in observing "fame" as owning it; smelling it, absorbing it, seeing its effect on myself and others as well as the way it was handled (tough outer confidence and outspokenness!) by the men and women who had worked so hard for it.

I appreciated their candor and indifference to livingroom approval ABOVE ALL because it meant deeper and more slashing communication in areas where the majority of people, however bright, are soul-cautious; they haven't been confirmed in their bones that they ARE the living truth as measured by the ecstatic spasms of others and the music of the cash register, no matter what gorgeous dreams for the future swell the air in their heads. But I also found in each case that a point scored in head-to-head flow, when you were seduced into opening up your most private bag by the candid assertions coming from the opposite chair, could suddenly be choked off by an arbitrary shrug, a pout, a putdown, intelligence and sincerity and the running tap of eager warmth coming from yourself could be cruelly stopped cold by the slightest ruffle in the celebrity's inner weather. In the case of Mailer this was always tempered by a kind of guilt, a violent tenderness in his awareness—never quite articulated but always present—of the impossibility of personal justice in this world, or even in the livingroom where he was then pontificating, given the anarchic forces that drove being. Mailer tried very hard to be sympatico and straight in the early stages of a social situation—very plain was his sense of appropriateness, consideration, adult realism, that quiet yet considerable quality of understanding so evident in his novella *The Man Who Studied Yoga* and so sobering to those who think of him primarily as a fireworks-salesman—but there was usually a turning point in my presence (around the third drink?) when the showboat cowboy in Mailer would start to ride high, bucking and broncking, particularly in the special company of our mutual funky friends.

These mff's were a gang of post-Beat kicks-oriented writer-fighters and wildassed gallants from P-town, the East Village and Washington (D.C.)—Bill Ward, Danny Banqo, underground moviemaker Rick Carrier, Lester Blakiston, Dick Dabney, Bill Walker—who admired Mailer as a guy who could more or less write like a bitch, drink like a cop, put his index finger up the System and still crack the headlines and bank the bread, a natural Jack Armstrong to raunchy scufflers who found bourgeois success as meaningless as an orange julius and needed a new White Nigger hope that coincided with their own roaring dissatisfactions. Mailer arm-wrestled, shadowboxed, sucked the pot, downed his Bellows, exploded energetically (I've seen him lift up a woman and windmill her around his head without sweat to either party) and generally had a ball in the shoulderpunching warmth of his barracksroom camaraderie; but he was also always conscious of being the dean of an after-hours school of tough talk and flowing booze, with fights, momentary flipouts, psychic confrontations, girl-stealing, crazy tensions, sometimes even murder threats finishing off one of these "existential" evenings. These were my friends, too, as was Norman, so my description is hardly a value judgment. In the early to mid 60s we all had urban Huck Finn eyes for this hardliving scene which crackled with real action, insight on the move, the faint presence of danger, the full presence of respect and sudden love—"You're beautiful!" said by one guy (or one chick) to another without shame after a telling small deed or gesture—when you earned it.

Part of the reason Mailer swung so well in this environment (more earthily than at the Flashy New York Upper-world parties which were always on his calendar but not as exclusively as they became after the advent of Lady Jean Campbell, his third wife, and appreciation from a grander new crowd of tailored winners: sports, theater, politics, journalism) was that he covered the human waterfront for this crew of literary outlaws. He had achievement and money as well as the physical gameness that was a trademark for the P-town–East Village battalion and it was the combination of Establishment SUBSTANCE side by side with bohemianpiracy that made him such a hot pistol in our setup. But I was always aware that if Mailer had not written a bestselling war (MAN's) novel and broken through to the gossipcolumn kingdom of The American Dream his friends and mine would not have felt they were swinging with a mythopoeic male who embodied all the contradictory colors that they themselves wanted to flaunt in this society. It was public certification that they lacked and public confirmation that Mailer possessed and even though they, along with Norman, mocked the sitting-duck Establishment and hated it for its sham their very sources of selfapproval seemed to need some of its bad blessing—especially as regarded their SEMAN (or names, spelled backward) which in our country today has become the symbol of a potent soul. Norman was of course the biggest name in our group, which conferred glamour on all the rest of us in the eyes of impressed outsiders; and although I could live with that as a fact of life even though I had always felt, and always will feel, every inch an equal to Mailer, I had to lock up these feelings in this quickly perceiving community of ours out of respect for the values of others.

If a loner like myself wanted the sense of SHARING and warmth generated in this freeform gang that floated north to Provincetown in the summer and south to the Village or D.C. in the fall (our emblem was the chaotic, surprisingly sharp, $-disastrous *Provincetown Review*, still going on no regular schedule, which was the first to print Hubert (*Last Exit*) Selby's toughest story plus Susan Sontag, Rosalyn Drexler, Alfred Chester, etc.) I had to see Norman with group eyes: namely, that it would have been phony for me to challenge his leadership when it was acknowledged as unchallengable by my friends' burning sensitivity to that very American

World on which he had scored a vital shot and at times seemed to have even "conquered" on his own terms. What ultimately became clear was that in the total society we all now participate in through the howling of the media and our own echoing inner voice if I or anyone wanted the "grace" that surrounded Norman he would have to make headlines for himself, match Mailer in trying to "hit the longest ball," "reach out and GRAB what he wants" (Jimmy Breslin)—become a hotshot competitor, in other words, in that eternal 100-yard dash which is either a necessary effort of adult life everywhere or a local disease that comes from living in our own unique 200 million-strong highschool. I had the highschool in me too, let there be no mistake, I also had college and graduate school; I was a stinkfinger kid and a Herr Professor in one suit; in fact I was a Civil War, updated, between ambition and soul, leadership and indifference, pride and prose, winning a popularity contest and glorying in my artistic apartheid, and there it stayed—unresolved, unspoken, Mailer once or twice clenching his fists when he smelled my own Presidential thoughts, me sneering coldly when he led "the team" on a drunken march to a High Wasp Truro restaurant where we were cooled off in the lounge (obviously) and even Norman the Awful couldn't bend them for so much as a fugging sandwich for the troops. Score one for my side. But nothing was settled for me by such microscopic oneupmanship except my stinging confidence that I had correctly targeted the problems as far as they pertained to me, that I knew the choices, that I was playing the good old American Postponement Game in my head instead of declaring myself in the race or out, in front or behind, genius or jelly; N.M. with good justification could have said I was sweating out one of his archetypal existential chessplays and except for that fact that I don't want to breathe comfortably inside the kid's metaphor (he's a year younger than I), I'd rather make my own in the high thin Mexico City air of my own quest, I'll say this—S.K. had to move, physically, emotionally, outwardly, frankly, and stop polishing that dime he stood on like a miser.

3

In the last four years Mailer and I have seen very little of each other: another Bourjaily novel therefore cocktail party at The Plaza, a Barney

Rosset spread on University & 11th St. for Michael McClure's *The Beard* where we just looked for a long beat at each other unspeaking but cool. Our "group" or gang, and the second word says it better, has fragmented into and out of jail, hospital, nomadism, marriage and a new generation of hipsweet kids unlike ourselves—no longer as tight or slashing-bright as a unit—and I now operate in my New York world in Jay (The Celebrity Checker) Landesman's phrase as a "semi-name." (And below 14th St. on my local East Village battleground as in fact a name: "You've at least got a name," *Provincetown Review* editor Bill Ward told me pensively in a verbal beer-sweep down at the south end of the St. Adrian Co.'s long bar the other night; "When you go to a party anywhere in New York at least one person there will know your name," a modest window-dressing fag told me wistfully at a sparse uptown Christmas gathering in the season just passed. He meant it as a darling compliment, not knowing that once started there is no security for you until the ENTIRE party stops as if shot at the sound of your—.)

When I moved off that dime I used my personality more consciously, expansively, deliberately, strongly on the public scene than I ever had up until then—writing for the dead but unforgotten *New York Herald Tribune*, advocating a style and point of view through editing (*Swank, Nugget, Show, Evergreen, Provincetown Review, New York Element*, etc.) and pushing work (Hubert Selby, Jan Cremer, Tom Wolfe, Leslie Garrett, Erie Ayden, Fielding Dawson, etc.) I believed in, teaching my faith in "creative nonfiction" from Columbia University down to a workshop in a deserted courthouse on the Lower East Side. I did nothing different in kind than I had in the 10 years before, but I was (and am!) acutely aware that in the society we live in—this U.S. earthship hurtling toward a new world—my intentions and would-be nobility of stance mean nothing compared to what I can impose on the scene around me. As frankly as I can put it, my sex life (I've been a bachelor for 17 years), my financial life, my relationships with friends, lovers, potential buyers of my talent on every level of American and even international life, depend on the impact I must make on the society I hear buzzing away each time my telephone rings. On the most hardnosed level I count for nothing out there except what I APPEAR TO BE TODAY in the status-clocking eyes of others: this is what 20 years of, from my view, intense, independent and risk-taking literary work and advocacy have boiled down to on the image-dominated marketplace (include in that marketplace the haughtiest universities, foundations, Knopf-type publishing houses, all danglers of the New Dollar while intellectuals sing and beg for their new green supper).

Within this superpopcommercial world that has mushroomed around me my own newly conscious "flair"—not stinting on color, boldness, selling yourself hard while keeping your words loose with each new performance—is my shield, apparently, when as much as anyone I've ever met or read about I wanted not flair but "truth" inscribed on it, "art" blazoned across its middle, "dedication" heralded at the top, "honor" quietly tucked in at the bottom, "integrity" bolting it together, etc. But in a new era with superstars rocketing across the sky of the mind, with the media blasting the faces of my friends across the globe and back, where am I to seek the purity I thought was my mission, where can I, the man, hide from the storm of unasked-for envy, career lust, the weakening or breaking of selfconfidence that each new emolument to the latest star heaps on all the rest of us—where except by staking out MY OWN territory and dirty-fighting for it like every other American savage of my generation? I am too exposed to everything as writer, guy, parched lover, genuine victim of the epic anxiety of democracy which drowns you with its flood of possibility and opens every pore to the slightest rustle on the ego-threatening wind, to find shelter anywhere unless I create it for myself by the power of my presence on this scene. Indeed I can sense myself as I write this pushing out a jaw that was once clean and memorable and now through the habit of defensive aggressiveness has become blunt and thickened, I can intuit the traps and pits of "celebrity hell" that were once moviecolumn hilarity to me becoming stronger as I nibble at the edge of the very name-fame trip I once stoically observed (and already know how the "secondrate" name burns in the glare of the "firstrate" one), I can see stretched out on the track of my imagination a future of desperate jockeying for billing on the marquee of literature which pays off in cash-prominence-veneration when I wanted Flaubertian sainthood, poverty be thou the bride, a religious quest in prose where Art was God and I pursued it like a driven priest.

But what kind of a nonabsurd holy man am I to be in the midst of a cultural orgasm where friends and contemporaries (Calder Willingham, James Baldwin, William Styron, James Jones, Herbert Gold) pull down advances in excess of a 100 or $200,000 on a single book, where Norman's *Barbary Shore* (which I have now reread and admire in patches but find a sealed crypt as a whole) is symbolic catnip that brings hippie pubis to its byline instead of a difficult headtrip that demands debate and thoughtful examination? In this unreal, inflating, sell-the-sizzle-and-not-the-steak scene how can I live, function, breathe freely without being forced out of selfdefense to hustle for that stardom myself, to drive the sweetest of my instincts to make that unsweet impact, to insulate myself against the victories of others by scoring for Seymour Krim and holding my own against an electronic wave that can smash your spirit no matter how high your inner flights? As a matter of fact, how do millions of us live with any niceness when neighbors, friends, even enemies, are churning up the turf and we eat clod as we watch their speed and curse ourselves down for tameness, highmindedness and lack of the competitive instinct?

Listen: I know we also are responsible to an American society with "real" problems of freedom, change, the necessary dignity owed to each citizen, an ideologically shriveled labor movement, a strident New Left, the technological revolution on every side—but it is the so-called soul of the man or woman underneath that I care about because I have to suffer it in my mortal way just as you do. And that soul if I'm any judge is now an ulcer of frustration in The Age Of The Glorified One no matter how straight your vision and tough your hide: face it, we live, hell, we CREATE with each passing minute a world that pays more attention to the myth-person who makes the deed than the deed itself. ("I'm THE Ronnie Tavel," said a young pop-camp playwright to me over the phone two weeks ago, giggling at his parody of himself but meaning it all the same, calling to find an agent.)

Can I, then, in my daily luncheonette-going, friend-seeing, check-writing, street-by-bar-by-cab New York life allow myself to be fucked up, put down, put uptight, made to writhe or joke or mask it at table when I hear Norman's name mentioned? Should I permit myself to bear that imprisonment to my own life-force and personality without fighting back with all of the brute weapons of success that Mailer has mortared my town with and which are now potentially available to me even if I once scorned them (truly?). Of course when I am alone in my small pad, right at this moment, I feel no resentment, no competitiveness, no feelings of being humbled, I wish Norman nothing but the best—conquer the world, baby! I mean it. Because here I have my yellow paper, my oldfashioned Corona, the dream, I'm King Shit here and the equal of any mind or soul in action anyplace on the planet. But in two inevitable hours I'll be hungry and walk down 10th St. to Second. Ave. and then up the block to Sonny's Pizza and there over meatballs and spaghetti I'll run into Jerry Roth or somebody from The Poetry Project at nearby St. Marks Church (where I teach) and he'll say, "F'Chrissake Krim why don't you get someone who's with it to guest-lecture, yeah some cat like Mailer . . ." and even though he'll wink because he perhaps senses my availability to pain I'll feel the metal harden in my blood, I'll wrack my head for a quick comeback and fail, and once again as in a script before my eyes I'll see my energy and imagination and every rich thing I believe I am or can be freeze so hard you could bounce a handball off it.

You see what I'm really asking is whether one man's public triumph— which abstractly I approve of, welcome, see as a sign of hope when it has been made out of the materials of truth—is to be another's heartache in this homeland of mine which puts such a premium on being IT that it even cripples those of us who should know better. I don't, I swear to you, want to write books like Norman Mailer. I don't want to write in his style; I've got my own, thanks. I don't want Mailer's social life, his Brooklyn Heights home with its crowsnest, his part-ownership of middleweight Joe Shaw and *The Village Voice,* his royalties, films, prizes, the works—I HONESTLY DO NOT WANT THEM. But I also don't want my friends, colleagues, women to bug me with his name, his doings, whether he frowned at Casey's (the West Village celebrity hangout) when he went over to Barney Rosset's table to speak to Harold Pinter, was he at his P-town house or in town over Easter?, this, that, the galling other. Slowly, unalterably, determinedly, to save my image of myself to myself, to relate to people I love WITH love and without hangups, to be the free man I know I am at my best and not a tense crank, TO GET NORMAN OUT OF MY GODDAMNED HEAD I must own a piece of this world more solidly than I ever have before, I can't rationalize it, I have no other choice. I ask you: Isn't that what's necessary to get the good tail, win respect from my media-impressed relatives (I was orphaned young and pine for it), be looked up to by the newspapermen and women I sentimentally cherish, have clout out on the 10th Streets and in the pizzerias of my time?

And yet if I lived in a less tight climate—out of the city, shacked, familied, not dependent on the underground bars and parties where we solo artists nakedly seek our opposite numbers to stave away the empty-bed blues—heart and head tell me that the task I was put here to plug at lies in a different direction for a conviction like mine. I want no less than to see the literary artist become inseparable from the leadership of history, I want to see him influence events by addressing his work to the people who make them, I want to see him take hold of the channels of communication marrying his vision to the news to recreate the meaning of reality in the interests of a New Day. My idealism, in other words, which is massive and genuine, has contempt for the Writer As Glamour Boy; I want the Writer As Saviour, if you will, and let him perish in the attempt if need be. But even as I say this and mean it I know as well as you that my words here are not primarily about literature. I am dealing with the agenbite of being,[2] emotional survival, living your 40s inside the heightened Manhattan crucible, all the loner necessities that must be coped with at every hour when I am not at my desk with the literary bag snugly over my head. And it is here that Norman, buzzing, perverse, challenging, decent to me with only occasional snot, Norman whom I have felt a brother to in the past, it is at these eight or more hours a day away from the role of writer-editor that I have learned to hate the sound of his overspoken name on the lips of our mutual friends, on the kazoos of our mutual generation.

Item: Did Mailer ever stop to think that his gigantic personal needs for being indiscriminately admired would help smear up a standardless period, seed an unbidden resentment and defensiveness and equal yen for the most whorish showbiz lights in others who once thought they were

---

2. *Agenbite* is an archaism meaning remorse.

content to work in the stacks all their lives and wear the good odor of library must like Spinoza and (N.M.'s beloved) Marx and Joyce before them?

Item: Did he ever imagine that his "longest ball," which he wanted to hit out of the private ache and need for dominance of his gut, would be a metaphor of romantic U.S. greed that would fly beyond his own smoking brain into the brains of men and women who are sharing his generational time—and further, across the sea, where narroweyed America-watchers are sardonically handicapping our future?

Item: Did he know or care that someone named Seymour Krim would be on the receiving end of this nonstop grandstand play and that this Seymour Krim would find his own existence brought to a crisis by Mailer's own lust for making stardom out of literature, money out of truth, personal power out of principle?

In other words, did Mailer ever see the implications of being Norman, which reach far beyond himself? Whether he did or didn't—and my more than educated guess is that he didn't, couldn't, wouldn't—it is still beautifully true that Mailer has defined me to myself, forced me and a horde of other under-50 writers to fight for our identities and rewards in every sense, in a way I would have dodged without him. Much as it stings to look in the mirror he has handed me out of the grit-and-sand of his own unashamed ego, I see how sensitive I am to recognition (I who was above it), cash (I who solemnly transcended it), how I crave the leverage of broad public muscle, influence, fulfilling myself in every conceivable public sense before I'm wiped out. Norman has brought these things out of me like a one-man Turkish bath and I suppose I can be grateful to him for having had a superior "animal sense of who has the power" (as he has written about James Jones) in order to shake me loose from a frozen image of The Writer and rub my shrinking nose in the competitive stink that so richly steams from the lockerroom of our generation. Norman, sweetheart, you have without a doubt slicked me down and toughened me up so that I can go my own way as ruthlessly and wholeheartedly as you have gone yours!

But even as I know that I now mean to have my share of the most striking notoriety, money, pussy, fun English shoes, TV interviews, the entire swinging menu while I still try in my inner temple to make THIS writer the significant figure in America's destiny that I believe our wordmen should be today—even as I attempt to mount a two-winged campaign that embraces my private career and also that of the artist in relation to this juggernaut which has never felt his full vision as a force in its day-by-day decisions—I know that what Mailer has done to me I WILL DO TO OTHERS whom I have never seen or heard of. If I succeed in becoming the public force that I must now become to protect myself from the Mailers of my time, what insane itch for the new name-fame powerplay will I implant in others, what jealousies and outraged thinskinned needs for capping me will I arouse in their all too human beings? Will my outward "success" be their failure unto themselves, will my stardom eclipse their inner faith, is this the only route we U.S. writers (born idealists who cynically learn that they must take care of themselves first) can follow to the end of our compulsive lives?

To tell the truth, as I see it, the best thing that could happen to me would be if I FAIL to make that booming public impact, if I eat my heart out in the shadows and if I follow my vision with total immunity to applause and try by example to show what the writer-in-action can do to counter-infect our history and change it by the new utilitarianism of his art. But as a man alive now, flung headlong into each day with only 170 pounds to confront the weight of the world, I don't have that ultimate cool, resistance, certainty, ability to stride through fire to the pools of the spirit up ahead. I have no armor when I have to walk down Norman's streets and in spite of my knowledge and foreboding of what I am doing, of the final futility of deifying my "I," the One, the Me, the paltriness of living for oneself in a scene of many, the pettiness of selfprotection compared to the grandeur that lies in selfless service to a concept bigger than oneself, the example to the young and unborn that I and every articulate American have or should have on our consciences, I can't help myself. I must therefore fight in this local Manhattan environment that Norman (more than anyone else) has created to protect what is mine, my words, my women, my status, my own greatness, and like a primitive with echoes in his mind of a civilization more beautiful which he can never entirely demonstrate because of the eat-or-be-eaten realities of his own life I must announce myself as another New Sonofabitch who dreams of peace—but only dreams. Thank you, Mr. Mailer, for everything!

12

Mario Puzo and Me

*In this article about Mario Puzo's post-*Godfather *success, Krim's sense of fail-ure is growing and that failure is multilayered. He did not make the big money, but that is not the worst of it. He also did not develop a mature personality. He feels he isn't hardboiled, tough, and the implication is clear that his debilitating tenderness has something to do with a disemboweled Jewish culture. But Krim, steeped in American literature, also touches on a theme central to the American novel: the relationship between the wide-eyed and the realist. The bildungsroman or coming-of-age story is a pillar of the novel, but in contemporary America the genre has been given a twist by casting middle-aged men as the maturing heroes. Over the last century, the day of reckoning in American novels has been con-tinually postponed. Huck Finn was an adolescent. Ishmael was college-aged. The* Great Gatsby *ends with Nick Carraway's thirtieth birthday. Saul Bellow's Moses Herzog was forty. Krim here is a superannuated Ishmael, a middle-aged Huck Finn, and the essay questions American romanticism and finds much to admire in realism. "Ah Mario, buddy New Yorker, fellow patriot, what a virgin boy I still am in my 50-year-old casing compared to yourself!"*

Mario Puzo is only two years older than I am, but it some-times seems like a hundred, and I don't mean that in the sense in which Mario put himself down for appearing physically aged when he had that nightclub face-off with the suntanned Frank Sinatra in Hollywood. I felt this difference in real, inner, human time when I read *The Godfather.* Mario talks about having "a thousand years of illiterate Nea-politan peasants" behind him, but whatever the head start he got in actual life and not moony theory it gives him a weight and an understanding of

161

cunning that makes me feel like an American Jewish boy scout whenever I read him.

Where are my 4,000 years of superior wisdom? It's a myth, I tell you. Like so many middle-class "reformed" Jews, I wiped the ancient Hebrew out of myself to become an American, a newborn babe of Democracy, and Mario has so far become a much more effective American than myself by plunging unashamedly into the pasta and coming out with red, white, and blue all over his napkin. He craved his life as if it were a fantastic meal even when it hurt the heart out of him; I ducked mine, intellectualized it, idealized it, and now at 50 I fly to London over the Christmas break to gamble my fantasies at the tables and in the streets, and right now I'm sitting in Mario's hotel rooms (two and a half) like a sensitive boy while he plays heavy pinochle with the two men who own the Tropicana Hotel in Las Vegas. My father's kind of pinochle.

I watch Mario as if I'm watching fate. We grew up 70-odd blocks from each other, we were each the sons of immigrants, but my people worriedly spared me every bruise they could except the major one of dying on me when I was barely 10 while Mario's threw him out on the streets of Hell's Kitchen and fed him with rough love and pasta after each day's excitement. And didn't die, wouldn't dream of it. Mario writes about his early days in *The Fortunate Pilgrim* (1965) with strength, with too much rosy sentiment for my taste, but with such unabashed warmth and appreciation that you'd think we grew up on different planets instead of in the same city at the same exact time. I write about mine in *Views of a Nearsighted Cannoneer* (1961) with hurt and bitterness, with frailty, with a kind of driving hysteria and enthusiasm and the pace of a stowaway on a rocketship trying to keep his head from blowing off. How could we be so different? We eager sons of immigrants? We new Americans, and for all I know the way things are going, we last Americans as well?

Mario is tender to me in the hotel room, almost as if he understood his advantages in the world of gravity. He is built closer to the ground than I am, with a huge gut, naked and glistening in the pinochle lamplight, telling me to take my shirt off too while he plays like a contented machine with the two bosses of the Tropicana. (They're over in London to audition talent as bait for the casino; Mario came along for the ride and the pinochle.) I loosen my tie, take my suit jacket off, but keep the shirt on—men like these two have turned me down for credit on days when I had to hitch a ride to the Vegas airport to get out of town, a month's salary down the toilet, and I can't forget it this quickly. Mario's eye is on the game but he tries to speak to me over the slap of cards. He only gets out of the house in Bayside, L.I., he's telling me deadpan, to fly to London or Vegas and back; otherwise he's a hermit. I laugh to myself while he talks, some hermit! He has married the haunted, bombed-out German heroine of his first novel, *The Dark Arena* (1955), fathered five children, and even more important for nonhermit engagement with the changing world, his big, deep, gaudy head is teeming with thousands of characters, scenes, events, some of whom swarmed out on the pages in *Godfather* with still more fantastic hordes to come in *Fools Die,* his new one, and those other books that are sure to follow. I remember William Burroughs saying that he could never be what other people call "lonely" even when he saw no one because he was surrounded by all these people who crowded his brain like a bedroom and I know it is true of Mario also. By hermit he only means that he hides until he explodes in print. If you're wired for the kind of big blast that Mario sets off in the world you can't carry your equipment around in the street, prey to every freak change of weather and chance jostle that would blow you up with your creation. Stay home, Mario! I cheer him on as he slaps down another card and grins, slightly, as he points to the little white pad with his stub pencil which shows that the two Tropicana bosses owe him $1,300 and the night's still young. Around 11:30 P.M. and this will go on till dawn.

Although I move in the world with the veteran poise of a headwaiter at this late date, I'm much more of a hermit than Mario will ever be. A DeMille cast doesn't storm the stage above my eyes although I've prayed for release from the bondage of a straight, literal reality. The only friends I have are flesh and my relationships are as delicate as flowers with needles in them. I take the echo of each meeting with another back into the cave of my psyche and dwell on it like a cannibal. I am only a person writing his way through life these days, not a writer with a personal life, and I have no wife, no family, no roots, no pasta, no bestseller, and like every common son of a bitch who walks the earth alone I am a deeper hermit than Mario will ever know.

But I knew Mario even before I met him for the first time earlier tonight at the Curzon House Club, where he bustled in like a zoot-suiter out of the 40s (complete with a looped pocket chain and pegged pants) to keep our date and blew a quick $150 at the baccarat table before we dodged the raindrops back to his hotel. I knew the smooth coiled spring of his prose, that same Italian-American suavity and control that anchors every portrait in oil that Gay Talese tears into with radical energy, except that in Mario there is even greater irony between the sure formal strokes of the writing and the savagery waiting below it. I knew what a human furnace Mario was inside, both from the bleak and bitter *The Dark Arena*, that grim and hopeless picture of what we American slobs were really like in postwar occupied Germany, and from that awesome scene in *The Godfather* when Mario's toughest, most vicious human prick forces the woman to throw the unwanted infant into the open furnace. I knew he had a stomach like a battleship for the scope of human cruelty and the unuttered plea of a priest for an end to blood, but without much hope. I knew he could be cheap with style, such as having his Ava Gardner woman toss her side-street screwing in the face of the singer/husband within the first six pages of *Godfather*, to work the reader like a carny man for a peep-show. And I even knew how tricks like this had become cynical second-nature to him during those long years free-lancing at the Martin Goodman Publications for *Male Adventure, Stag*, etc., the names are interchangeable, when he became the best hack in the crap-magazine business in order to support the writing of those two comparatively unknown fine books, *The Dark Arena* and *The Fortunate Pilgrim*, which earned him a total of $6,500 over 20 years of labor.

Yes, and I knew too that he thought *The Godfather* the worst of his books, that he defiantly said, "I was 45 years old and tired of being an artist, besides, I owed $20,000 to relatives, finance companies, banks and assorted bookmakers and shylocks," that he then wildly said, "I'm one of the best technicians in the Western world," to somehow come to terms with the book's success. I knew he was as uneasy as a call girl who has spent half her life in a convent when the book became some kind of international fascination, and I, a stranger, had even rammed out five paragraphs of copy in the *Chicago Sun-Times* to tell Mario in the spring of this year that he had nothing to be ashamed of, everything to be proud of, if he accepted the fact that his destiny was to be a major popular novelist instead of a Joyce or Proust and that we were tremendously appreciative of the massive class and dignity and insight he had brought to a form that others treat like shlock. I knew that his occasional "cheapness" in *Godfather* was the price that the good old butcher-shop world asks of its powerhouse entertainers and it never fazed me in the least in my loyal stranger's respect because I knew the blood dues Mario had paid and I wanted him to get every reward there was. I knew he had seen himself as a fat funny little guy who even to this day won't allow a publicity picture of himself at his publisher's, will not appear on TV, who thought he was an ugly man, who had taken that self-consciousness and cold protectiveness towards women into the most desperate kind of gambling, just as I had recently—the most public kind of masturbation there is—and I wanted him to know that he was loved because he was bigger than his weaknesses and much stronger that his sorrows. In fact by his sheer fucking guts he had become without a doubt the latest Italian-American cut along authentic heroic lines. To the names of LaGuardia, Sinatra, DiMaggio, Rocky Marciano, Vince Lombardi, Father James Groppi, and even the Newark strongboy, Tony Imperiale, you could add Mario and everyone knew it.

But I say none of this to him and he says nothing except, "Have a steak, Seymour, have some Scotch, bourbon—please have anything you want," his left hand poised over the room-service phone while his right slaps down the cards methodically as the Tropicana boys assess their own hands with a bit of lip-licking and brow-wrinkling. Puzo likes this world. He got to know these guys over the years of uncontrollable Vegas gambling. Now he is an equal in their league, VIP suites on the house when he does his Vegas ceremony, fresh-cut flowers, all the magazines and papers, no longer the squat little John, the sucker, "the professor," as I have smirkingly been called by pit-bosses from London to San Juan. The professor with a sickness, dropping the money he doesn't have on those cool green tables like semen. And now I hear that "they" (his family, his accountant) ration Mario to $10,000 or so when he does a gaming weekend in London or Vegas, putting a lock on his fantasies.

Yet it was those same fabulous sexual growths of the mind and not primarily the pants that went into his stateside Roman carnival, into *The Godfather* which is now blitzing them all over London in the movie version even as I write, and you wouldn't have had the one without the excesses of the other. It is the triumph of excess in Mario's case, one in a million, and he is a beautiful marvel to me because he has blackjacked over the rules of society, he has hit the final number that every romantic debt-ridden gambler revolves like a sex diamond in his head, it has all come true through Mario for every autoerotic/slob/loser everywhere.

Richard Harris, the game actor, and his nice, hotshot London Jewish agent come into the rooms to talk pleasant international bullshit before a singing date that Harris is going to play for the first time three weeks from now at the Tropicana. They thank Mario for six autographed copies of the London edition of *Godfather* for themselves and their wives and kids. Mario is gracious and cool, showing only the slightest bit of tough when the agent flings his chutzpa too far trying to cram an actor from his stable down Mario's taste on a picture Puzo is thinking of producing with the Tropicana men. I watch Mario expressionless when the agent says he won't let Richard gamble when he plays his date. Richard has no eyes for it anyway. He doesn't live inside his imagination as do Puzo and myself, he is not a hermit, a re-creator of other people's lives, a sad and determined vicarious experiencer, a man whose mind contains multitudes like a Breughel riot and whose body is soft and undeveloped. Richard is out front all the way, telling us with a big grin that his son's cock is nine inches long (sic), much bigger than his own, that the birds are already beginning to mob the young fucker; that for sport he, Richard, rented a big transatlantic jet for a weekend at a cost of £8,000 with all his pals buck-naked aboard screwing, drinking, smoking weed, and it was fun to see so-and-so, a colorful Irish bar owner and radio/TV personality who most of us know in New York, running around the plane with a tiny little thing on him a quarter the size of his 16-year-old son's.

Richard acts out his fantasies while Puzo and I have to make ours up, actually prefer it, are not actors in the total actual sense that Harris is. He seems to act everything out right to the edge of the roof. His nose, he tells us, was built up out of a rib after the original was smashed apart in a wild Irish saloon fight and you believe him without a second thought. (Mario says nothing, the fights he knows in his heart are for death and drastic humiliation and never for sport.) Richard's got the real flat-belly machismo and I respond warmly to him, to his violent authenticity, the fine set of his shoulders, even the kid-thrust of his jaw which says, "I'm a competitor, no man fucks with me," but then I see him steered and suited by his agent from job to job and I know that his independence is theatrical, real but for show at a price, and I also know that Mario's celebrity is all of his own making from the very foulest sewer-bottom up. Nobody's gonna steer him nowhere, leave the driving to me is written in steel on his very pumpkin ass.

But I can say none of this noble shit. He wouldn't want to hear it, couldn't relate to it now, in fact on the sheer talk and "Have a steak, Seymour"-level I'm badly let down by the ordinariness of our contact, the superficiality of it, but thank god I know the work like a *fanatico* knows his bullfights and the surface reticence and even the banality just drives me down deeper to a grudging appreciation of the amazing inner life and drive of the man who is coming on like beer-can Joe Citizen on the other side of the room. (The pinochle has stopped for 10 minutes so everyone can eat and guzzle.) It's not affectation, I don't think. It's a kind of sad weariness with everyone else's games and tolerant but not that forgiving observation of the falteringness of their would-be strengths. I used to occasionally date the girlfriend of Joey Gallo when he was in prison and she would repeatedly tell me, still fascinated by him, still pussy-whipped in love with him, cool in the nice sense with me but concerned that one of his lieutenants would spot us from a nearby roof sipping wine and getting high in her apartment, that he had the mind of a "genius"—that if he had gone straight he could have been a great labor leader, a general, an organizer supreme. Perhaps this is the heritage of Caesar in every male Italian-American, don't write it off. Because underneath the neutral, unrevealing, *Daily News* talk, Mario might very well be regarding us all, Harris, myself, the agent, probably not the Tropicana bosses whom he acts most natural with, as adolescents and fumblers; good but naïve people, not made of the manual labor and concrete and garbage that great builders have to use to impose their greater wills on a conventional and insincere world.

Mario's constructions are his books. But you should see them as having the span, the foundations, the strength of big bridges meant to handle the heaviest thundering traffic and not shake. He is a natural, breathing builder who loves risk without underestimating danger, not unlike every superior Italian construction crew in the country. I am not a builder. I am a lover and a listener as I get older, a sufferer and a loner of human stature by my own hard standards, even a speechmaker with some inspirational qualities I've been told, but not a builder. I would therefore work in Mario's construction gang any time he called and not feel demeaned, dig the physical pressures of building, the vision behind the sweat. I admire what I'm not and will always go after it to try and fill myself out in the simplest, loveliest, most elementary American desire to be more than you are right up to the bloody wire. Ah Mario, buddy New Yorker, fellow patriot, what a virgin boy I still am in my 50-year-old casing compared to yourself! Back to your game, baby. I'll see you around the ballpark.

13

The One & Only
Million-Dollar Jewboy Caper

There has been no shortage of soul-searching, hand-wringing, and grandstanding about the use and abuse of the racist N-word, but in this essay Krim has the territory to himself when it comes to "Jewboy."

This is the true story of what happened when a Krim article in the New York Times *quoted famed reporter Jimmy Breslin using the slur. Breslin said he flew to Los Angeles to sell the film rights to his novel* The Gang That Couldn't Shoot Straight, *and "got a quarter of a million bucks from these two Jewboys." Breslin saw his words in an advance copy of the* Times, *raised hell, and the paper sent "an army of chisel-wielding gnomes" to the plant to scratch Jew off the plates, leaving only "boys."*

Krim makes hay with this rich subject, touching on the role of ethnic street-tough slang, anti-Semitism, taboos, and Jewish timidity. "The Times *was appeasing Breslin by the minute, Jewish nervousness was racing with Jewish masochism to see which could butter his ass most eagerly." But it earns its place in the literature of success and failure by honestly assessing how this incident expelled Krim from the world of legitimate writers to the failure department. As with the Mailer article (see chapter 11), Krim again put his working life at risk to write about his own pettiness, the pettiness of others, and the high stakes of success that prompt everyone to behave shabbily.*

It cost me no proud blood to write a passionate, extra-bases review of Jimmy Breslin's *World Without End, Amen* for the *Chicago Sun-Times* and then to crib my own words and sock the message even harder in the *San Juan Star* so that all the heavy-drinking statesiders down here (where I'm teaching) could see the dark star of Breslin's talent in the bottom of the bottle. I wanted to alert people everywhere that Jimmy the non-Greek was writing better than ever, that the words sizzled and struck out at you like grease being tormented on a griddle, that line for line and play by play he was a New York Ace who had come through with a super-bitch of a performance. And I can use the word "performance" easily and unself-consciously in telling you about it, even though the ads for his book have been carrying a tagline also calling it a "dynamite performance," because I knocked off the original lyrics for the *Sun-Times*. Those two selling words in the ad came from me.

You see, I was as close to this book which is going to build into a national phenom as a neurotic is to his own obsession, reviewing Breslin for two or, hell, twenty newspapers was a psychological necessity for me, and being able to honestly and totally shout my admiration in public for this deeply lived and stunning print-bomb with its beautiful grave title, yes *Amen* Jimmy, has cleaned me out and made a free man of me for the first time in almost four years. In relation to Breslin. So get ready for a story.

In 1970 I published a piece in *The New York Times Book Review* saying that I thought Breslin had betrayed the tremendous possibilities of his own New Journalism by birdieing out, probably for money, with a cutesy romance about the real, ball-breaking, skull-kicking, shit-thinking Gallo Gang from Brooklyn. As you know, the book was called *The Gang That Couldn't Shoot Straight* and it was entertaining and successful to a lot of people outside jungle New York, including the most impartial and serious book journal in the English-speaking world, the *Times Literary Supplement* of London. I was amazed, yet forced into a big head-shaking grin of respect by the transatlantic muscle of what I thought had been Breslin's hype; I knew I'd have to rethink my stand in a second piece or end up some kind of crank/fanatic croaking over a closed circuit I didn't want. I wanted truth with all the portholes open. But the damage had already been done, if damage is the right word for the nightmare I walked into, and instead of Breslin having kissed off his responsibilities to the truth as I had it in my article the script was turned around and I was suddenly tagged as the smalltime Judas to his pop, commercial Christ. Every straight impulse I had in trying to lens-wipe Jimmy and others to the real power for change I thought a New Journalism could rifle into the minds of men, causing them to act with armed vision on the basis of true stories written with the insight of the older fiction, causing them to hug literature as their own very skin and not a remote lip-service thing, was immediately knocked down by Breslin and his twerps to a cheap attack by Seymour Loser who was jealous of his book, money, fame, big juicy cockarisma on the scene we live in. The Breslin Rubberhead Corporation took one hard, dumb, demeaning line that unwavered like lead for the next 18 months and it was essentially this: Don't hand us that highminded intellectual baloney, Krim. We know what goes on in that beady, crooked, vengeful brain of yours. You want what we've got and what EVERYBODY creams for, momser,[1] and since you can't cut it for yourself you've got your tin blade out for every big duke around. Self-destruct, parasite!

In case you think I'm laying it on, paranoiding, that it all sounds too vicious/simplistic/naïve for a man like Breslin to attribute such salivating one-dimensional motives to a man like myself, someone he had brothered and, yes, even loved when I was his mate on the *Herald Tribune,* hang on until you hear the whole story. But the important thing to say right here is that I didn't know what a World War I was getting into when I banged out my original piece. It taught me to respect the firepower of Breslin's cannons until the day I die. I had known Jimmy for six intense months on the *Trib* before it collapsed in April 1966, and then we met occasionally in his hangouts (Mutchie's, Weston's, Toots Shor's) and rapped more often on the phone until I left the country three years later, but even though I knew the man and loved his work, I was too blind to see he wasn't kidding with all his gangster bullshit. I had seen him slap (not punch) red into the face of a girl secretary at a high-boozing *Tribune* farewell party, just like a haughty, manicured, slightly effeminate Mafioso Don teaching an underling an S&M lesson, and then have his Brooklyn "soldiers" form a ring of steel around him when three drunken *Trib* reporters tried to get at him. I thought it was all pure theater at the time and even admired

---

1. *Momser* is Yiddish for bastard.

him for his crazy balls in breaching the weak liberalism that would have turned the rest of us to stone if we tried a stunt like that, but that was before The Treatment was turned my way. When that happened it wasn't his crazy balls I was admiring, believe it; I was fighting for my basic bones as a human being and a free voice against a sudden enemy who wanted to wipe me out in exactly the same way that Jimmy's arsonists, heist-men, hit-men, cops on the take, all the types that once seemed so beautifully pricky to us, do a number. Breslin can write them better than anyone because he instinctively thinks and acts like they do when his ass is against the wall.

It had never been my primary intention to put Breslin on the defensive in that *Times* piece. He knew very fucking well I thought he was the big fundamental journalist of our time in New York and that in my own zealous, John Brown way I was trying to call him home from dollar-bill hamming to the scorched harvest of his own reality. But in spite or because of the damn emotion in my writing voice ("that was a hell of a love-letter you wrote Breslin"—Gordon Lish, unmet Fiction Editor of *Esquire*, scribbling off an innocent note to me before hate ruled the day), I went overboard on at least two counts in the piece which gave Jimmy all the excuse he needed to get into his King Kong suit and go ape after me from the top of *The New York Times* Building all the way to London and Paris. I'll explain.

The first count was my overconviction in crackling positive tones that straight fiction was not his bag and in fact a waste for Breslin when he had such an obvious head start over most alienated novelist-types in dealing with the real world. I was dead wrong, not having the foresight to see that he would be using the novel in future books (*Amen*) as a more penetrating news/reality medium than any he had taken on before. And having just worked like a trooper on his first one, no matter how cute or transparent his motives in cooking it up, it was predictable that he would defend his labor and always sharp skill from some penniless idealist who thought the stuff second-rate. For all I know, he had felt uneasy all along about writing a burlesque gangster camp when he knew the soiled backstage story, and my piece merely prodded his shame. I don't know. But I do know that my second count really drove him to murderville with such an epic glotz of rage,[2] guilt, exaggeration, hood threat, and wounded rhetoric that it would have made a hell of a patriotic home movie if it hadn't scared the shit out of so many people and hung over my own life for over a year like that well-known death sword.

What happened was this. In the last phone talk I had with Breslin before I split the States in April, 1969, he told me happy and mellow at high noon that he had just pulled off the most beautiful caper of his career; he had gone out to the Coast himself and sold the move rights to *The Gang That Couldn't Shoot Straight* on the basis of only two sweet little chapters. "I got a quarter of a million bucks out of these two Jewboys," he husked in my ear, triumphant, and I knew exactly what he was grinning about. Jimmy had a healthy respect for money and a healthy respect for Jews; if he could make that kind of score out of two smart J's he had to be good. As for the Jewboy business, it was a sign of cruel honesty between us. Not only had the *Trib* been the roughest, toughest-talking shop that a reporter could hope to work in, not only did Breslin have the most inspired street language of any man I'd ever met, I had the rep in Jimmy's eyes of being a renegade Jew who could be detached about the usual digs that the non-Jewish part of the humanoid scene occasionally gets off on. Jewboy was in if you had any taste for the brown of life, which I did and which Breslin certainly did.

When I came to write my piece I stuck in the phone call to punctuate the fact, rub in the fact, that here was a major man more interested in pulling a swiftie on Hollywood and running his fingers through the bread than in sculpting what I then thought had to be his stone destiny: big, graphic, nonfiction truth books written with the punch of old-fashioned fiction. My old song! I don't feel totally clean about it, however, and if I were doing the piece again four years ago I wouldn't use it. I was sore at Breslin for that cynical streak which to my mind had made him cop out on the best part of his gift and I wanted to get under his skin by giving him a mirror-image of What Makes Jimmy Run. What I didn't understand was that to the streetboy still in him "Jewboy" was still a dirty word, he

2. *Glotz* means eye-popping; it's from the Yiddish.

hadn't really come to terms yet with the ethnic guilt/violence at his back-alley core, and when he used it with me it was not the hip, secret grip of brotherhood I had once thought but more like a puritan speaking dirty to a whore. Perhaps I knew this unconsciously and I stuck it in because I didn't want to be Jimmy's dirty lay. I'm not sure. But it wasn't vital to my argument, I was showing off, and the little "Jewboy" became the pimple on the nose of the piece that almost did the big one in.

Anyway, the article went through the then-cautious *Times Book Review* without a murmur, all the Jewish boys who worked on the Sunday edition were so glazed by euphemism that not one was insulted by this little shot of funky energy. But then Breslin the Beast roared in after seeing an advance copy and must have threatened to have Marvin the Torch fire-bomb the building or Sam the Tool Man go to work on (publisher) Punch Sulzberger's jewels unless the terrible "Jewboy" was forever plowed under. I don't know what he said, I was in London poised to fly across the channel for one last beautiful fling in the newspaper business on the *International Herald Tribune*, but sudden word sputtered to me over the transatlantic wire from an awed voice in New York that whatever Breslin had said, hundreds of printers were now down in the bowels of the Times Building hacking at my copy. Like an army of chisel-wielding gnomes, they were scratching the word "Jew" from the plates so they could print the remaining 700,000 copies of the *Book Review* with the nice whitebread phrase, "I got a quarter of a million bucks out of these two . . . boys." All of this done by hand, dig it! The *Times* was appeasing Breslin by the minute, Jewish nervousness was racing with Jewish masochism to see which could butter his ass most eagerly, but Jimmy, god love him, stood by his principles. Since 800,000 copies of the book review had already been printed and he was now bared to the world for being an honest roughneck with his mouth, if not especially his book, this naked integrity was just too much for an unofficial mayor-type like Breslin to put up with.

He could lose the father-figure patronage of all those wise old cynical Jewish state senators and judges who loved him like a mascot in Toots Shor's. His radical third-party run with Mailer in '69 for mayor and president of the city council would seem a Nazi sham. Oy! That prick Krim knew he was more of a Jew-lover than Krim himself and the perverse atheist was trying to disgrace him. It probably never occurred to Breslin that any possible disgrace in that piece had more to do with his ducking reality (even such as "Jewboy") rather than embracing it on the level we knew was in him, that nobody gave a particular crap in a time that was spawning Kinky Friedman and His Texas Jewboys, and that for all the folklore about Jewish neurotics carrying on like caricatures, nobody can hold a candle to a guilt-bombed Irish ex-Catholic. Breslin on March 4, 1970 sued me and the *Times* for a nice round $1 million for libel, saying the whole bloody intention of my piece was to depict him as "anti-Semitic" and "a hypocrite."

Like a movie, all this million-dollar stuff was shaking in N.Y. the exact day I landed in Paris broke, patched bag and beaten typewriter in sweaty hand, my fucked-up Italian girl waiting for a join-me signal in London, hoping against hope I could cut it on the *International Trib* copy desk (no reporter jobs, this is a tight editor's paper fed by the pick of the wires) and continue to push for a Newspaper as Literature. Perhaps you know, I was and am a three-decade committed literary man who fell hard for daily reporting at the screwy age of 43 and would have happily given up writing books if the old *Trib* had lasted or another writer's paper called. It hadn't happened. I had written another book, an ad for the cover actually sock-ing it to you from the back of this paper, and here I was now at 21, Rue de Berri, anxiously waiting to get the O.K. from Editor Buddy Weiss to hit the lowly, gorgeous desk when Weiss came out of his office and silently threw me a piece of folded yellow paper. It was an open telex from Breslin that had been sitting there two days and must have been read by everyone in the joint except the French janitor and the finger-popping black copyboy. The gut paragraph read: SEYMOUR, WHO DO YOU THINK YOU ARE? YOU'RE A LITTLE, RESENTFUL FAILURE, GOING AROUND JUDGING EVERYONE ELSE'S LIFE AND ABILITIES AND YOU HAVE NONE OF EITHER. IT IS THE CRUMMIEST STUNT I EVER HEARD OF.

"I don't like Breslin," Weiss told me, looking me in the eye, "but I love him."

I went to work that afternoon editing wire-service copy and writing headlines with sick fingers and inside of 13 days I was fired for slowness, incompetence, and general human sadness by the same team that had told me in N.Y. on the old *Trib* that I was a natural. I wired Rafaella some of the money they paid me off with in bribe-crisp U.S. dollars, not even a bookkeeping record that I had ever worked there, Jesus, my journalistic wonderland, and taxied over to James Jones's house on Isle San Louis and asked him for a gun. He told me straightforwardly he'd give me one and three bullets too if I still wanted it in 72 hours. This was his policy. His mature grisly directness straightened me up like a goddamn jackknife and after speaking to the *Times* long-distance, telling them I'd start preparing the miles of defense evidence they wanted, I left Paris for grimy London as if this whole gaudy insane show had happened to another Seymour Krim. I went back to America six months later and began teaching; Rafaella took a Land Rover caravan to Mother India when I came home and has disappeared from the face of the earth. . . .

So after almost two years of legal farting around, during which the well-heeled *Times* would fly me in to New York from Iowa City and Chicago and places like that, Jimmy finally dropped the case without saying boo. He told Dotson Rader at some WPIX speak-your-mind program that the thing had mainly been a joke. Fun-ny! Rader believed him, but I remembered the *Times*'s attorneys hammering at me across the overseas phone wanting to know if I had a tape of the chewboy and commanding me to fly home; I could quote the humiliating unanswered letters I wrote to Breslin in Dublin offering to fight, talk it out, anything except go to hairy million-dollar law; I remember Buddy Weiss, Rafaella, the Paris *Trib*, the gun (Breslin has a great moment about a gun being dipped in mashed potatoes in his new book), the mutual friends I haven't seen since the "joke" started, the loneliness I feel for that whole roaring wiseguy crew headed by the big sick joker himself. But I'll tell you this. Breslin's book is every inch and more the one I thought was in him. It is "fiction" in its plotting, and in that sense I was wrong, but the sting of life is real, super-real, super brown, and I can't help thinking I goaded him into his best. In case you think that's bullshit vanity, and you're wrong, tell me how many million-dollar Jewboy lawsuits including the crummiest stunts you ever heard of have you been in lately? They leave a deep nonorthodox circumcision that lasts the rest of your life. I'll always be in Breslin's head and he'll be in mine until a nicer, easier world comes around the corner.

14

For My Brothers and Sisters
in the Failure Business

Phillip Lopate included "For My Brothers and Sisters in the Failure Business"
in The Art of the Personal Essay: An Anthology from the Classical Era to
the Present *(1994), and it stands up to the competition offered by George Orwell,*
Henry David Thoreau, F. Scott Fitzgerald, and H. L. Mencken. "Failure Busi-
ness" is a moving analysis of Krim's—and America's—obsession with success
and failure. Less obviously, it is also a farewell to a Jewish-American type.

Alfred Kazin wrote how he was intoxicated by America, how he fell under the
spell of the country that "would soon be the greatest power instrument in history"
(1979, 21). Mailer was drunk on America when he declared he would settle for
nothing less than making "a revolution in the consciousness of our time" (1959,
17). The poet Delmore Schwartz had equally outrageous ambitions. "The heroic
appealed to his grandiose imagination" and he dreamed of becoming a "great ath-
lete, statesman, actor, drama critic, and intellectual" (Atlas 1977, 17). Allen Gins-
berg, to his credit, mocked this penchant for outrageous demands by comically
asking in his poem "America," "When can I go into the supermarket and buy
what I need with my good looks?" (1983, 31).

In "Failure Business," Krim understands the syndrome. "America was my
carnival at an earlier age than most and I wanted to be everything in it that turned
me on, like a youth bouncing around crazed on a boardwalk. I mean literally
everything." This ambition produced unstable personalities that more often led to
failure than success. The love and enthusiasm that Krim and his contemporaries
brought to being Americans exacted a high price, but one that Krim feels was
worth paying.

> He dreamed that he was actually the hero of a legend, going back to
> his sophomore year at Columbia and taking the football team on to
> glory at the Rose Bowl, following with an A in Chemistry, running the
> fastest mile ever run in Madison Square Garden, being scouted by the
> Yankees for their baseball team, becoming a great actor playing King
> Lear, impressing Madison Avenue by writing "a book so golden and
> so purchased with magic that everybody smacks their brows," and
> ending up knocking out Joe Louis and becoming the world's heavy-
> weight champion.
>
> —*Kerouac* by Ann Charters

We are all victims of the imagination in this country. The American Dream may sometimes seem like a dirty joke these days, but it was internalized long ago by our fevered little minds and it remains to haunt us as we fumble with the unglamorous pennies of life during the illusionless middle years. At 51, believe it or not, or believe it and pity me if you are young and swift, I still don't know truly "what I want to be." I've published several serious books. I rate an inch in Who's Who in America. I teach at a so-called respected university. But in that profuse upstairs delicatessen of mine I'm as open to every wild possibility as I was at 13, although even I know that the chances of acting them out diminish with each heartbeat.

One life was never quite enough for what I had in mind.

At 50 my father was as built-in as a concrete foundation and at 55 he was crushed out of existence by the superstructure of his life. I have no superstructure except possibly in my head. I literally live alone with my fierce dreams, and my possessions are few. My father knew where he stood or thought he did, having originally come from an iron-cross Europe, but I only know that I stand on today with a silent prayer that tomorrow will bring to me my revelation and miraculize me.

That's because I come from America, which has to be the classic, ulti-mate, then-they-broke-the-mold incubator of not knowing who you are until you find out. I have never really found out and I expect what remains of my life to be one long search party for the final me. I don't kid myself that I'm alone in this, hardly, and I don't really think that the great day will ever come when I hold a finished me in my fist and say here you are, congratulations. I'm talking primarily about the expression of that me in the world, the shape it takes, the profile it zings out, the "work" it does.

You may sometimes think everyone lives in the crotch of the pleasure principle these days except you, but you have company, friend. I live under the same pressures you do. It is still your work or role that finally gives you your definition in our society, and the thousands upon thousands of people who I believe are like me are those who have never found the professional skin to fit the riot in their souls. Many never will. I think what I have to say here will speak for some of their secret life and for that other sad America you don't hear too much about. This isn't presumption so much as a voice of scars and stars talking. I've lived it and will probably go on living it until they take away my hotdog.

Consider (as the noble Dickens used to say about just such a lad as I) a boy at the turn of the 30s growing up in this land without parents, discipline, any religion to speak of, yet with a famished need that almost unconsciously filled the vacuum where the solid family heart should be, the dizzying spectacle of his senses. America was my carnival at an earlier age than most and I wanted to be everything in it that turned me on, like a youth bouncing around crazed on a boardwalk. I mean literally everything. I was as unanchored a kid as you can conceive of, an open fuse-box of blind yearning, and out of what I now assume was unimaginable loneliness and human hunger I greedily tried on the personalities of every type on the national scene as picked up through newspapers, magazines, movies, radio, and just nosing around.

And what a juicy parade through any inexperienced and wildly applauding mind America was then, what a nonstop variety show of heroes, adventurers, fabulous kinds of human beings to hook on to if you were totally on your own without any guidance and looking for your star in a society that almost drove you batty with desire. In my earnest role-playing the philosophical tramp and the cool millionaire-playboy were second nature to me, as were the style and stance of ballplayers, barnstorming pilots, polar explorers, radio personalities (how can I ever forget you, gorgeous-voiced Ted Husing?), generals, bridge-building engineers, treasure-hunters, crooners, inventors. I wanted to be and actually was Glenn Cunningham, Joe E. Penner, Kid Chocolate, Chandu the Magician,

Eugene O'Neill, a Gangbuster. If you're old enough, tick off the names of the rotogravure big-shots of the time and see Seymour impersonating them in his private magic theater. And later on when I had lost my adolescent shame and knew myself to be a freak of the imagination, even wallowed in it, I identified with women like Amelia Earhart and even the hot ripe early pinup girl, Iris Adrian, and transvestited my mind to see the world through their long lashes and tough lace. Democracy means democracy of the fantasy life, too, there are no cops crouching in the corridors of the brain. Dr. Freud's superego hasn't been able to pull its old country rank over here, even though it's tried like a mother, or should I say a father?

But my point is this: what a great fitting-room for experimentation, a huge sci-fi lab for making the self you wanted, America was for those of us who needed models, forms, shapes we could throw ourselves into. Obviously, everyone from my generation didn't chuck caution out the window even if they felt the lure, as I did, of a new make-your-own-lifesize-man era. Some of my more realistic contemporaries narrowed it all down early and became the comparative successes they are today. Whether it's making a lot of money selling scrap in a junkyard (Ed Feinberg) or writing thrillers for connoisseurs of kinkiness (Patricia Highsmith), they all had to focus clearly, work hard. As traps and frustrations of 51 close down around me, with all the small defects and petty hurts that sometimes seem to choke away all thoughts of the unique homeric journey of the inner person in America, everyone's inner person, I salute them for achieving some of what they wanted. Nobody gets it all. But I salute anyone in this bewildering dreamland of a nation who has managed to cut through the wilderness of tangled trails to some definite cabin of achievement and reward.

Yet those of us who have never really nailed it down, who have charged through life from enthusiasm to enthusiasm, from new project to new project, even from personality-revolution to personality-revolution, have a secret also. I'm sorry to say it isn't the kind that desperate people can use to improve themselves, like those ads in the newspaper. Sadly enough, it IS the kind that people in my seven-league but very leaky boots often take to psychiatrists, hoping to simplify their experience because they can't cope with the murderous tangle of it. But for those of us who have lived through each twist and turn, the psychiatry sessions, the occasional abyss, the endless review of our lives to see where we went wrong, and then come to see our natures as strange and special manifestations of a time and place that will never come again, there is a wonder in it that almost makes up for the beating we are beginning to take at the hands of the professional heavyweight world.

Our secret is that we still have an epic longing to be more than what we are, to multiply ourselves, to integrate all the identities and action-fantasies we have experienced, above all to keep experimenting with our lives all the way to Forest Lawn to see how much we can make real out of that prolific American Dream machine within. Let me say it plainly: our true projects have finally been ourselves. It's as if we had taken literally the old cornball Land of Opportunity slogan and incorporated it into the pit of the being instead of the space around us; and fallen so much in love with the ongoing excitement of becoming, even the illusion of becoming, that our pants often fall down and reveal our dirty skivvies and skinny legs. The laughter hurts, believe me, but it doesn't stop us for very long. We were hooked early.

What it comes down to is that the America of the pioneer has been made subjective by us. The endless rolling back of the frontier goes on within our heads all the time. We are the updated Daniel Boones of American inner space. Each of our lives, for those of us in this country-wide fraternity, seems to us a novel or a play or a movie in itself, draining our energy but then at other moments lifting us up to spectacular highs, yet always moving, the big wagon-train of great new possibilities always crushing on. The fact that all of this is private doesn't make it any less real. What it does do is make us ache with hopelessness at times as to how to find a vocation for this private super-adventure serial out on the streets of life.

I know for a fact that I wanted to become a novelist in my teens just so that I could be all these different personalities and events that it was physically impossible for me to be any other way. As a matter of fact, I feel that the writing of the realistic/romantic novel in America (and they were usually one and the same, with the hairy details just used to tack down the sweep of imagination) came out of these basic human needs to transcend the one body and temperament you were born with in order to mingle imaginatively with a cast of thousands that could only exist in a monster-country like ours. Others wanted to become actors for much the same reason, to impersonate all the people they could not be, but in my case I wanted to compose the script itself so that I could participate in the minds as well as the outward actions of characters who were all extensions of myself and my own mad love affair with the fabulous diversity of this society.

I never accepted the discipline or, finally, the belief in a pure fiction separate from myself and never became the marvelous novelist of my teenage ambition. But I was an inward one, just as so many young kids today shoot movies in their heads with themselves as the leading character. I think it was just an accident of history that made me good at words instead of the sounds and pictures which are the newest language, but I feel little superiority at being able to pitch a word or two compared to those like myself in other ways who are tongue-tied. What unites us all is that we never knew except in bits and pieces how to find a total expression, appreciated by our peers, in which we could deliver ourselves of all the huge and contradictory desires we felt within. The country was too rich and confusing for us to want to be one thing at the expense of another. We were the victims of our enormous appreciation of it all.

Even though, with words coming easily to me, I began in my 20s that long string of never totally satisfying jobs as Office of War Information rewrite man, assistant pulp editor, motion-picture publicity writer, motion-picture script reader, book reviewer, finally editor of a magazine, I was always looking past them. When I heard a great black blues singer, I wanted to incorporate that sound in me and even tried singing in Greenwich Village. When I saw a handsome movie star close up, I thought that was my birthright also and went to a plastic surgeon to try and make me look more like this example of male beauty. When I had saturated myself with the brilliant records of Lenny Bruce and Lord Buckley, I thought that I too should improvise in a nightclub and even played a small engagement in the Midwest to painfully act this dream out. Whatever I saw that was good in others and which I didn't possess, I tried literally to add to my nature, graft on to the living flesh. It seemed to me, and I'm sure to those like me who haven't yet spoken, that American society was essentially a launching pad for the endless development of the Self.

We cared more about trying to enlarge and extend the boundaries of being what we were, of demonically sucking all of the country's possibilities into ourselves, than we did about perfecting a single craft or profession. As I've said, it was a beautiful, breathless eagerness for all the life we could hold inside, packed layer on layer like a bulging quart container of ice cream. Granted that in a way it was the most rank kind of selfishness and self-absorption, yet this too was forecast and made part of the national inheritance in 1870 when Walt Whitman chanted, "One's-self I sing—a simple, separate person; yet utter the word Democratic, the word En-Masse." That's what this democracy was for us, a huge supermarket of mass man where we could take a piece here and a piece there to make our personalities for ourselves instead of putting up with what was given at the beginning.

But this lovely idea became for some of us a tragedy, or at least a terrible confusion that wasn't counted on at the beginning. When do you stop making a personality? When do you stop fantasizing an endless you and try to make it with what you've got? The answer is never, really. You keep adding and subtracting from that creation which is yourself until the last moment. Once begun, it is not a habit that can be given up easily. Some people who started off this risky life-game with high hopes found that after a while they were unable to live with the self they began with and unable to come close to the self, or selves, they desired to be. They live in pain, and some are no longer living at all, having found it too bitter to take.

In my own case, because of the fluency with words, I was able to express my own longings and desires with personal statements in print as the years went by, and thus I wasn't as completely frustrated as those other dreamers I know who have run the gamut of jobs and flings at movies, writing, dancing, politics, and yet have never found a home to match their imaginations. Simply put, they never found a form to contain them, or have only caught it momentarily, and then it was gone.

During my 20s and 30s, even into my 40s, it was exhilarating to learn and be involved at this and then that steaming source—the *Partisan Review* brigade of radical intellectuals, then the Beat Generation, then a wonderful fling at daily newspaper reporting on the *New York Herald Tribune,* then the breakthrough (to my mind) of the New Journalism. I was confident as are all American nomads of the jeweled highways of the imagination that there would be a sudden confluence of all the roads at some fated point and then I would put it all together with a gorgeous thunderclap. No soap. Actually all of this can conceivably happen, but the mathematics are against you as time goes on. Yet time is just that factor we don't want to hear about until it elbows us in the nose.

We know all along that time is squeezing us into a corner while we mentally rocket to each new star that flares across our sky, and yet we can't help ourselves. We forget that our contemporaries are building up wealth of one kind or another, reputations, consistency, credit in the world, and that it counts for more as age settles down around all of us, the very age we have denied or ignored. In a way, those of us who have lived higher in the mind than on the sidewalk making and revising our salad of possibilities have stayed younger than we should have. We have even been sealed off from our own image as it's seen by others.

Yet each one of us sooner or later gets the elbow that reminds us that the "real world" we have postponed making a deal with, in fact played with like Chaplin kicking the globe around in *The Great Dictator,* has been evaluating us with a different set of standards than the ones we have been applying to ourselves. If we have been snotty towards ordinary success, proud and mysterious as we followed the inner light, even making thoughtless cracks about those who settle for little, then the day always comes when our own inability to put it all together is seen by another who wants to cut us down to size and our lives suddenly explode in our faces. Mine came in February of 1970 when a brash, unshy public personality I know, an ex-pal who came hungry and swinging off the city streets, reacted violently to a piece of public comment I made about him and a book he wrote and sent me a bitter telegram calling me a "failure" who spent his sniveling days carving up his betters. My payoff after all those invisible high-flying years!

I was living in Europe at the time, where the attitude towards personal success and failure is much less of a real distinction than over here because of the evenhanded wounds of recent history. Everyone was badly hurt by the war. Even today one man or woman's fate counts for less than some kind of minimum well-being for masses of people who are trapped by political and economic circumstances beyond their control and must learn to live, cheerfully if possible, without much hope for large personal triumphs. It is a relief for Americans who come from a society that glorifies individual achievement to the aching and breaking point to live over there for a while, and try to recuperate from the American heat in a different psychological climate. In fact many of our permanent expatriates are just the kind of people I have been talking about all through this communication, a band who have never found themselves by our official standards and perhaps never will, but who can live more at peace beyond our shores with less money and less strain than at home.

I, too, had been unkinked in this easier, we're-all-fucked-together-so-let's-make-the-best-of-it environment, self-lulled into thinking I was as rich and potential a human gold mine as I always believed—as all of us in my camp want to believe—when the dirty American word "failure" winged its way across the water and hit me where it hurts. It was obviously not the way I saw myself, the way any of us saw ourselves, always living on the lip of hope, the great configuration of our many possibilities always within an inch of being jigsawed together, the intensity of our days denying to us that we had wasted them. But I wanted to face the word in all of the ugliness it stirred up for anyone who came out of the middle class, which means most of us. It suddenly and brutally defined to me the price I had paid for my bid to be everything that proposed itself to my imagination. Maybe I never had a choice, and would have been an uncertain performer at whatever I did, but my decision to aim at the stars had been a conscious one and this was the way it was being weighed on the common man's do-it-or-shut-up scale. (My ex-friend's strength as a personality and writer is precisely his common-Joe instincts; ditto for what he doesn't see.)

I don't know if my fellow visionaries will tolerate the word "failure" when members of their blood families, looking to them for money, status, some tangible outer sign of the golden inner constellations they claim to have traveled, fling this ancient curse at them. Perhaps they should not accept it in any sense and preserve the innocence that started them on a quest beyond materialism, petty achievement, the reduction of their many selves into one Kodak-pure white shirtfront on which a conventional medal can be pinned. Perhaps.

But I personally am not ashamed of the tag, although it tore a hole through my pride. As Jack Lemmon said recently, "Success is always somebody else's opinion and not your own," and so it is with failure as well. Obviously the majority of skeptical life-scarred adults who have seen their own illusions go down the drain will not be as sympathetic as we were to the lavish possibilities we envisioned in our minds, the many shapes we wanted to translate this into, the difficulty of using our American birthright to the full in a totally exploratory way. They want results as time tightens its grip on all of us. And it is only partial results, inconclusive, shifting, mistake-riddled, unfinished, that we mostly have to show as we start the final lap. So it is foolish not to admit that they are right as far as they go, the hardboiled dockers of money, product, prestige, the pragmatists who check off winners and losers only and not what-might-have-beens or any fancy complexity of motives.

But if you are a proud, searching "failure" in this society, and we can take ironic comfort in the fact that there are hundreds of thousands of us, then it is smart and honorable to know what you attempted and why you are now vulnerable to the body blows of those who once saw you robed in the glow of your vision and now only see an unmade bed and a few unwashed cups on the bare wooden table of a gray day. What we usually refuse to acknowledge in our increasingly defensive posture is that we chose our royal inner trip out of an excess of blind faith, out of a reach beyond what we might have had if our desires had been less grandiose. I can't really criticize this, I think it is inherent in the American mystique to want to go all the way to the limit of your imagination, but if we are straight about it we must accept that we are in large part responsible for the jam we are now in.

In my own situation I know only too well that from childhood and adolescence on I clutched at the habit of dreaming up a glittering future, always, instead of putting my head down and slugging my way through the present. I must confess that in an almost reflexive sense I still find myself doing this childish number, as do so many of those other poor lovely romantics who are like me. It's a primitive method so native to us by now that it is part of us. What was once a psychological choice when we were young, in other words, has now become for many of us a habit as hard to kick as junk. The handy magic of relying on the future, on tomorrow, to knit together all the parts of a self that we hoarded up for a lifetime can't be stopped at this late date, or won't be stopped, because our frame of mind was always that of a long-odds gambler. One day it would all pay off. But for most of us, I'm afraid that day will never come—the original hopes, their extravagant range and spaciousness, and yes, their lack of specific clarity and specific definition, were beyond translation into deed. They dramatized our lives for a good long while and then turned slightly sour when people began to ask for proof.

For a minority, and I still believe this, the special form they seek to pull it all together will unexpectedly click into place after years of turning the key this way and that. And as for myself, I am lucky I guess in that I can write about this very phenomenon that I live while others who experience it just as toughly, maybe even more so, are without the words to tell you what they have gone through. Maybe that is my "revelation," the final "me," my purpose in the schemelessness of things after looking so strenuously in all directions and being so discontented with what I can apparently do without strain.

But this is a poor second to what I wanted and I will never be satisfied with sketching my own portrait and that of those like me when it was action we finally craved, after all those dress rehearsals in the mind, and not self-analysis. America worked on us too hard, when you get right down to it. We imaginatively lived out all the mythic possibilities, all the personal turnon of practically superhuman accomplishment, stimulated by the fables of the media. We were the perfect big-eyed consumers of this country's four-color ad to the universe, wanting to be one tempting thing and then another and ending up, most of us, with little but the sadly smiling hope that time would somehow solve our situation. When I've been brave, I've told my friends who share my plight that this is no longer a true possibility to hang on to. Time will most likely repeat itself. We will most likely repeat ourselves. Most of my friends agree, with that hard twinkle in the eye that unites all of us who have earned it.

But you cannot separate us from the deepest promise of the country as it was lived within by very sensitive poets without a tongue, so to speak, and perhaps the ultimate failure of the country. This last is not an easy thing to say, even in a time in which America-baiting is the rage. Like most of us in the failure business, I am, we are, patriots so outrageously old-fashioned that we incorporated the spirit of the country in our very heads, took literally its every invitation to the greatest kind of self-fulfillment ever known. There's something beautiful about being an American sucker, even if you pay for it with tears and worse. We were millionaires of the spirit for at least 20 adult years before we felt the lowering of the boom, and in the last analysis it is the spirit, the attitude within, a quality of soul, that this country has to offer to history much more than its tangible steel and the bright blood too often accompanying it.

It might be, and this is the tragic point of intersection between our lives and that of the land that produced us, that America in its ultimate sense was never anything but promise, the future, the hope of one day putting it all together—just like us—and that the reality has always been disappointment after that initial fairy-tale spring rain upon the green longings of its children. I don't mean this in a sour-grape sense, please accept that such a motive is beneath me; I would never damn the country as a whole because I have not gotten out of it what I so fervently wanted. But I truly think that the Idea of America was so overwhelming to those of us who bit right to the core of the infinitely juicy hope that it had to let us down on a sheer reality-level, even if we had come close to acting out the wondrous. We, like the nation itself, were so impressed with our potential that we took victory in everything for granted. And both of us have been pounded into pretty fair philosophers as a result of recent events.

Those of us who climbed the hill on the basis of our country's promise, and are now going down the other side, can't reclaim any of the years spent in the most exalted daydreaming. All we can do is suggest other values to our kids which will in turn be passed on to theirs. But perhaps we fed our visions into the atmosphere, and added to the depth and richness of a different new America to come. Perhaps this seeding of the air will one day be credited to us, the mostly unknown soldiers of the last innocent battalion who fought for the American Dream on the most intimate level it can be conceived of. It was too immense not to embrace.

PART FOUR

15

The Menahem Begin Image

Krim's battles with the various models life offered him—Village intellectual, Beatnik, success, and failure—were secondary to the unhappy but unavoidable knowledge that being a Jew was his true and inescapable fate. In these next four essays, Krim's writing emits less anxiety because of the use of a new pronoun: "we." When Krim speaks of the Jews he includes himself in a way he rarely does when he writes about other topics (except perhaps failure).

Nearly every major American-Jewish writer has been irked by the designation. As Woody Allen once remarked about calling man mortal, it is obviously not a compliment (1981, 83). Outpourings of Jewish creativity, combined with a Jewish eagerness to escape Jewish parochialism and hit the big time, produced in America a paradox that everyone recognizes but only Stephen J. Whitfield formulated: "The American Jewish subculture looks drab in the light of an American culture that Jews have helped to energize, a mass culture that has dazzled the world" (1993, 11). Krim, like many of his Jewish contemporaries, wanted to dazzle the world. Norman Mailer and others managed it. Krim did not. But Krim's smaller talent was not the only hindrance to such achievement. He also was fated to a smaller realm by his attachment to the American-Jewish subculture. Whether writing about intellectuals, blacks, Mailer, Puzo, Breslin, success, or failure, Krim wrote about Jews.

In the following essays, Krim writes solely about Jews. And from one article to the next he expands the Jewish circle that he feels himself part of. He even opens his arms to the unfashionable and right-wing Israeli prime minister Menahem Begin.

This is a strictly inside-page style note on the way Menahem Begin's manner, looks, voice and fierce identification with Old Testament Father Abraham, as if 6,000 years ago were yesterday, is bound to shake up assimilated American Jews when he comes over here.

Unless Menahem pulls his punches as a guest, that vast majority of American middle-class Jews is set to experience an implosion under the vest ranging from tormented blushes to secret pride when Begin starts to do his thing on the evening news.

Here is the intact, unashamed, brilliant and sometimes scathing old-world relative they've done their best to forget. Here, without contact lenses, tinted airplane glasses, nose job, hair weave, rep tie or Brooks suit, is the image that might have belonged to Grandpa down on Hester Street 60 years ago; but certainly not the new ritzy generation of Ivy League lawyers, doctors, skiers, swingers, and tennis-playing English profs.

For Begin, the one time I heard him interviewed from Tel Aviv, by an ABC correspondent who literally could not get a word in—Grandpa all over again!—exults in his Jewish down-home style without any attempt to clean it up.

He is a Majority Jew, not a Minority one like his American cousins, and he doesn't have to look over his shoulder to check out what the goyish crowd is thinking. He is the cutting edge of the crowd in his own small country.

He could step right out of Irving Howe's *World of Our Fathers,* except he didn't emigrate to the United States from a little shtetl in Poland but instead went right from Russia to the land of his biblical fathers and helped dynamite the state of Israel into existence.

Yet he is a throwback to American Jews who have been here for more than a generation. He is no good-looking, could-be fraternity man like ex–Prime Minister Rabin. He slaps down stupid questions like flies. He suffers fools ungladly. He believes in what he believes to the point of contempt. I can hear my concerned aunt up in Manchester, N.H. asking—I can hear everyone's concerned aunt asking: "Is it good for the Jews?"

The answer will be debated for months after Menahem goes, but as one pro-American member of the ancient family tree who has already been exposed to the Begin Blast, I can tell you there will be no consensus. I can also tell you that the emotional ripples, vibrating everything hidden in the American-Jewish soul, will lead to self-examination of a searing kind.

Some American Jews—who can blame them?—will want no identification with this embodiment of all the conspicuous "Jewish traits" that made them fight shame as young Americans, with new images of a high-kicking future in their star-spangled eyes. Others will undergo reconversion, feel they have betrayed the solid Jew in themselves with mod disguises, feel that Menahem is in holy touch with roots they've let wither out of ignorance or double-martini worldliness.

Either way, no one who still thinks of himself as a Jew in America (or is thought by others!) is likely to get off the hook that Menahem Begin is shining up for us just by being what he is, coming from where he did, standing for what he does.

Yet I personally think it was always inevitable, forced to define yourself this way, and Menahem's pointing finger goes all the way down to the most protected personal depths. Ex–Prime Minister Rabin seemed an imitation American compared to this implacable gent. American Jews could see him blending out on the ecumenical links without thinking twice about the man until he got in trouble.

But Menahem is the face in the mirror we don't want to see—anti-movie-star, heavy glasses, the accent that sent H*y*m*a*n K*a*p*l*a*n to night school: the ghetto heritage according to our helpless media standards. But then he begins to speak, actually to think aloud through that Lower East Side litany. The Jew suppressed in all of us steps forward, alert. Agree or disagree with Menahem, intelligence ignites in the ears, ideas crumble image—"we see not with but through the eye," said William Blake—admiration tentatively climbs over the fallen body of self-consciousness and the shock of recognition . . .

Mr. Raw Conscience is coming to America to put all middle-class American Jews on the existential spot. He comes for reasons other than the subjective turmoil he'll leave behind from New York to Los Angeles, but to many of us hitched forever to America that will be the main impact of his visit. Our private lives are the most inviolate reality we have, like every other United States citizen. He will enter each one like an avenging ghost you can't keep out.

16

Sitting *Shiva* for Henry Miller

Krim has enough pride in the designation of Jew to bestow the label upon Henry Miller, who Krim feels would agree that it can be a compliment. Like the "Menahem Begin" piece in the last chapter, this essay argues for a Jewish tent big enough to include every Jew and every friend of the Jews. And again like the "Begin" article, Krim here establishes a litmus test of Jewish authenticity that snubs the uptown Jews in favor of the downtown Jews, gritty and plain. This tension over the nature of Jewish-American identity is a theme of the American Jewish novel. In Bellow's Herzog, *the character Shapiro condemns himself by exclaiming, "How delightful!" which is seen as inauthentic for the son of an immigrant apple peddler (1976a, 90). In Philip Roth's* Goodbye, Columbus, *the hero Neil Klugman has a momentary lapse into spiritual solemnity while resting his feet in St. Patrick's Cathedral, asking God "Which prize is You?" Once back on Fifth Avenue, the world gives him a Jewish rebuke that he interprets as "Which prize do you think, schmuck?" (Roth 1982, 71). Krim's generation of Jewish writers rejected polite refinement as bad medicine. Krim also has little use for it, and in Miller's disdain for it Krim finds a Jewish soul mate.*

I am writing this four days after we got the news that Henry Miller finally cashed it in out in Santa Monica, at the Old Testament age of 88, and the ghetto is sad. That was Henry's name for his favorite part of Manhattan, from Astor Place over to the East River and south to around Broome Street. "The ghetto is the only part of New York which is dear to me," he once wrote. "The rest of the city is an abstraction, cold, geometrical, rigid as *rigor mortis,* and, I may as well add, insane."

This notion of insanity outside the ghetto walls strikes a particularly apt note right now, even in the midst of the solemn handshakes that some of us are giving each other on our own "Little Broadway," Second Avenue. We stop and shake hands almost as if an older brother or a father has died. Last night Joseph Resnick, who runs the National Book Store at 20 Astor Place, shook my hand with more quiet eloquence than he ever has in the 15 years we've known each other.

"What a marvelous man," he said. I nodded, no words necessary between us. "Even if he was a little mystical, that was his right." I nodded again. We Jews who drank in reason like devoted alcoholics to try and figure out this wild world that sometimes exploded in our faces could forgive Henry almost anything. Even his mystiques, his astrologies, his long-shot gambler's taste for magic.

The only person who has been missing, of course, is Irving Stettner, who must be in hiding. It was Irv who published everything Henry wrote these last two or three years in his magazine, *Stroker* ("Every word like a Crackerjack box—with a surprise!"), it was Irv whose own life was transformed by becoming the last great friend of Henry's final days. Henry chanted Irving's poems 3000 miles away and bought his watercolors. Henry gave him the faith we all need, just as Stettner has passed that faith on to the ex-convict Tommy Trantino, and the Arab hash blower Mohammed Mrabet, and even to the now bifocaled Nearsighted Cannoneer, Seymour Krim, by printing them in the pages of his magazine.

But Irving is nowhere to be seen, and I don't blame him. It was he, the poorest of us all, who made those recent trips out to the coast to see Henry and to spur him on. It was he who brought back the news of Henry's going functionally blind in one eye, of how he couldn't read anymore (this "barbarian" who had read more books than any member of his generation), but also how he kept painting like a whistling kid right to the very end. It's right that Irv Stettner shouldn't be around *On the 2nd Avenue Patrol,* the title of his book of poems, to stick out a hand to console or be consoled. Henry's death was much more inexpressibly personal for him than it could ever be for us.

But let's get back to that reckless brush-stroke of "insanity" that Henry Miller characteristically flung over the rest of Manhattan. Obviously I don't really think the other parts of the city have any squatter's rights on madness, but here we are practically sitting *shiva* for Miller in the ghetto, when with almost perfect grotesque timing Roger W. Straus, Jr. popped up in *The New York Times Book Review* a week before Henry died and accused him of being an anti-Semite. Just to refresh your memory, Roger is the Straus in Farrar, Straus & Giroux; he is also a member of the Guggenheim family, and he is most definitely not a ghetto type, no how, no way.

Roger is a townhouse guy, very upright and robust, a kind of Jewish Teddy Roosevelt, and he used the Letters column in the June 1 *TBR* to tell us self-righteously how he refused to buy the original manuscript of one of the two *Tropic* books when Henry was dead broke.

"I disliked the anti-Semitism running through those books," said Straight Arrow Roger, clapping himself on his medals.

Down here in the ghetto today, where we are still stunned by the inevitable, I looked back over Roger Straus's letter and couldn't help but think that it did in fact represent another New York that was actually hallucinating with a reality we never questioned. Henry the anti-Semite—when his greatest American champions have all, without exception, been Jews? "I call Henry Miller the greatest living author because he is," Karl Shapiro has told everyone who would listen. "A genius, a giant, and a great artist," says Norman Mailer, "who has had perhaps the largest stylistic influence of any 20th century author." "The Daddy of us all," is Erica Mann Jong's testimony, or words very much like that but wittier (I haven't been able to track down the exact quote so far).

Why then did a Jewish stuffed-shirt like Roger Straus take such offense at the reference to Jews in *Tropic of Cancer, Tropic of Capricorn,* and probably *Black Spring,* all written during those blazing Paris days in the early 30s when Henry was kicking down the stalls that had excluded him from his rightful place in world literature? I think I know. Henry treated us familiarly as family, just as we have always treated him. He told the truth about us in the same frank way that we tell the truth to each other. But he had an added Gentile perspective, existentially denied to every Jew, and we could recognize its justness in a flash. It tickled us because we knew it was all being said by a friend, yet it had the bite of reality that we always welcome in a world where we are as much of a baffling mystery story to ourselves as we can be to others.

For example, here is one of the quotes from *Tropic of Cancer* that probably burned Roger Straus's ears, yet it is a delight to Karl Shapiro and to this ghetto-boy as well: "I sometimes ask myself how it happens that I attract nothing but crackbrained individuals, neurasthenics, neurotics, psychopaths—and Jews, especially. There must be something in a healthy Gentile that excites the Jewish mind, like when he sees sour black bread."

Here is another from *Cancer:* "Carl was jumping around like a cockroach. He has enough Jew in him to lose his head over an idea. . . ."

And one from *Black Spring,* the kind that can make us blush, but not in the least obliterate the truthfulness of the observation and the rough respect, even love, that lies behind it: "The Jew who pronounced his name for me had thick lips; he could not say Vladivostok, for instance, nor Carpathians—but he could say Dostoievski divinely. Even now, when I say Dostoievski, I see again his big blubbery lips and thin spread of spittle stretching like a rubber band as he pronounced the word. Between his two front teeth there was more than usual space; it was exactly in the middle of this cavity that the Dostoievski quivered and stretched, a thin, iridescent film of sputum in which all the gold of twilight had collected. . . ."

Is it this that Roger Straus, and all the other Roger Strauses out there, consider anti-Semitic? I'm not unsympathetic. I can understand his, and their, discomfort, unless we recall that Henry was born in 1891 right in the middle of the great waves of Eastern European Jewish immigration to New York. From his earliest years he saw these raw Torah-toters come right out of the classic ghettos to our streets. They were Jews alone, to Henry, not Jewish-Americans or any of the smoother designations that are now properly part of our sensitive vocabularies. What would Roger, of old and dignified German-Jewish stock, want Henry to call them? Eskimos? But more important, can't he and all the "Our Crowd" Jews in the fancier precincts of this town see and feel that Henry embraced Jews for being exactly what they were, without amputating his eyes ("sad Jewish faces trimmed with soft beards") and ears out of some hypocritical sense of politeness?

Henry Miller's life and work, so broad and yet so curiously unofficial in this country's modern history that it hasn't yet been truly tallied, was more intimately wrapped up with Jews than that of any major, non-Jewish

U.S. writer I can think of. His meeting with Emma Goldman in San Diego, in 1913, changed his life by his own word. Jack Kahane of the Obelisk Press had the courage to publish the first edition of *Tropic of Cancer* in Paris, Barney Rosset took up the cudgels from there. Alfred Perles, Max Fraenkel and Lowenfels were his great buddies and sparring partners of the Paris/Clichy years. Abraham Rattner toured America with him on his return, Leon Shamroy was the first to encourage and collect his watercolors, Irv Stettner became the sweet son and younger brother of his ebbing days. . . .

No, the distortion of anti-Semitism comes from some overly proud, vulnerable place in Mr. Straus himself, not from Henry Miller. He described his complex and incredibly human Jewish relationships with zest, honesty, sometimes even a gust of unnecessary breeziness that can seem like cheek, but always with deep concern and even reverence for the specific individual. I can't very well say that Henry finally became a Jew himself, but down here in his favorite ghetto on this unhappy day, let me say for Henry what Hemingway in another context once said for himself.

"I am proud to be an honorary Negro," Hemingway declared. Henry, you are an honorary Jew, and the next time we tear into the chopped liver and the Dr. Brown's at the Second Avenue Deli you'll be there in the extra, unused chair. But for god-sakes, behave yourself!

17

My Sister, Joyce Brothers

In the late 1960s, the New York Times *assigned Krim to interview Dr. Joyce Brothers and write a feature on her for the Sunday paper. But Krim met Brothers with poison in his heart, the interview died, and the story never got written.*

Ten years later, Krim wrote this intelligent and moving article about his own prejudices as a Greenwich Village intellectual contemptuous of Joyce Brothers but also jealous of her accomplishments, discipline, and integrity. The essay ends with Krim seeing himself and Brothers as two poles of the American Jewish experience. Krim salutes Brothers as his "straight, smart JAP sister who has survived on a rougher track than I could ever play on."

I once spooked Dr. Joyce Brothers, the most formidable JAP (Jewish American Princess) in the country, and she has haunted my life ever since in revenge. I know she'll never stop until I do her justice.

When I call the Weather Bureau, they plug Dr. Joyce after the temperature and tell me I'll find hope if I call 936-4444 ("Hello, I'm Dr. Joyce Brothers: Medically speaking, there is no such thing as a nervous breakdown."). When I grab my *New York Post* fix each noon, there on page 24 is "America's foremost psychologist" smiling up at me like a tireless light bulb. When I teach one night a week at Columbia, it is in a building only two doors away from where Dr. J. was a psychology assistant, 1948–1952.

And when I won $1638 during a Vegas gambling weekend in the mid 1970s, I spread the money out on the bed of the same Ramada Inn room where Brothers was to be robbed of $220 at gunpoint, then briefly locked in the same john where I exultantly drank cognac under the shower. I found this out later.

I can't get away from Joyce Brothers, either as a man, American, writer, reader, viewer, listener, thinker, feeler. For more than 10 years I have lived her life almost as if it were my own to try to understand her and understand myself. We symbolize opposite poles of New York Jewish need and intensity that practically led to civil war when we met, yet there was bitter, grudging respect on each side. Let me tell you what I mean.

When I was orphaned and rebellious at age 10 in Washington Heights, Joyce Diane Bauer grew up in Queens the shining apple of her lawyer-parents' eyes (both Morris and Estelle Bauer were successful attorneys). And where I was expelled from DeWitt Clinton HS for publishing a dirty-word lit magazine called *expression* and at 17 had to kiss ass for readmission, Joyce Bauer was graduating from Far Rockaway HS with the best marks in her class. While I was flunking out of the U. of North Carolina and drifting through the WWII years proud, defiant and dreamy as a poem, Dr. Joyce was getting her B.S. from Cornell at 20. No poetic license for this cool cookie!

At 22, she had already wrapped up in marriage the indisputable target of every ambitious JAP—Dr. Milton Brothers, boy intern. At 23, she had her M.A. from Columbia in experimental psychology ("An Analysis of the Enzyme Activity of the Conditioned Salivary Response in Human Subjects"). At 26, her Ph.D. ("An Experimental Investigation of Avoidance, Anxiety and Escape Behavior in Humans as Measured by Action Potentials in Muscles"). At 28, Dr. Joyce became nationally known by winning top prize on the first leg of the *$64,000 Question,* telling 20 million viewers that *"cestus"* was the name of the leather glove worn by ancient Roman boxers.

That was the same year I cracked like an eggshell and watched Dr. J. bring down the house from a folding wooden chair in Bellevue. I was wearing a white robe, like a fighter, the subject that finally brought her a total of $134,000 after she had memorized the *Ring Encyclopedia* and watched every "Great Fight of the Century."

I patched myself together, dreams intact but scarred with vinegar, while Dr. Joyce quickly converted her victory into an avalanche of radio and pop psychology shows, a *Good Housekeeping* column ("make your marriage a love affair") and a syndicated newspaper column, and bought

Milty a practice. "I was supposed to be a 'Joseph' and not a 'Joyce'—my parents were expecting a boy," she told Joe Wershba of the *Post*. "So to some extent I've been trying to prove I'm better than a Joseph. I'm enormously organized."

Your reporter was not enormously organized. I was passionate, raw, nose-thumbing, bourgeois-baiting, hoping to turn America on its ear with words shot from a cannon, but Joyce Brothers and I needed each other like uptight brother and sister. The mass audience and status I snubbed but couldn't live without led me to her. The mass-ier audience and money and fame she loved without shame led her to me. Here is the way it happened.

On a managing editor's gamble, I had become a counter-culture general assignment reporter for the respectable *New York Herald Tribune* before it sank. I wrote handcuffed but light and sassy pieces that Dr. Joyce clipped in her Yorkville apartment and filed in her famous yellow-and-white metal cabinets. (She has filed the world in those cabinets.) I could be useful to her, although I didn't know it. She, in turn, was to become my lifeline to keeping my name in uptown print. She didn't know that, either.

The *Trib* suddenly collapsed one Tuesday in the late '60s. Two days later Seymour Peck of the Sunday *Times* telegraphed me at home to do a feature on her for the Arts & Leisure section. "She's made for you," he said when I called him. I agreed. What a plum, this little "Dr." Goody Two-Shoes who was prostituting the honor of the unknown soldiers of science, who had groomed her, so she could have a signed photo in the window of Lindy's Broadway deli! The only member of the American Psychology Association who was "repped" by General Artists Corp., which said in the handout Peck gave me for background: "She looks like Loretta Young, walks like Marilyn Monroe and talks like Dr. Freud." I rubbed my hands while setting up the interview with a perfumed NBC publicity eunuch.

But I knew in a flash, when I first saw Joyce walking toward me on the second floor of 30 Rockefeller Plaza, that this was not going to work out the way I had fantasized. It was as if we had seen into each other's secret hearts before saying a word. The air was charged with invisible bayonets: tall man vs. tiny woman, Village intellectual vs. Madison Avenue money player, hired gun vs. the network darling. "Hiya, Doc," said two jaunty announcers coming from their stint in the next-door studio, as we stood there hypocritically shaking hands, and I couldn't help notice the way she beamed.

You want to be loved, don't you, Dr. Joyce? I thought, never once conceding that I wanted exactly the same response for my smartass image as she did for her comforting one. My calculating, note-taking eye saw her left hand tremble slightly as she semi-disguised the hornrims she was holding while we struggled for something to say, waiting for the elevator. I wouldn't acknowledge that my hand was shaking also as I lit a smoke.

We squared off in the well-known NBC coffee shop, Greentrees, my notepaper on the Formica table. Dr. Joyce frozen-faced in the outfit that had become her trademark: light blue blouse, skirt and eentsy blue loafers to match her eyes (which were now staring unflinchingly past the enemy). I plunged right in, driven by my pounding pulses.

What was a behavioral psychologist like herself doing handing out psychotherapy over the airwaves? Why had a reputable scientist with a Columbia Ph.D. shaved a year off her age in every public printout? (*Who's Who* lists her as born October 20, 1928; her typewritten Ph.D. thesis, which I had had in these very hands in the Columbia Psych Library, says in her own words that her birthdate is October 20, 1927.)

Why did she cheapen her credibility by, among other things, playing foil to Johnny Carson? And now that Charles Van Doren and Teddy Nadler had come clean, surely as one adult to another she could admit she got at least an inch of help on the *$64,000 Question?*

Dr. Joyce looked down at her coffee, three or four delicate beads of perspiration sprouting on her upper lip. ("Studies show that sweat prepares animals to cope with danger," she once wrote. "Diet, pace yourself, keep an emotional diary.") This is the gist of what she said in that small, unwavering, adolescent-girl voice:

"Johnny is very gentle with me on his show. I respect and like him. At 12 I lied about my age to get a counselor job in a camp for problem children. I don't consider it a sin if there's a legitimate purpose behind it. In this case the ability to reach many people in a youth-obsessed culture where I could conceivably be penalized for my age. I've always been interested in people, even when I did lab work. A tremendous amount of material in the field of psychology is being researched and developed. It's my purpose to take this new understanding and bring it in clear form to the average person.

"Yes, my training was essentially in experimental psychology (you call it behavioral), but I will never offer advice that has not been susceptible to verification. I definitely wanted the fame and fun and money of this new world of mass communication. But I never received the hint of an answer as a contestant, it was completely and utterly honest, they even tried to squeeze me off the show and failed! I get 2000 letters a week and try to read each one. When I'm given a problem, I refer to the psychological research, boil down the language, give a layman's answer. I've spent as much as 15 hours preparing for a 15-minute show, I've rewritten a page as much as 16 times."

Then she looked up at me, the shadow of a tear fleeting across her pale blue eyes: "You're out to do a hatchet job."

"Not so. My questions just hold a mirror up to your contradictions."

"No, you have contempt for me," she said quietly. She looked down at the cold coffee and said that when the *Trib* collapsed she had called the city room and tried to get my number. She had read my stuff and wanted me to work with her on a "sound but light-hearted" follow-up to her first book, *10 Days to a Successful Memory,* since she was not really a writer. But obviously that was a mistake, she now saw.

Dr. Joyce left a dollar on the table and stood up, all five feet of her ("Experts agree that a smaller girl has an easier time of it, people are usually more protective"), saying that if I needed more information her assistant would give it to me. Then she walked out of the coffee shop. Not like Marilyn Monroe, but like a small, determined woman who has just learned that her dog has been run over and she has to cope.

I tore up my yellow-paper notes and 10 minutes later was at the *Times* building on West 43rd St., grimly taking the elevator (no armed guard at the desk in those days) and walking right over to where Seymour Peck sat in shirtsleeves.

"I can't do the Brothers," I said, slapping down the packet of background clips he'd given me. "You don't have to pay me a cent." (He paid me in full.)

"Take it easy, Seymour No. 2." Our little joke. "What happened?"

"She's obviously a fraud," I said, "but I can't undress her in public. It's too goddamned cruel. You have to get somebody else."

He calmly nodded without quite understanding, the intuition of a good editor, and I found myself glowing with rosy-cheeked blood at the lie. Sure Dr. Joyce was a high-ego powerhouse who loved the spotlight, just like a certain small-time writer I knew, but I also knew in my gut that she had never once dipped beneath her scrupulous code in this new league. I might detest the skin-deep seriousness of the media game she accepted without a murmur, but not her. She had worked harder and more conscientiously than I ever had, for all my anti-Establishment thunder, and I knew she had never really harmed anyone with her capsules of informed common sense. She was also enough of a 'street' psychologist to have seen through me like a shot.

A decade has rolled by, I've been too proud to write Joyce Brothers and tell her the truth about that meeting: that she is my straight, smart JAP sister who has survived on a rougher track than I could ever play on and once caught her smartass brother with his juvenile, scarlet-envy pants down. Straights and non-straights can never be totally at ease together. But I think now Dr. J. will give me some peace, even when I bump into her in every crazy corner of this new 24-hour, total communications world she helped create: "Studies show if you're the kind of person who makes others uneasy, people will like you better if you do something clumsy like spill your drink, trip over the rug, enter a room with a smudge on your face."

Yes, sweetheart, next time!

18

Epitaph for a Canadian Kike

This essay begs to be read aloud. It is one of Krim's most Jewish articles, not just exploring a Jewish theme but reveling in a Jewish tone of voice, indulging in Jewish-isms such as "Mr. Disgusting," and employing off-color Yiddish phrases such as momser *(bastard) and priceless Jewish mother understatements such as the one-word sentence "Nice" in response to the news that the subject of this essay, shit sculptor extraordinaire Sam Goodman, told a potential buyer, "I shit on you, too." Krim brings the obscure Goodman vividly to life as a knowing Jewish knave and scoundrel thoroughly at home with the dirty facts of life and gleefully eager to rub your nose in them. Krim's easy, fluent, street-corner use of four-letter words enliv-ens, joyously, this portrait of an unmannered son-of-a-bitch, and it is a testament to Krim's skill that it is impossible to know for certain whether this 1969 article was inspired by Philip Roth's* Portnoy's Complaint, *which appeared at the beginning of the same year. That's what Picasso meant when he said that great artists steal.*

This essay is in many ways a Jewish version of the "Black English" piece (chapter 9) that examines how blacks use obscenities, and the similarities between them suggest that the Jews' affinity for black life stems from a shared anger. Just as Krim understood black cursing as a regurgitation of the foulness blacks had been forced to swallow in America, Krim views Sam Goodman as a deliberate offender who offered gifts of excrement to a world that had fed the same to the Jews. The similarity between the two essays goes further. Krim's sympathy for black cursing and Goodman's art cannot overcome his distaste and condemnation of both. Krim makes no special pleading for Goodman out of Jewish brotherhood. He provides a hilarious and brilliant interpretation of Goodman and his art, but rejects the man nevertheless, just as his understanding of black foul language does not make him a defender of it.

How much of what I'm going to say about Sam Goodman—yes, Sam, I'm trying to come to terms with you at last, you prick, you enduring pain in the world's ass!—is "true," actual, the way it really was, and how much is my own anxiety-specked creation I don't know, ultimately; but if God existed and he wanted a view of Sam on earth (or Sam on concrete since I only knew him in N.Y.), as heaving and personal as anyone else's protests today, I would tell him what I am about to tell you and, in working it out, myself. Was it the tough old Arab-boy-fucker Gide who said we write things down to define them for ourselves?—he did, but so did half a dozen others whose names do not come to mind in this gloomy instant and they were all correct. I've buried Sam far down in my safety-seeking head until now, refused to acknowledge that accusing corpse, been afraid of what I'd find in myself as much as in Sam. But that's all over. I've shed my shame. Let come out what will, what must—that's my motto for tonight, alone here in an empty Madrid apartment, far from my roots, home, N.Y., America, alone with the sneering ghost of Goodman. Some ghost, believe me, I can feel him mocking me as I write, but feverishly wanting the publicity also: "You know fucking-A I deserve it, Krim, now where is it going to be published—when?—and do you have pictures? There's a very good one of me . . ."

Good one of you? Don't make me laugh or I might actually, legitimately, throw up. Let me do this my way, momser, user, Mr. Disgusting, or I won't tell it at all . . . yet I have to, eventually, so you win again you—you—cheap hustler! No. You were both more than that and less effective.

To get on with it: all I can do is sketch what I saw and felt, take my chances, and I certainly had a lot of shooting, unexpected feelings in the dozen or so times I was around Sam. Different body-pulls traveling all over the place and causing me pain, mostly. Boris had introduced me to S. in his studio one night in late 1963 or early '64 and the three of us went out and had a bite of supper, as I recall, or perhaps just a drink or two (Scotch) at Boris's whitewashed, police-locked miniature fortress over on E. 6th St. I wasn't too impressed with Sam as a person, that's putting it mildly, like Ovaltine, although I had more than liked those ingenious, surefingered, excellently crafted little horrors of his in the "Vulgar" and "Doom" shows at the March Gallery on E. 10th St. in the early 60s. They seemed beautifully apt to me, these neo-sculptured distortions and garish monstrosities that ridiculed "plastic" America, before the kids discovered that all-purpose epithet, and the galloping technological environment that was already treating us as numbers in its stainless-steel brain.

That was the work, or part of it, and I was always to be fascinated by those dextrous, deadly hands and eyes of Sam's as they showed their vicious skill in the artifacts he turned out. But the man, oh dearie me, the man! THAT was something else, wasn't it? First, foremost, most obvious I guess and therefore unworthy—but then I am as unworthy as you, my hypocrite readers, and as nine tenths of humanity, so we all make a team, don't we?—there was this eerie likeness to the Hitler caricature of the slimy Jew about Sam. (Did he know he was a caricature, was that why he had earned his living cartooning in second-class nightclubs in Buffalo and Miami before hitting the Village?) And before I go into this, which I must, keep in mind what I said at the top about questioning how much one reveals of oneself when writing or speaking about another, how much one imposes the terrors of one's own existence onto others, staining them with your own black sweat. For example: no matter what I might be now, perhaps even unafraid to go down and down into my own unsavory past like a diver, learned by the efforts of living which are superhuman even for the most trivial of us, my style then was fleetfooted Jewish middle-class American—get away fast! My first wife was Waspy, I never got bar-mitzvahed (confirmed), had plastic surgery done to my eaglebeak, wanted to integrate like a beaver and leave that Old World Rotten Jew Stigma disintegrating into never-to-be-missed little pieces behind me. I'm oversimplifying, obviously, and abbreviating the complexity of the whole thing, but that was the essence of it—I could accept being "Jewish" very nicely if I didn't look like one, "act" like one, fit any of Adolf's brilliant visualizations (another kind of artist!) which had wrung the heart out of me as a mirror-hypnotized lad in the 30s and which I vowed then to escape from for the rest of my life.

And here was Sammie Goodman who brought me back to my own self-persecution dreads, rubbed my new button nose in it, just by being himself. Why did he have to be born or at least why appear in my carefully ordered life of all goddamn places?

Sam looked and talked like the all-time mockie, there's no other word. Short, belly sticking out, hooked schnozzola, the inevitable myopic glasses (maybe slightly crosseyed too), going bald, he REPELLED my eyes, I'm sorry; and my ears and sensibilities too—he was crude, whining, wheedling, criticizing, going hardon-crazy at the sight of any ass gyrating down the street, licking his cherry joolips when he talked about IT like some cornball silent-movie creep. I was ashamed to be seen with him. I wanted to be elsewhere. I wanted to shrink up and disappear, and I was then—when Boris introduced us—a man (?) over 40. No doubt, not a doubt in the world, this says more about me than it does about Sam, perhaps you're already putting me down as another yellow U.S. yiddlediddle who hasn't the stomach to accept himself ("your heart has turned to cunt," an ex-buddy once attacked me with—maybe all the charges are true?), but for me to write candidly about Sam I must take the lid off the packed shit in myself as well and this is surely the way it was, the way I'm telling it. Sam at this time, after our muttered meeting, was preparing the famous Shit Show at Gertrude Stein's Gallery in the East 80s, formally called the "No-Sculpture Show" I believe, and I would taxi up to the deserted gallery three or four days a week after my stint at *Nugget* magazine as a kind of literary standby to Sam and Boris's efforts. (And after supper and talk, or defending myself from Goodman's conscious and unconscious violations, I'd charge back to *Nugget* and sweat out my frustrations on a pile of 30 or so manuscripts until far into the deserted night.)

By this, the "literary standby" business, I mean that Boris Lurie, who was the organizer and downtown Trotsky for the thrust of this movement (himself, Goodman, Stanley Fisher at the core), needed psychological support right now. He was going out on a frail scaffolding 17 floors above the street, above the fashion to which he was more sensitively calibrated than supposedly knowing trend-types realized, and even though this was to be Sam's Show in an important sense—the end-product of his scorn, perhaps—Boris as usual was calculating and fretting and working his peter off too getting the thing in order and giving pointers to Sam, in fact sharing the labor on the pieces themselves that later were all subsumed under the Goodman snarl.

I was badgered by these two about press releases, the phrasing of come-on sentences to publications and critics—getting people like Tom Wolfe and Brian O'Doherty if I could to make the opening and write immediate blazing articles (sickening in memory how Goodman slavered at the imminence of publicity, like now, Sam, eh?), things of that sort. As one afternoon close to zero hour, opening night, I saw the canvas coverings taken off that red-veined sculpture which looked like the ultimate bowel movement for the human stable, I was—well, practically knocked across the room, this was the height (or the depths, depending on where you stood) of Sam's style and I told him so with defenseless enthusiasm.

He greeted my praise with hooded eyes and a slight trace of crooked grin. He was shy and condescending both. His expression said to me as clearly as any words: "Thanks, Krim, but I deserve it, you know, all those bastards with so-called names—critics, artists (ha!), parasites, they aren't in my class and I've always known it. So thanks, old man, for spelling it out but don't expect me to pat your behind for your compliment, it's merely correct." His arrogant cool turned me to ice, then rage. Insulted what I thought was my sincerity, generosity, goodwill, even selflessness. Didn't I have a stronger rep in the hip world (Manhattan highbrow) than this smalltime bitching Canadian mockie who was always downgrading the U.S. in the most cowardly fashion, yes, shamelessly lusting for its goodies and then biting, no, shitting all over the hands that fed him? Oh baby, fuck you, Sam Goodman, fuck you good, was my reaction, and not the last time I was to think it either. He grated on me, this fishbellied whiner— "This lousy country of yours deserves to be bombed, incinerated, for its sins"—and I bitterly regretted my compliment, wanted to grab it back out of the air for my own self-respect's sake. He took and he didn't give, the prick, the sawed-off lout, and I wanted to haul off and smack him, literally, drive his yellowed teeth down his throat. But even though I was bigger, taller anyway (the animal was heavyset), I was afraid. Not only that he'd give me a fight—there was something oblique, ominous, about that air of private power—but that he'd be laughing at me. I swallowed my pride, my outrage at his stinky little superiority game, and would go out and catch a bite with both of them (Boris had averted his eyes) at a Child's or Schrafft's, I believe, on Madison not too far from Gertrude's place.

Goodman was funny and sharp over food—a nibble maybe, I did the substantial eating, this was my legitimate supper hour while it was just shmoozing for them (they ate at insane hours)—and after a drink I'd even permit a smile, especially when he'd satirize the itch for power among the Abstract Expressionists masquerading as cowboy innocence. He was smart, goddamn him. But while I could appreciate the quick crap-player's brain that was forever scheming away in Goodman's head and even the "sweetness" that came out of him when he wanted to be liked—and he wanted me to like him, some desperate crack opened in his warped machinery and a flower tentatively stuck its head out—I never took to him for more than a minute. Which was rare for me, because I have more than my share of male friends, perhaps a sublimation of that unconscious homosexuality which a novelist (American) I know here in Spain tells me gets obvious when I become drunk; or perhaps, as I choose to think—without particularly contradicting the novelist, adding to his observation—because I was without family as a boy and feel an ache for brothers my age and not those fatherly ones that life gave me, something like that. Anyway, Goodman even made overtures to me, snotty behavior notwithstanding, calling me up at home late one afternoon and inviting me down to the Champagne Gallery in the Village where he was having an opening of some less monumental work, "American Death Show" (what else?), before the Big Shit was set to slither out uptown. I never went, obviously. "Get down here and write something about it, you're a writer, aren't you?" is what my inner ear heard, rightly or wrongly, defensively at this point, but I hate to be ordered around and used, gentlemen, hate it! Yet this opportunist, user, this pushcart Yid—that's what I thought, let the League of Jewish Women Voters sue me—wants to get cozy with me without having the least concern for what my human needs are. Stay away from me, don't call me, you self-consumed little shyster, I thought, you loser—get yourself a derby and a pawnshop, that's where you belong!

I said loser to myself and say it now because Sam wore all the tags of that bad name, overbearing pride without visible foundation, handicaps piled one on the other, jealousy streaking the air around him, etc., etc., and when he died in pain and bodily waste in May 1967 (guilt gnawed at me for not having the soldierliness to visit him in the hospital where he lay helpless, then guilt got covered over with the usual mental muck of tonight's and tomorrow's survival and disappeared), he didn't, I don't think, even rate a one-paragraph obit in the *Times.* Everything about him smelled like a loser, take my word for it, all those freaky little Village emporiums—he even half-owned one called the "Caricature" (natch!) on McDougal St. with a mysterious "wife" whom we never saw and to whom, I later found out, he was never married—where he held forth like a sideshow prophet. He reminded me in that sense of Harvey Matusow, the clown of all avant-garde dodges who is now truly swinging in London, making it in a healthy sense for the first time since he got out of the federal slammer after his McCarthy Period bust, but who then in the mid-60s used to finagle amateurish 10-minute standup comedian gigs in places like the Champagne Gallery for no money, only yocks, prayerfully, from the straggler audience, and who always invited me to watch him strut his dubious stuff down there, and where I never went. It was a form of J.D. Salinger Manhattan snobbery, I guess, but it was also a reaction against crumminess, pathetic little tinhorn forms of egotism, blat-splat-bleep, look-at-me! and I felt there was something basically wrong-o about Goodman in that he should produce smooth daggers of artwork, pieces that cut and brought blood, and yet have to hustle them in the most phony part of the Square Trap, McDougal St., without dignity or even significant indignity. Just fourth-rate carnival exhibitionism like geeks biting off chickenheads for a quarter.

When Boris later told me that Goodman was the son of a Polish Jewish junk dealer who had come over from the other side in his stained vest and settled in Toronto, that Sam came out of crap and garbage and fuck-your-brother-in-law shadowy little deals, haggling price over a lousy piece of tin with dried mud and phlegm on it, it all made sense to me, did it ever. But when I later learned that Goodman, before I knew him, in the early 60s, "could not pass up a street garbage can," "was obsessed with junk as an artist," "even started dressing like garbage" (all this told me by an informant), THAT didn't fit my picture at all. That was something else, wasn't it? the demon in Goodman that dredged for materials out of his own contemptible past, the contemptuous imagination in the man that made him reach into the toiletbowl of his own life and come up with steaming turds in his knobbed hands from his own gross experience. He threw me a curve, you see? Even dead, but not quite to me or anyone else who suffered him, the bedbug keeps throwing curves, doesn't he?

When we'd have these drinks and sandwiches (for them) and my evening meal at Schrafft's, while he and Boris were mounting the SS, the walk to the restaurant—and do I remember accurately Goodman's paranoia about the German-accented waiter hovering over us at that hour, what did the scum want from us?—would take us past one of the fancy chiselhurst young-cunt finishing schools in the upper 70s. I remember the slightly pukey feeling that swept my stomach and chest, for real, when Sam started fucking them all with his mouth, looking at the windows and then gobbling away out on the street. Then the stories, how he had picked one up from the same school three months before (she had wandered into Gertrude's gallery) and how she had practically grabbed his cock out of his pants and started blowing him in the back room, after that wanting to fuck him on his lap right on Park Ave. in the taxi ride downtown, how she was crazy about him, offering money (she had monthly trust-fund checks), everything, this silverblonde Connecticut moaner of 16 or 17. She couldn't get enough of it, and he was thinking he'd have to throw her back in the teenybopper fishbowl to save his energy, sanity, when her divorced mother took her out of school, suddenly, to go and live in Beverly Hills.

Again, hearing this, the contempt button went wild in my mind—who the fuck did this comicstrip type think he was kidding, did he really take me for a mark, me, Seymour Krim, buying his homely bastard's fantasies, an attractive well-setup swinger like myself who had been plowing N.Y. ass for just about a quarter of a century? It would have been pathetic except that Goodman spoke with such assurance, confidence, that the pathos you have for a cripple's feeble lies turned (with me, anyway) into scorn, anger. I put him on:

"Want to go in the lobby, man, and we'll pick a couple up?"

"Terrific! Come on."

Boris turned away modestly, a slight smile on that neatly mustached mouth, this wasn't for him, but he knew Goodman, I didn't. He knew what a steel walking cock the man thought he was. Insane. Goodman took me firmly by the arm and we started moving to the entrance of the school.

At the last minute I got out of it, scared. It had been years since I'd tried to pick up somebody that young on a dead-cold gamble like this. I wasn't about to be put down, laughed at, shaken. But Goodman didn't give a damn, he wanted a stand-up mate he could hunt pussy with, even use as a foil to get at it, I saw it all in a flash—Boris wasn't tuned to it (between the appetite and the act falls Boris's shadow)—and I WAS AFRAID.

"When I have more time, Sam."

"Anything you say, Krim."

The glint of the killer was flickering in those eyeglasses he wore and I looked at him secretly as we redirected ourselves to the restaurant and wondered with a shiver about the shiksa golden girl of 16 who knelt before his schlang as if it were a scepter: could all of this be real then? Had Goodman transcended his really cartoon Yid turnoff style, somehow transmitted his inner charge and apparently luminous vision to snatch by some great courage of the balls that was light-years ahead of me, still worrying about the flawed scalpel dip at the right side of the bridge of my nose, the reflection of harsh light on my carefully doctored thick glasses wearing my hopeful appeal to women (each previous lay was an accident, cried my stuttering soul!) as a brittle portrait painting out front while Goodman was giving them zap zap expressionism right from the fly of his pants? Again he'd outplayed me, outpunched me, outgutsed me; he was the better man with crotch-honey because he was unashamed, unself-conscious, it seemed, and I resented this too, I burned again, not just because I sensed that red-eyed dick of his driving for every bush on the street but because he made you swallow his bullshit airs because they were backed up by a certain reality. I of course never told him this, never complimented him again, I'd be damned if I'd confide an inch of pure feeling to a monster like this one after the first time he'd closed me out, but it took root in spite of. The pig had harpooned me where it hurts.

There were stories, lots of them, about Goodman after the Shit Show finally came off in May of '64 (funny, he died in a May too and that's the month of my birth); and although none of us knew it, least of all Goodman, the cancer of throat and mouth that was to waste and kill him—and I shed no tears at the gruesome one's death, I shed nothing except a feeling of relief that he was out of the way, frankly—was already poisoning him just when he'd pulled off his biggest or at least most spectacular feat (fart?) of artistic nastiness. Or was it more of just that same craving for attention at any price? One of the stories was that he told the *Art Voices* critic who covered the opening, referring to those gorgeous mounds of liquid plaster-stone shit, with that hemorrhoidal red tracing on the top and sides which I'll never forget, "This is what I think of the art world after spending 30 years in it." Also: "I'm thinking of naming each sculpture after a well-known New York artist."

That's our boy Goodman, yes sir, I have no doubt as to the authenticity of the story. (I was at the opening but getting high in the john to insulate myself), duplicated by yet another one in which in front of witnesses he told a notorious pop collector-investor, who was bargaining with his "adjutant" over doing some buying—and Sam madly wanted to be bought—"I shit on you, too." Nice. And also as compulsively self-defeating as everything else about this human mess except where you knew he topped you, but we won't go into that, a few embarrassments per night is enough, agreed? Then there are a few anti-Goodman stories which are less dramatic, less punchy, concerning this show, the best of them told to me by Tom Wolfe, who covered Goodman's last Shit Show for the late *Herald Tribune* but couldn't manage to get it into the paper in all of its splendid beige (Sam's shit was subtle as well as all-pervasive, I've got to admit) and so nothing was printed. According to the usually accurate Wolfe, who grew up wanting to be a fastball pitcher for the Yankees and is a fiend for control underneath the glitter, Sam was annoyed because Brian O'Doherty, then doing his brisk art reporting for the *Times,* was cooly undisturbed by the exhibition; refused to be shocked in any sense because Brian had been a certified medical man, a doctor, before getting into the arts and saw the whole diarrhetic explosion laid out on Gertrude's floor with medical objectivity. Goodman sulked all over the place, according to Wolfe, even though O'Doherty's report was cleanly and clearly favorable. I like that.

I never saw Goodman in the flesh again after the SS, although it was no surprise to me when I heard that all the fecal matter boomeranged in his suitable kisser, no sales, no money, more enemies, everything you'd expect from this piece of bad news incorporated. Because he had self-righteously and big-mouthedly screwed himself out of all the attention and big bread he so thirstily craved, he apparently wound up back in the cheapest part of the Village cursing the de Koonings and Warhols and grubbing around in phonyville until the end, when the cancer set in. Boris tells me he was actually, factually, rocking and rolling with more of his obsessive pussy than probably ever before right at the end, also, although he was getting too feeble to handle it—consistent, oh yes, you miserable shmuck! Boris (who had broken with Goodman by then) also says—and I've learned to trust his skullhard objectivity, his (at his best) truly without-fear-or-favor eye—that even though Goodman had these modest michelangelesque ideas of being a great master and bragged about his invention of the "long stroke" (he actually used a hockeystick to spread paint on the canvas during his AbEx days), some of his boasting was disquietingly true, "I can mention names who learned the 'long stroke' from him. . . ." Ah Boris, Boris, I KNOW IT, you don't have to tell me, anyone as odious as Goodman had to have a gun in his blood somewhere to make me back up the way I did. When you tell me "the Jews in the N.Y. artworld disliked him because he reminded them too much of what they were trying to get away from, the Jewish haberdasher without 'esthetic beauty,'" well, baby, I find that the understatement of the year! I know what you're saying right down in the privacy of my carefully controlled little-girl feelings. What a throwback Goodman was, a blot on the pop-glamour picture of Manhattan, what an animal. Oy. And yet wasn't it true, Boris, that all of you who fueled this "movement"—you, Goodman, Stan Fisher, with your "Doom" (and "Gloom") and "Vulgar" and "No" and "Shit" exhibitions—can't be separated, as people, as artists, from this whole miserable, real, unending twentieth-century Jewish business?

In other words, Boris Lurie came from the borders of Russia and served time as another Bad Jew in a concentration camp during the war; Goodman was a Hebrew outsider in the tough Canadian Army and got a cushy berth with the film board during the fighting but used to kick himself, afterwards, for not having gone overseas and wrenched open the incinerators where but for the grace of geography he might have been cooking; Fisher was the only American-born member of the three, but he was just as alienated as the other two from the goyishe jamboree of American life.

In fact, I remember a story he once told me of a Germany infantry lad giving him, the bright Brooklyn J-boy, a pair of warm boots in Germany right before the surrender or just after it. A loving gift from persecutor to victim to persecutor, and the look of tenderness that touched Fisher's eyes when he told me this in a soft voice . . . Am I imagining this? No, Fisher told me all right, and he, the least Jew-conscious of the three men, the most screwball Ammurrican. And yet all of them, in this sour, drastic, accusatory, almost hysterically moral work of theirs, tossed their bum stinkbombs at U.S. life from the experience of the war in Europe, with charred Jews down at the bottom of the entire pyramid that ended with Uncle Sam boogie-woogieing before the whole globe on the triumphant top. They were inflamed Jewish WAR artists, it suddenly occurs to me, who carried on their jehovahianism against America the Moloch, those collages of mass graves with pinup tits by Betty Grable jiggling above the skeletons—no wonder Goodman couldn't separate his prick from his skullcap, his sense of holy mission (ha!) from pussy!

Certainly he was fighting a perpetual losing war, against Boris finally, even me, the collectors, the galleries, the hated "big names," himself. And think how your correspondent felt watching him crap on this country which in spite of its terrible sicknesses has made me what I am (terribly sick? is that what you say?) and is indivisible from my being and protection, wanting its money and its cunt, shitting on it—yes, I'm tired of that word too, but it was HIS show, his display—while he wiped his unattractive ass with all its small favors. Yes, think if you will what emotions I felt towards mine brudder-Jew, brother-artist (if I may), brother-in-arms for the same impossible vision of truth and justice, amen. I despised him and I admired him, that's the ticket, double ticket for our time, admired this human louse, know that his bright savage work isn't done (wait for the great retrospective Goodman "Kike Show," he would have loved that, wouldn't he?), that he'll emerge from this sick period of artistic mannequins and male models and, yes, cynical urbanites like myself with his just vinegar due running down his greedy little memory. They never grow, these grotesques who stick when the smoothies wilt into the void, never grow but crooked, misshapen, distorted ("Don't you dig distortion?" sincerely asked the bop musician showing off his humpback chick to an embarrassed buddy),

EVIL, baby. Sam to me was as evil a mother as any paranoid Jewish phantom that ever gave Adolf his nightmares but remember I only saw him from the outside, with my insides, yet within that tension he certainly matches up, oh does he! "Shy, slightly stuttering in public, humble with his friends"—I've heard that too in my grudging researches to "round out the picture," to show the WHOLE man as magazine editors smugly say, to surmount the nasty subjectivity which I warned you about at the start, but for me this so-called shyness was a cover for superiority, arrogance, snot, as a certain kind of shyness so often is. I used to want to take a metaphysical shower when I left Goodman, good and hot with strong black tar soap, but I could never expunge that sarcastic mockie from my veins, no, never, in fact I never want to get him out of my system now because he was a sharper and more spicy and authentic being than I was although I'll NEVER LET MY SECRET ENVY SHOW LIKE GOODMAN DID, one has one's pride, doesn't one? Fuck genuine people when they're alive if they're a hideous embarrassment to us, right? I say Sam deserved his constant failure and is better off dead so we can "appreciate" him in memory, not hold our noses, avert our eyes, be put uptight and shattered, so we can go about our proud unembarrassed business without being murdered in a dozen different ways, correct? Come on, be honest, admit it, who wants a grinning, unbreakable, unendurable, gross, homely, egomaniacal, insane, self-exalted, cutting . . . who needs it???

Yes, except time catches up and passes us all and the dead, a few, overtake the living and eat their vitals away by the strength of an appetite that roars from the other side. Losers can even become winners with the years and it's winner take all, dead OR alive, better believe it! and know thyself to be a petty, apologetic little windbreaker compared to the Real Shits of this world—fuck off, Goodman, stop eavesdropping and preening wherever you are, you undeserving anti-hero, true stinker for an age!

Appendix

. . .

Works Cited

. . .

Index

APPENDIX

Seymour Krim Bibliography

Books

Krim, Seymour, ed. 1954. *Manhattan: Stories from the Heart of a Great City.* New York: Bantam.

———, ed. 1960. *The Beats.* New York: Gold Medal.

———. 1961. *Views of a Nearsighted Cannoneer.* New York: Excelsior Press.

———. 1968. *Views of a Nearsighted Cannoneer.* New York: E. P. Dutton.

———. 1970. *Shake It for the World, Smartass.* New York: Dial Press.

———. 1974. *You & Me.* New York: Holt, Rinehart and Winston.

———. 1991. *What's This Cat's Story? The Best of Seymour Krim,* edited by Peggy Brooks. New York: Paragon House.

Lurie, Boris, and Seymour Krim, eds. 1988. *NO!art: Pin-ups, Excrement, Protest, Jew-art.* Berlin: Edition Hundertmark.

Recordings

Interview with Seymour Krim. 1984. Columbia, MO: American Audio Prose Library.

Seymour Krim Reading "Siege." 1984. Columbia, MO: American Audio Prose Library.

Archival and Unpublished

Seymour Krim's papers are held in the Special Collections Department, University of Iowa Libraries, Iowa City, Iowa. The collection includes Krim's many book reviews, drafts and typescripts of his articles, and also correspondence he received from dozens of writers and critics, including Gregory Corso, Norman Mailer, C. P. Snow, James Dickey, Gay Talese, Allen Ginsberg, and Tom Wolfe. The papers include Krim's unpublished prose-poem *Chaos,* also called *Siege.* An excellent overview of the Krim papers is available online at http://www.lib.uiowa.edu/speccoll/MSC/ToMsc400/MsC367/MsC367_Krim.html.

Further Reading

Gornick, Vivian. 2001. *The Situation and the Story: The Art of Personal Narrative.* New York: Farrar, Straus and Giroux.

Wakefield, Dan. 1992. *New York in the Fifties.* Boston: Houghton Mifflin/Seymour Lawrence.

Wenke, Joseph. 1983. "Seymour Krim." In *The Beats: Literary Bohemians in Postwar America,* edited by Ann Charters, 316–20. Detroit, MI: Gale Research.

Works Cited

Allen, Woody. 1981. *Side Effects*. New York: Ballantine Books.

Atlas, James. 1977. *Delmore Schwartz: The Life of an American Poet*. New York: Farrar Straus Giroux.

Baldwin, James. 1961. "Review of *Views of a Nearsighted Cannoneer*, by Seymour Krim." *Village Voice*, July 13, 1961, 6.

Baraka, Imamu Amiri. 1976. "Babylon Revisited." In *Modern Poems: An Introduction to Poetry*, edited by Richard Ellman and Robert O'Clair, 467–68. New York: W. W. Norton & Co.

Bellow, Saul. 1953. *The Adventures of Augie March*. New York: Viking.

———. 1976a. *Herzog*. New York: Avon Books.

———. 1976b. *Humboldt's Gift*. New York: Avon Books.

———. 1995. *It All Adds Up: From the Dim Past to the Uncertain Future*. New York: Penguin Books.

Bellow, Saul, and Keith Botsford, eds. 1961. "What's *This* Cat's Story?" *Noble Savage* 3:201–22.

———. 2001. *Editors: The Best of Five Decades*. London: Toby Press.

Bloom, Alexander. 1986. *Prodigal Sons: The New York Intellectuals & Their World*. New York: Oxford Univ. Press.

Boyarin, Jonathan, and Daniel Boyarin, eds. 1997. *Jews and Other Differences: The New Jewish Cultural Studies*. Minneapolis: Univ. of Minnesota Press.

Breslin, Jimmy. 1969. *The Gang That Couldn't Shoot Straight*. New York: Viking.

Brown, Kenneth H. 2001. "Krim's Way." *News from the Republic of Letters* 10:18–19.

Cohen, Mark. 2008. "Saul Bellow's Favorite Thought on Herzog? The Evidence of an Unpublished Bellow Letter." *Notes on Contemporary Literature* 38, no. 4:10—12.

Chapman, Abraham. 1974. *Jewish-American Literature: An Anthology*. New York: Mentor.

Charters, Ann. 1992. *The Portable Beat Reader.* New York: Penguin.

Damon, Maria. 1997. "Jazz-Jews, Jive, and Gender: The Ethnic Politics of Jazz Argot." In *Jews and Other Differences: The New Jewish Cultural Studies,* edited by Jonathan Boyarin and Daniel Boyarin, 150–74. Minneapolis: Univ. of Minnesota Press.

Dean, Maury. 2003. *Rock 'n' Roll Gold Rush: A Singles Un-cyclopedia.* New York: Algora.

Dylan, Bob. 1985. *Lyrics, 1962–1985.* New York: Alfred A. Knopf.

Endelman, Todd M. 2001. "In Defense of Jewish Social History." *Jewish Social Studies* 7, no. 3:52–67.

Forman, Seth. 1998. *Blacks in the Jewish Mind: A Crisis of Liberalism.* New York: New York Univ. Press.

Friedman, Murray. 1998. "The Civil Rights Movement and the Reemergence of the Left." In *African Americans and Jews in the Twentieth Century: Studies in Convergence and Conflict,* edited by V. P. Franklin, Nancy L. Grant, Harold M. Kletnick, and Genna Rae McNeil, 102–22. Columbia: Univ. of Missouri Press.

George-Warren, Holly. 1999. *Rolling Stone Book of the Beats: The Beat Generation and American Culture.* New York: Hyperion.

Ginsberg, Allen. 1961. *Kaddish and Other Poems, 1958–1960.* San Francisco: City Lights Books.

———. 1983. "America." In *Howl and Other Poems,* by Allen Ginsberg, 31–34. San Francisco: City Lights Books.

Hill, Herbert. 1998. "Black-Jewish Conflict in the Labor Context: Race, Jobs, and Institutional Power." In *African Americans and Jews in the Twentieth Century: Studies in Convergence and Conflict,* edited by V. P. Franklin, Nancy L. Grant, Harold M. Kletnick, and Genna Rae McNeil, 264–92. Columbia: Univ. of Missouri Press.

Howe, Irving, ed. 1977. *Jewish-American Stories.* New York: Mentor.

Itzkovitz, Daniel. 2005. "Race and Jews in America: An Introduction." *Shofar* 23, no. 4:1–8.

Katz, Shlomo. 1963. "My Father Was a Hero." In *Breakthrough: A Treasury of Contemporary American-Jewish Literature,* edited by Irving Malin and Irwin Stark, 267–77. Philadelphia: Jewish Publication Society of America.

Kazin, Alfred. 1958. *A Walker in the City.* New York: Grove Press.

———. 1963. "The Kitchen." In *Breakthrough: A Treasury of Contemporary American-Jewish Literature,* edited by Irving Malin and Irwin Stark, 254–58. Philadelphia: Jewish Publication Society of America.

————. 1979. *New York Jew*. New York: Vintage Books.

Kerouac, Jack. 1957. *On the Road*. New York: Viking.

Krim, Seymour. 1938. "Two Photographers in Search of a Subject." *Magpie* 22, no. 2:20. http://newdeal.feri.org/magpie/docs/3806p20.htm.

————, ed. 1954. *Manhattan: Stories from the Heart of a Great City*. New York: Bantam.

————, ed. 1960. *The Beats*. New York: Gold Medal.

————. 1960. "Making It!" In *The Beat Scene*, edited by Elias Wilentz, 75–83. New York: Citadel Press.

————. 1961. *Views of a Nearsighted Cannoneer*. New York: Excelsior Press.

————. 1968. *Views of a Nearsighted Cannoneer*. New York: E. P. Dutton.

————. 1970. *Shake It for the World, Smartass*. New York: Dial Press.

————. 1974. *You & Me*. New York: Holt, Rinehart and Winston.

————. 1984. *Interview with Seymour Krim*. Columbia, MO: American Audio Prose Library.

————. 1991. *What's This Cat's Story? The Best of Seymour Krim*, edited by Peggy Brooks. New York: Paragon House.

————. 1994. "For My Brothers and Sisters in the Failure Business." In *The Art of the Personal Essay: An Anthology from the Classical Era to the Present*, edited by Phillip Lopate, 577–86. New York: Anchor Books.

————. 2001. "What's *This* Cat's Story?" In *Editors: The Best of Five Decades*, edited by Saul Bellow and Keith Botsford, 367–87. London: Toby Press.

Lee, Don L. 1975. "The Revolutionary Screw." In *The Norton Anthology of Poetry*, edited by Alexander W. Allison, Herbert Barrows, Caesar R. Blake, Arthur J. Carr, Arthur M. Eastman, and Hubert M. English Jr., 1296. New York: W. W. Norton & Co.

Liebling, A. J. 1982. *The Sweet Science*. New York: Viking Press.

Lopate, Phillip. 1994. *The Art of the Personal Essay: An Anthology from the Classical Era to the Present*. New York: Anchor Books.

Mailer, Norman. 1957/1959. "The White Negro." In *Advertisements for Myself*, 337–58. New York: G. P. Putnam's Sons.

————. 1961. Foreword to *Views of a Nearsighted Cannoneer*, by Seymour Krim, 6. New York: Excelsior Press.

————. 1968. *The Armies of the Night*. New York: Signet Books.

Malin, Irving. 1996. "Review of *What's This Cat's Story? The Best of Seymour Krim*." *Journal of Modern Literature* 19, no. 3–4:490.

Malin, Irving, and Irwin Stark, eds. 1963. *Breakthrough: A Treasury of Contemporary American-Jewish Literature.* Philadelphia: Jewish Publication Society of America.

Marx, Groucho. 1974. "Groucho and Me." In *Jewish-American Literature: An Anthology,* edited by Abraham Chapman, 254–61. New York: Mentor.

Menand, Louis. 2009. "It Took a Village: How the *Voice* Changed Journalism." *New Yorker,* Jan. 5, 36–45.

Mezzrow, Milton, and Bernard Wolfe. 1946. *Really the Blues.* New York: Random House.

New York Times. 2005. Dec. 7, E10.

Nicosia, Gerald. 1989. "Seymour Krim: Making Every Word Count." *Washington Post Book World,* Oct. 29, 1, 10.

Podhoretz, Norman. 1966. "My Negro Problem—And Ours." In *Doings and Undoings: The Fifties and After in American Writing,* by Norman Podhoretz, 354–71. New York: Farrar, Straus & Giroux.

———. 1967. *Making It.* New York: Random House.

———. 1978. "The Rise and Fall of the American Jewish Novelist." In *Jewish Life in America: Historical Perspectives,* edited by Gladys Rosen, 141–50. New York: Ktav Publishing House.

Reznikoff, Charles. 1986. *By the Waters of Manhattan.* New York: Markus Wiener Publishing.

Rischin, Moses. 1978. "The Jews and Pluralism: Toward an American Freedom Symphony." In *Jewish Life in America: Historical Perspectives,* edited by Gladys Rosen, 61–91. New York: Ktav Publishing House.

Rosenfeld, Isaac. 1963. "America, Land of the Sad Millionaire." In *Breakthrough: A Treasury of Contemporary American-Jewish Literature,* edited by Irving Malin and Irwin Stark, 259–66. Philadelphia: Jewish Publication Society of America.

Roth, Philip. 1969. *Portnoy's Complaint.* New York: Random House.

———. 1982. *Goodbye, Columbus.* New York: Bantam.

———. 1985. *Reading Myself and Others.* New York: Penguin Books.

Solotaroff, Theodore. 1959/1963. "Philip Roth and the Jewish Moralists." In *Breakthrough: A Treasury of Contemporary American-Jewish Literature,* edited by Irving Malin and Irwin Stark, 354–66. Philadelphia: Jewish Publication Society of America.

Sundquist, Eric J. 2005. *Strangers in the Land: Blacks, Jews, Post-Holocaust America.* Cambridge, MA: Belknap Press of Harvard Univ. Press.

Tallmer, Jerry. 1989. "Fiercely Independent." *Village Voice,* Sept. 19, 21.

Wakefield, Dan. 1992. *New York in the Fifties*. Boston: Houghton Mifflin/Seymour Lawrence.

Waldman, Anne. 1996. *The Beat Book: Writings from the Beat Generation*. Boston: Shambhala.

Watson, Steven. 1995. *The Birth of the Beat Generation: Visionaries, Rebels, and Hipsters, 1944–1960*. New York: Pantheon Books.

Weingarten, Marc. 2005. *The Gang That Wouldn't Write Straight: Wolfe, Thompson, Didion, and the New Journalism Revolution*. New York: Crown Publishers.

Whitfield, Stephen J. 1993. *The Paradoxes of American Jewish Culture*. Ann Arbor: Jean and Samuel Frankel Center for Judaic Studies, Univ. of Michigan.

Whitman, Walt. 1944. *Leaves of Grass*. New York: Random House.

Wilentz, Elias, ed. 1960. *The Beat Scene*. New York: Citadel Press.

Index

Agee, James, 6, 8, 30, 70

America: and blacks, 96, 112, 117–28; and
    failure, 177–89; and Jews, 16, 43–44,
    112, 162, 194, 201, 209, 217; Krim's love
    for, xxiii, 16, 43, 59, 194; and New
    Journalism, xx, 75–76; and the novel,
    44, 58–68; and success, 134, 143, 145,
    149–50, 168

American Jewish Committee, 10

Amundsen, Roald, 62

anarchists, 4

Anderson, Sherwood, 44, 60, 122

Ayden, Erje, 74

Baez, Joan, 147

Baker, Dorothy, 60

Baldwin, James, xix, xxiv, xxvii, 51, 94,
    111, 147, 157

Baraka, Amiri (LeRoi Jones), 117, 125

Barrett, Will, 6

Bazelon, Dave, 6

Beats, the: Allen Ginsberg and, xxxiii;
    and Jewish writing, xxxiii; Krim and,
    xxv–xxvii, 121

Begin, Menahem, xxxii, 193–95

Bellow, Saul: intellectuals and, 3, 6, 83;
    as Jewish writer, xxix, xxxii, xxxv,
    xxxviii; *Noble Savage* and, 3; and

similarities with Krim, xviii, xix, xxiv,
    3, 78, 95, 131, 161, 196

Berkeley, 121

Bible, 41, 45

Blackmur, R. P., xxi, 9, 13, 33

blacks: angry at whites, 119–20, 125; anxi-
    eties of discussing, 101; in Harlem,
    97, 104–6, 114–16; and intellectuals,
    122–23; and jazz, xxvi, 95–99; Jewish
    camaraderie with, 93, 103, 114–15;
    Jewish perception of, 103, 112; Jews'
    imitation of, 96, 99; and Krim, 100–116;
    Krim's view of, xxvi; Krim's vindica-
    tion regarding, xxvii; and manliness,
    107, 109; and obscenities, 106, 116,
    117–28; racism toward, 113, 120; sarto-
    rial style of, 106; as sex object, 103; and
    slang, 96; social pathologies of, 96–97,
    110, 115; suffering of, 111–12, 124; white
    attraction to, 114–15; white imitation
    of, 98, 102, 121–22; white romanticiz-
    ing of, 97, 99

Blake, William, 8, 31, 49, 71, 195

Breslin, Jimmy, xx, 153, 169–76

Breuer, Bessie, 60

Brighton Beach, 47

Bronx, xxiii, 4, 41, 46

Brooklyn, 40, 45, 84, 146, 170, 218

Brooklyn College, 46, 84

231

Brooks, Peggy, xxxvii, 138
Brossard, Chandler, 6, 32, 51
Brothers, Joyce, 201–6
Broyard, Anatole, 6, 40, 52, 55, 57
Bruce, Lenny, xxxv, 123, 150, 182
Buber, Martin, 10
Burroughs, William, 71, 123, 163
Byrd, Admiral, 62

Cain, James, 58, 63, 67
Caldwell, Erskine, 59
Cape Cod, 40
CCNY (City College of New York), 46
Central Park West, 45
Chase, Richard, 10
Chayefsky, Paddy, xxiii, 70
Clancy, Bill, 9, 14
Cleaver, Eldridge, 121
Cohen, Elliot, 28
Collier's, 5
Columbia University, 35, 46, 154, 201
Commentary, x, xxv, 6, 8, 10, 16, 56, 83
Commonweal, x, xxv, 9–10
Congdon, Don, 5
Conroy, Frank, 74
Crane, Hart, 33, 40
Cremer, Jan, 74, 154
Crosby, Bing, 98, 102

Depression, the, xxiii
DeWitt Clinton High School, xxiii, 4, 62, 202
di Donato, Pietro, 60
Donne, John, 32, 49
Dos Passos, John, 58, 147
Dreiser, Theodore, 7, 12, 24, 38, 42, 45, 60
Dylan, Bob, xxv, xxxviii, 147

East Village Other, 124
Einstein, Albert, 53
Eliot, T. S., 9–10, 33
Ellison, Ralph, 71, 122, 142
Esquire, 46, 61, 172
Exodus, xxvi, 20

failure: and America, 64, 177–89; causes of, 184–85; disdain for, 133–34, 145, 171; fear of, 13, 133; greatness standards and, 17, 26; and Jewish identity, 131, 147, 162; Krim and, xx, xxi, 13, 69, 175; meaning of, 186; pain of, 136, 184–86, 188–89; and self-hatred, 157; as sin, 133; value of, 160; writing as revenge for, 65–66
Fante, John, 60
Farber, Manny, 6
Farber, Marjorie, 8
Farrell, James T., 24, 58, 61, 72, 122, 147
Faulkner, William, xxii, 7, 44, 58, 61, 63, 71, 137
Felker, Clay, 79, 138
Fiedler, Leslie, 10
Fineman, Irving, 60
Fuchs, Daniel, xxxiv, 60

Gallo, Joey, 167, 170
Ginsberg, Allen, xxvi, xxxiii–xxxiv, 51, 122, 147, 177
Gold, Herbert, xxxiv, 156
Goldman, Emma, 200
Goyen, Bill, 51
Graves, Robert, 13
Greenberg, Clement, 6, 84–85
Greenwich Village: artists in, 87; blacks in, 104; hedonism of, 104; hipsters and,

48; intellectuals in, 6, 22, 53, 83–84; Jews in, 46–47; Krim in, 29–30, 93

Hall, Oakley, 60
Halper, Albert, 60
Harris, Richard, 166–67
Harvard, 46
Hemingway, Ernest, xxi, xxiv, 7, 33, 44, 58, 72, 200
Hentoff, Nat, 146
Herbst, Josephine, 60
Hitler, Adolf, 209
Holiday, Billie, 30
Hudson Review, xxi, 11, 13, 54
Huntington Hartford Foundation, 5

intellectuals: vs. anti-intellectualism, 3; blacks and, 122, 126; European influence on, 7–9; greatness standards and, 16–17, 22, 54–55, 57; and jazz, 95; Jews and, 3, 6, 15–16, 24, 42–45; and Milton Klonsky, 28–57; Krim and, 19, 21, 24, 184, 203; mooniness of, 107; *New York Times* and, 78; Harold Rosenberg and, 83–88; scorn for, 171; success and, 132; and talking, 18; vanity among, 21, 108
Israel, xxi, xxxviii, 194

Jews: American culture and, xxix; anger of, 217–18; assimilation and, 46–47, 194; Menahem Begin and, 193–95; and blacks, 103, 113; bohemian and straight, 201–6; *Commentary* and, 8; and cultural studies, xxix; downtown vs. uptown, 196–98; and emotional intensity, 50; ethnic slurs about, 173;

intellectuals and, 5, 8, 15–16, 22, 41; and Jewish studies, xxxiv; and Krim, xxiii, xxx, 6, 8, 14–15, 23, 29, 42–46, 58; Krim's identity as, 42–45, 47, 50, 209–10; Krim's interest in, xxvii–xviii, xxx–xxxii, xxxvii; middle-class vs. poor, 45–47; Henry Miller and, 196–200; and *New York Times,* 81, 176; nonfiction by, xxxv; social history of, xxix; as white, 91–93; writing by, xxvi
Jones, James, 51, 123, 137, 150, 159, 176
Joyce, James, 7, 8, 17, 33

Kafka, Franz, 8, 17, 29, 33
Kazin, Alfred, xxiii, xxxv, 6, 58, 177
Kees, Weldon, 5
Kenyon Review, 11
Kerouac, Jack, 38, 51, 178
Klonsky, Milton, xxi, xxx, 6, 28–57
Klonsky and Schwartz, 28
Krim, Seymour: as actor, xxxvii; and America, 177–89; American literature and, 7, 23–24, 42, 58–77; and awards, xxi, 5; Beats and, xxv–xxvii, 12–13, 121; blacks and, 100–116; book reviewing and, 8; in childhood, xxii; 4, 42, 62, 101–2, 118, 202; drugs and, xx, 36; as editor, xxv–xxvi; education and, xxiii, 4, 46, 70, 202; employment and, 4, 171, 178, 182, 184, 210; enemies of, xx; and failure, xx–xxi, 17–18, 69, 175, 177–89; family of, xxii–xxiii, 36, 46, 59, 101–2, 140, 162, 179, 202; fans of, xxiv; fiction by, xxii; and gambling, xx, 163, 165, 201; Greenwich Village and, 6, 22, 29–30, 101; health of, xxxviii; in high school, xxiii, 4, 44, 58, 62; homosexuality and, xix, 52–53, 212; intellectuals

Krim, Seymour (*cont.*)
  and, 6, 14, 15, 16–19, 24, 33–34, 38, 42,
  83–88; and Jewish anger, 65–66; Jewish assimilation and, 43, 45–47, 162,
  209; Jewish identity and, xxxiii, 42–45,
  47, 66, 92, 113, 174; and Jewish studies,
  xxxiv; as Jewish writer, xxx, xxxviii–
  xxxix, 24, 146; Jews and, xxviii,
  xxx–xxxii, 4, 8, 14–15, 23, 29, 45–46,
  140; literary criticism and, xxi, xxiv, 9,
  14–15, 19; mental breakdown and, 5,
  19, 49, 202; and New Journalism, xx,
  70–77, 144, 157, 171, 175; as New Yorker,
  141, 168; novel and, 7, 42, 58–68; in
  Peace and Freedom Party, 121; and
  plastic surgery, 43, 104, 115, 182, 209;
  and Provincetown group, 151–53;
  psychoanalysis and, 31, 43, 49; reading
  habits of, 42, 58, 60, 78–82; suicide and,
  xxxviii, 20, 112, 176; women and, xxiv,
  30, 35, 103–4, 138–39, 166, 175, 214; and
  writing, xxi, xxv, xxxix, 14, 23, 142,
  154, 157, 165, 183, 203

Lawrence, D. H., 8, 18, 122
Lewis, Sinclair, xxiv, 44
Liebling, A. J., xviii, 3
Lowell, Robert, 15, 142
Lurie, Boris, 208, 210–15, 217

Macdonald, Dwight, 10, 84
Macdonald, Nancy, xxxvii
Mailer, Norman, xviii, xix, xxx, xxxviii,
  3, 55, 74, 94, 121, 138–60, 169, 174, 177,
  193, 198
Mamet, David, xxxv
Marcus, Steven, 10
Marvell, Andrew, 7, 32, 38, 40, 49

Maugham, Somerset, 21
Melville, Herman, 8, 147
Mezzrow, Mezz, xxvii, xxxi, 95, 96
Miller, Henry, 24, 122, 196–200
Moore, Marianne, 41
Morgan, Fred, 13, 14
Morris, Willie, 74
Moss, Howard, 40
Murray, Albert L., 122

New Criticism, 69
New Directions, 61
New Journalism: cultural studies and,
  xxix; early, xvii; and Jewish New
  Journalism, xxix, xxxii; Krim on, xx,
  70–77, 144, 159–60, 173, 203; and Krim's
  success, xxi; Krim teaches, xxi; and
  social history, xxix; vs. traditional
  nonfiction, xxxv; *Village Voice* and, xix
New Masses, 61
New York (magazine), xxi, 80, 138
New York City, 131
New Yorker, xix, 4, 40, 61, 81, 83, 84, 86–88,
  106
New York Herald Tribune, 184, 203
New York Post, 201
New York Times, xxi, xxiv, 8, 28, 79–82, 169,
  170, 198, 201
Noble Savage, The (Bellow), xix, 3

Odets, Clifford, 61, 70
O'Hara, John, 58, 63–64
Oursler, Stephanie, 122
OWI (Office of War Information), 4, 31

Partisan Review, xxi, 3, 6, 9, 11, 84, 88, 132, 184
Phillips, William, 10

Podhoretz, Norman, x, xxx, xxxii, xxxvi, 10, 28, 74
Pollock, Jackson, 86, 137
Poster, Herb, 6, 50
Poster, Willie, 6, 8
Pound, Ezra, 13, 33
Princeton University, 13, 46, 106
Prokosch, Frederic, 60
Proust, Marcel, 17, 29, 165
Puzo, Mario, xxxi, 161–68

Rahv, Philip, 84
Ransom, John Crowe, 9, 13
Rattner, Abraham, 200
Reed, Ishmael, 124
Rimbaud, 31, 33, 86
Rorem, Ned, 74
Rosenberg, Harold, 83–88
Rosenfeld, Isaac, xxxiv, xxxv, 6, 8, 32, 50
Rosenthal, A. M., 79
Rosset, Barney, 154, 157, 200
Roth, Philip, xxviii, xxx, xxxv, 95, 196, 207

Sanders, Ed, 123
Saroyan, William, 59, 61, 150
Saturday Review of Literature, 61, 67, 87
Schlesinger, Arthur, Jr., 40
Schlesinger, Tess, 60
Schmidt, Gladys, 60
Schwartz, Delmore, xxxix, 6, 28, 41, 55, 58, 140, 177
SDS (Students for a Democratic Society), 121
Seide, Michael, 19
Selby, Hubert, 71, 122, 152
Sewanee Review, 11
Shakespeare, William, 41
Shepp, Archie, 125

Smart, Christopher, 32
Smith, Robert Paul, 60
Stein, Gertrude, 20
Steinbeck, John, 44, 58
Stettner, Irving, 197
Stevens, Wallace, 13, 33
Story, 61
success: and America, 143, 155, 168; as antidote to confusion, 135, 149–50; and art, 156; and celebrity, 136–37, 149–50; corrupting power of, 137, 142–43, 155–56, 160; cynicism and drive for, 132–36; despair and, 136; and failure, 133; and image, 145–46; insight afforded by, 147–48, 167; and Jews, 140; language of, 131–32; and lost ideals, 132–36; magic of, 147, 166, 168; Norman Mailer as, 138–60; necessity of, 153–55; new attraction of, 132; New York and, 132, 139; power of, 149–50, 156–57; price of, 164; superficiality of, 136

Talese, Gay, 164
Tallmer, Jerry, xix, 14
Tate, Allen, 8, 33, 40
Tolstoy, Leo, 26, 53
Trilling, Lionel, 9, 33
Trotsky, Leon, 7, 210

Up Against the Wall Motherfuckers, 121

Village Voice, xviii, xix, xxv, xxvi–xxvii, 14, 20, 96, 121, 146, 157

Wakefield, Dan, ix–xi, 74
Warshow, Bob, 8

Weidman, Jerome, 59, 61

West, Nathanael, 60

Wharton, Edith, 42

White Horse Tavern, xxv, 12

whites: beauty standard set by, 114–15; black rage at, 118–21; blacks as seen by, 102–4, 115, 121, 123, 125; in Harlem, 105, 109, 114; imitating blacks, 95–99, 102, 121–22; and Jews, xxxi, 46, 91; and Krim, 66, 91; mockery of, 91–93; obscenities and, 123; racism and its benefits, 113, 120; sartorial style of, 106–7; vanity of, 108

Whitman, Walt, xxi, 12, 23, 45, 78, 183

Winchell, Walter, 45

Winters, Yvor, 13

Wolfe, Thomas, xxiii, 4, 25, 41, 45, 54, 58, 64, 72

Wolfe, Tom, xvii, 74, 86, 154, 211, 216

Wright, Richard, xxiii, 58, 61, 111

Yaddo, xxiv, 5

Yale University, 46, 84, 106

Yeats, William Butler, 17, 33

Yippies, 121